The Age
of the UFO

The Age of the UFO

Edited by Peter Brookesmith

BLACK CAT

Acknowledgments

Photographs were supplied by AP, Aerofilms, Aerospace Publishing, Agence France Press, Airviews Ltd, Aldus Archive, C. Berlita, British Army Magazine, Bufora, Centre for UFO Studies, Centre National D'Etudes Spatiales, Bill Chalker/Australian Centre for UFO Studies, Charnwood Audio Visual, Chronicle Publishing, Bruce Coleman, Philip Daly, Arnold Desser, Paul Devereux, EFE, ET Archive, Robert Estall, Europa Press, Euston Films, Mary Evans Picture Library, Examiner, Ferranti, French Government Tourist Office, Joel Finler, Flying Saucer Review, Fortean Picture Library, Fort Worth Star Telegraph, Foto Monsted, GEOS, Gamma, John Glover, Goodyear Co, Henry Gris, Ground Saucer Watch, Robert Harding Associates, Hawker-Siddeley Aviation, Betty Hill, Michael Holford, Mike Hooks, Robert Hunt Library, Anwar Hussein, Nat Irvine, Guy Jouhaud, Kobal Collection, Frank Lane, A. Lawson/Mary Evans Picture Library, Library of Congress, London Express, MARS, Colin Mahar, Manchester International Airport, Marconi Research, Martin Aircraft Co, McDonnell Douglas Corp, GT Meaden, NASA, Personality Picture Library, John Pett, Photri, M. Piccin, Popperfoto, Press Association, Probe, Jenny Randles and P. Whetnall, Rex Features, August C. Roberts, D. Scott Rogo, Rolls Royce, Roswell Daily Record, Santus-Dumont, Science Museum London, Science Photo Library, J. Schuessler, Robert Sheaffer, Paul Snelgrove, Space Frontiers, Spectrum Colour Library, Steiger Agency, Johan Taylor, John Topham Picture Library UPI, United International Pictures, United Nations, United States Air Force, Valle Collection, Velstein, T. Verdal, Peter Warrington Library, Westland Helicopters, J.J. Wheeler, ZEFA.

Consultants	**Deputy Editor**	**Picture Researchers**	**Designer**
Professor A.J. Ellison	Lynn Picknett	Anne Horton	Richard Burgess
Dr J. Allen Hynek	**Executive Editor**	Paul Snelgrove	**Art Buyer**
Brian Inglis	Lesley Riley	Frances Vargo	Jean Morley
Colin Wilson	**Sub Editors**	**Editorial Manager**	**Production Co-ordinator**
Editorial Director	Mitzi Bales	Clare Byatt	Nicky Bowden
Brian Innes	Chris Cooper	**Art Editor**	**Volume Editor**
Editor	Jenny Dawson	Stephen Westcott	Lorrie Mack
Peter Brookesmith	Hildi Hawkins		

The publishers would like to thank the following authors for contributing to this book:
Charles Bowen 178–197; Peter Brookesmith 41–43; Paul Devereux 72–80; Robert S. Digby 90–93; Hilary Evans 10–11, 23–31, 44–54, 144–152, 165–176; W.A. Harbinson 105–117; Douglas Hill 131–134; Charles Lock 68–71; Kevin McClure 119–130; Ian Mrzyglod 20–22; Jenny Randles 12–19, 55–66, 94–104, 135–142; John Schuessler 153–164; William H. Spaulding 32–40; 81–89.

Printed and bound in Czechoslovakia by Aventinum
50836/01

ISBN 0 7481 0311 2

Contents

Introduction

No mystery, ancient or modern, has so profoundly intrigued people all over the world as the mystery of the UFOs. It is a mystery that is with us here and now; it is not something that happened centuries ago and has subsequently become hoary with layers of unverifiable assertion, taking on the status of legend. It is a living enigma that can be examined in the bright light of the present – yet it has defied all the knowledge and skill of modern scientists.

It is a mystery, too, in which the reader can become actively involved. There is no need to consult musty manuscripts; the diligent student can talk and work directly with those who claim to have witnessed UFOs – even to have experienced a 'close encounter' with their occupants. And it is easy to keep abreast of UFO investigations around the world through the numerous publications devoted to the subject. UFO research organisations exist in almost every country, too, and generally welcome anyone with a serious interest in the subject.

What, then, *is* the UFO mystery?

We are confronted by the fact that many people, of good repute, in good standing in their communities, and often with considerable technical expertise (such as pilots or engineers) have reported – often with reluctance – witnessing certain extraordinary phenomena, in the air or on the ground: coloured lights, often very intense; 'craft'; and sometimes apparently intelligent 'entities'.

The mystery lies in the origin and behaviour of the UFOs. That behaviour is often bizarre and an outrage to common sense. As reported by the witnesses it is unexplainable by present-day science and, largely for that reason, unacceptable to scientists. Seemingly physical in nature, UFOs do not behave as we expect physical things to behave. (You will find many examples of this in the following pages). They act more like the Cheshire Cat that Alice encountered in Wonderland: that mysterious creature, you will remember, appeared without warning, apparently with a definite purpose, remained visible for a short time and then disappeared just as inexplicably. UFOs likewise tend to appear suddenly and, according to most witnesses, seem to be fully aware of their audience (which is almost always remarkably small). They remain visible for a relatively short time (UFOs that can be seen for more than 10 minutes are the exception). Then they vanish, sometimes just 'blinking out', sometimes departing at enormous speeds. But where do they go? Unlike ordinary physical objects – but like the Cheshire Cat – the UFO, once it has left one spot, cannot be located anywhere else.

This apparent coming into and going out of existence is the conspicuous 'trademark' of the UFO. Yet, outstanding as it is, this feature is ignored by the most popular theory of UFOs: the 'extraterrestrial hypothesis'.

To most people, influenced no doubt by science fiction and the media, UFOs are synonymous with 'little green men' from outer space – or, to give them a more dignified title, 'extraterrestrial entities'. So prevalent is this common interpretation of UFOs that it has been an obstacle to research into other possibilities.

Scientists, especially astronomers, are far more fully aware than the public of the truly awesome distances that separate the stars. The majority of them dismiss the extraterrestrial hypothesis as utterly impossible – and thereby, in the opinion of many, throw out the baby with the bathwater. Ardent defenders of the theory hold that we must not think in terms of our current science and technology: rather, we must assume that other civilisations in space, far more advanced than we are, have learned how to overcome these formidable distances in a manner incomprehensible to us - perhaps by means that we would call paranormal. Some pursue these ideas into the realms of the ancient teachings concerning 'planes of existence' beyond the physical – 'parallel realities' not subject to ordinary physical law. But once such ideas are entertained, anything becomes possible!

Suffice it to say that there is sufficient mystery in the UFO phenomenon to satisfy anyone's craving for the unknown. In the pages that follow this will become amply evident. The reader can spend delightful hours in pondering various theories and stretching his imagination far beyond the confines of everyday life.

Of course, it must be recognised that such tapestries of the imagination depend entirely on whether the claims of UFO witnesses can be believed. Delving into these matters, one soon comes to the sobering realisation that the first question in ufology is not 'Where are they from?' or 'What is their propulsion system?' but 'Did things happen as the witness says they did?' With the very important exception of radar and photographic data, and of the occasional physical evidence of a UFO's presence, the case for UFOs rests on human testimony and therefore, finally, on the integrity and probity of the witnesses. Some sceptics maintain that even an honest witness may, through purely subjective processes, become convinced that he has seen a UFO and that it physically affected not only him but his car, his dog and his immediate environment. But such explanations of UFOs as 'all in the mind' are forced to postulate psychological processes almost as mysterious as a genuine, objectively existing UFO would be.

Every mystery has its sceptics and its 'debunkers'; they play a healthy role in the search for truth. Matters as bizarre and controversial as the UFO phenomenon need watchdogs to guard against trespass by fantasy, superstition and charlatanism. Still, it has been interesting to observe the frustration of the sceptics in this matter of UFOs, as they have attempted to sweep away the mystery with 'common-sense' explanations that have often been extremely far-fetched. They have had their greatest successes in showing that the great majority of the initial or 'raw' reports have been caused by the misidentification of planets, satellites, balloons, and so on – often by people who sorely want to see a UFO and let wishful thinking take them over.

Such cases are termed 'IFOs', or 'identified flying objects', and experienced UFO investigators are fully versed in weeding them out. The general public is simply not aware of the host of unmysterious objects that can be seen in the sky and that can trap the unwary into thinking they have seen something 'out of this world'.

But the residue, after the IFOs have been removed from the collected reports, appears to represent a true challenge to science and perhaps to all mankind. The complexity of the subject, which becomes apparent only after considerable study, is astounding. It is far from certain that UFOs represent a single phenomenon, despite the simi-larity in patterns of reports from all over the world. It is this commonality in the sorts of things reported as UFOs that is quite noteworthy. The Center for UFO studies, in the United States, has amassed a database of more than 100,000 UFO reports from some 140 countries. The same patterns, broadly speaking, appear all over the globe.

It is of considerable interest to note what these worldwide reports do *not* contain. If all UFO reports were the products of overstimulated imaginations, as some sceptics maintain, then it is surprising that there is such a poverty of imagination. In the database there are no reports of flying pink elephants, of fiery dragons, of brilliant golden octopuses! But roughly the same kinds of things *are* reported from around the world, regardless of the ideology, culture or religion of the countries from which they come. And they have been so reported for several decades past without any drastic change in the content of the reports. It would seem that the UFO mystery is very real and enduring.

Perhaps I may presume to intrude my own opinion on these matters, based on more than 30 years of study. I believe that the UFO phenomenon is in some way directing us to consider an aspect of reality of which we have hitherto been largely unaware – an aspect, indeed, that may eventually be incorporated into our science and may prove to be of great value to the progress of mankind.

J. Allen Hynek
Center for UFO Studies
Evanston, Illinois

UFO tracking

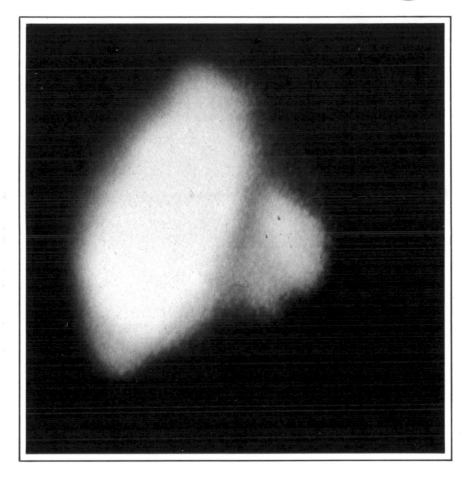

Each year more and more people report seeing mysterious objects overhead. The dossier of cases mounts up as evidence is investigated by scientists and disinterested laymen alike, and found to be inexplicable in terms of our present knowledge. Yet government and military agencies refuse even to acknowledge the existence of UFOs. Is there a cover-up?

The UFO paradox

Only the most hardened sceptic can still pretend that UFOs do not exist. But in what way are they real? An examination of this vexed question indicates that there may be more than one answer

'THEY FLEW LIKE A SAUCER would if you skipped it across the water.' This is how, on 24 June 1947, American airman Kenneth Arnold, an experienced pilot, described some unusual flying craft he had seen over the mountains of America's west coast. Newspapermen applied his phrase to the craft themselves, and the misleading label 'flying saucer' has followed the UFO ever since, like a tin can tied to a cat's tail.

This fanciful name has deepened the reluctance of professional scientists to take the UFO seriously. Only a few have taken the trouble to investigate this bizarre phenomenon, which surely qualifies as the strangest of our time. Even that phrase, 'of our time', is a subject of controversy: many people claim that the UFO has been with mankind throughout history. But the evidence they offer is meagre and their case far from proven. There seems little doubt that our earliest ancestors were considerably more advanced than has generally been supposed, but that is a long way from the theory that our planet was long ago visited by extraterrestrial voyagers.

Whether or not UFOs existed in the past, there is no doubt that UFO sightings have proliferated in astonishing numbers over the past 30 years. This fact seems to be in some way linked with man's first steps towards exploring space, and this connection is undoubtedly an important clue in trying to explain the UFO.

Estimates of the total number of UFO sightings vary so widely as to be meaningless; more helpful figures are provided by the catalogues of reported sightings prepared by individual investigative organisations. Recently a French team catalogued more than 600 encounter cases in France alone, each vouched for by responsible investigators; how many more were not reported or investigated? In the early 1970s UFO investigators made lists of all reported landing cases for particular countries: 923 were recorded in the United States, 200 in Spain.

Are UFOs real in the sense that, say, spacecraft are real? The surest proof would be actually to get hold of one, and there are persistent rumours that certain governments, notably that of the United States, have indeed obtained a UFO, which is kept in total secrecy. However this remains mere conjecture, despite the sworn affidavits of alleged witnesses. Indeed, the whole matter of governmental involvement – or the lack of it – is a further and fascinating aspect of the UFO controversy.

In the absence of a real UFO that we can touch and examine, there is a great deal of evidence of the phenomenon in the form of a

The COMING of the SAUCERS

By Kenneth Arnold & Ray Palmer

Above: Kenneth Arnold's book, first published in 1952, was the first full study of UFOs. Arnold began collecting accounts of UFO sightings after he saw several disc-shaped objects in the sky in June 1947

mass of photographs and a handful of movies. The majority are undoubtedly fakes. Those with good credentials are so blurred, so distant or so ambiguous that they simply add a further dimension to the problem: why, if UFOs exist, and in an age when many people carry cameras with them most of the time, have we not obtained better photographic evidence?

Perhaps the strongest evidence we have is from the effects caused by UFOs on surrounding objects, particularly machinery. In November 1967 a truck and a car approaching each other on a Hampshire road in the early hours of the morning simultaneously suffered engine failure when a large egg-shaped object crossed the road between them. The police, and subsequently the Ministry of Defence, investigated the incident, but no official explanation was ever issued. Such a case may leave investigators puzzled, but it makes one thing certain: if they can cause physical effects, UFOs must be physically real.

If they are physical objects, UFOs must originate from somewhere. When the first UFOs of the current era were seen, back in the 1940s, it was assumed they came from somewhere on Earth. The Americans suspected they were a Russian secret device, perhaps developed using the expertise of German scientists captured at the end of the Second World War.

But as more reports came in it became clear that no nation on Earth could be responsible. Nor was there sufficient evidence to support other ingenious theories – that they came from the Himalayas, long a favoured source of secret wisdom, or Antarctica, where unexplored tracts of land and climatic anomalies provide a shaky foundation for speculation. Instead, ufologists began to look beyond the Earth, encouraged by the fact that our own space exploration programme was just beginning. We were starting to take an active interest in worlds beyond, and it seemed reasonable that other civilizations might have a similar interest in us.

However, although the number of potential sources of life in the Universe is virtually infinite, the probability of any civilisation being at a stage of development appropriate for space travel is very small. The fact that no solid evidence has been found for the extraterrestrial hypothesis is discouraging. Although it is the best available explanation, it remains no more than speculation.

Messages from outer space?

Today it is recognised that the UFO poses a problem not only for the astronomer and the engineer, but also for the behavioural scientist. The psychologist confirms that an individual's response to a sighting is conditioned by his psychological make-up, while the sociologist places such responses in a wider social context and relates them to cultural patterns. The anthropologist detects parallels with myth and traditional belief, while the parapsychologist notes how frequently sightings are accompanied by such psychic manifestations as precognition and poltergeist phenomena.

This is particularly true of 'encounter' cases in which the observer claims to have had actual meetings with UFO occupants. The entities are generally described as extraterrestrial aliens, often ambassadors from an inter-galactic power; their purpose is to examine human beings, to warn us of misuse of resources and to bring reassuring messages from some cosmic brotherhood. With only one or two such cases on record they could be dismissed as fantasy, but there are hundreds of such cases on file.

If a single one of these cases could be shown to be based on fact, the UFO problem would be established on solid foundations and serious scientific interest assured. But in every instance it remains an open question whether the incident actually occurred or is simply a fabrication – deliberate, unconscious, or perhaps induced by some external force. Hypotheses range from brainwashing by extraterrestrial invaders, to deliberate invention by the CIA.

Almost certainly, UFOs exist on both the physical and the psychological level. Somehow we have got to recognise that, although they are real, they are not what they seem. This is the paradox that lies at the heart of the UFO mystery, which we examine in the classic UFO case histories that follow.

Right: this photograph was taken at Taormina, Sicily, in 1954. Sceptics claim the 'objects' are nothing more than lenticular clouds, or even the result of lens flare

Below: a shot taken from Skylab III in 1973. The object rotated for several minutes before disappearing. UFOs have been reported by almost all astronauts

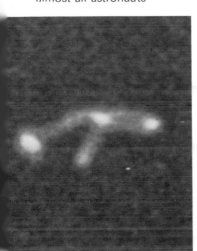

A bird, a plane - or a UFO?

Weird lights in the night sky, strange silvery shapes flashing through the sunlight – these are the stuff of UFO reports, but they often have a perfectly rational explanation. This chapter explains how to recognise unusual objects in the sky – including true UFOs

ON THE AFTERNOON of 7 January 1948, a strange bright light was seen to hover for several hours over Godman Airfield, Kentucky, USA. In due course, a team of F-51 aircraft appeared in the area, led by Captain Thomas Mantell. Though on a routine mission, Mantell agreed to divert his planes to investigate the glittering intruder. One by one, however, the pilots were forced down – lacking proper oxygen equipment to travel above a limited height. But Mantell himself continued climbing. At 20,000 feet (6000 metres) he reported seeing a metallic object, ahead and above him. Minutes later the wreckage of his F-51 was found scattered over a wide area. According to a report at the time, which has persisted to the present day, Mantell had been shot down by a UFO.

On 31 December 1978 two police officers in Hertfordshire, England, watched in amazement as an incredible object passed silently overhead. It had a cigar-shaped, silvery body with what looked like windows along the side. Behind trailed shimmering orange-coloured streamers. The thing moved slowly away out of sight and, alarmed by what they had seen, they radioed their headquarters.

Unknown to the policemen, hundreds of other people, including airline pilots and coastguards, had reported seeing the same thing in many parts of Britain. Many believed that it was connected with the piece of film taken by a television crew off the coast of New Zealand the day before; a film that was already receiving massive world-wide publicity. As with the first case, there was a

Above: Allan Hendry, whose study of UFO identification, *The UFO handbook*, has become a classic of its kind

Below: friction creates a blaze of light around the Apollo 11 space capsule as it re-enters the Earth's atmosphere on returning from a mission to the Moon. Debris from satellites and other space vehicles can cause similar displays – but because they are unexpected they are often mistaken for UFOs

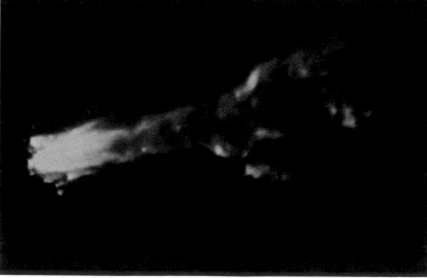

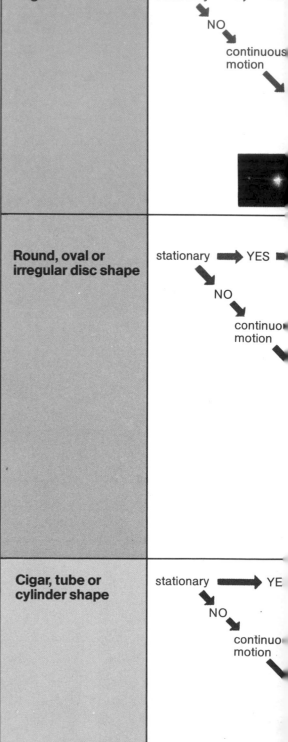

Lights	stationary → YES
	NO ↓ continuous motion
Round, oval or irregular disc shape	stationary → YES
	NO ↓ continuous motion
Cigar, tube or cylinder shape	stationary → YES
	NO ↓ continuous motion

If you think you've seen a UFO, check the features of your sightings on the chart below. This shows the three major categories of the man-made and natural objects that are most often mistaken for UFOs and enables you to eliminate them from the investigation

widespread belief that the 'object' was a UFO.

On closer investigation many cases of UFO spotting turn out to have a perfectly ordinary explanation. Yet it seems to be fairly easy to misidentify a perfectly normal object, under certain conditions, as a UFO. Strange objects in the sky, especially when seen at night in a deserted area, can be alarming. There is the case, for example, of a woman who locked herself in her bedroom and hid under the bed

for an hour, terrified by seeing an object she believed to be a UFO, but that turned out to be a star. In America, ufologist Allan Hendry has described how one man was in such a panic after seeing a well-lit aircraft, believing it to be a UFO, that he ripped his neighbour's door off its hinges, so anxious was he to escape. These examples may sound funny, but it would be wrong to assume that such people are idiots.

Jimmy Carter, for example, when Governor of Georgia, reported seeing a brilliant light in the sky in 1973. The light, which changed colour, was seen to hover silently for 10 minutes at a height of 300 feet (90 metres) before descending to roof-top level. After performing various manoeuvres, it moved on. Twelve other people witnessed the same event, and despite the 'official' explanation – that it was in fact the planet Venus – the belief still lingers that it was a UFO. Especially since Carter, a trained scientist and former naval commander used to navigation by stars, was perfectly able to recognise Venus.

To help witnesses distinguish between what is and what is not a UFO, the term 'true UFO' is used for something that does not appear, after investigation, to be a case of mistaken identity. If the object seen turns out not to be a UFO but has a recognisable identity, then the term IFO – identified flying object – is used.

Ufologists divide UFO reports into several categories. But, more often than not, the reports tend to fall into two simple classes. These are often called 'low-definition' and 'medium-definition' experiences.

Low-definition experiences – 45 per cent of all UFO reports – involve seeing a light or a highly amorphous phenomenon with no distinctive shape. The colour of the light is not of great importance. In most cases it is white, but there are many different coloured light sources that can be seen, and the presence of thin cloud or smoke in the atmosphere can subtly alter what is seen. If you see an unidentified light in the sky there are a number of things you can do.

First, note whether the light remains stationary or if it moves. If stationary, the chances are that it is a star or planet. Stars and planets are among the most common sources of UFO misidentification. Of course they are not really stationary, but their motion is so slow relative to an observer that it is not usually noticed except over a period of hours. This is an excellent tell-tale sign. If a light is visible in the night sky for over an hour or more, and hardly moves at all, then it is probably a star. You can check by looking at a map showing the positions of stars and planets in the night sky for that time of year.

Venus is a common source of misidentification. It is the brightest object in the night sky and at certain times of the year is very close to Earth. It can be seen even in daylight, as a bright white speck, if one

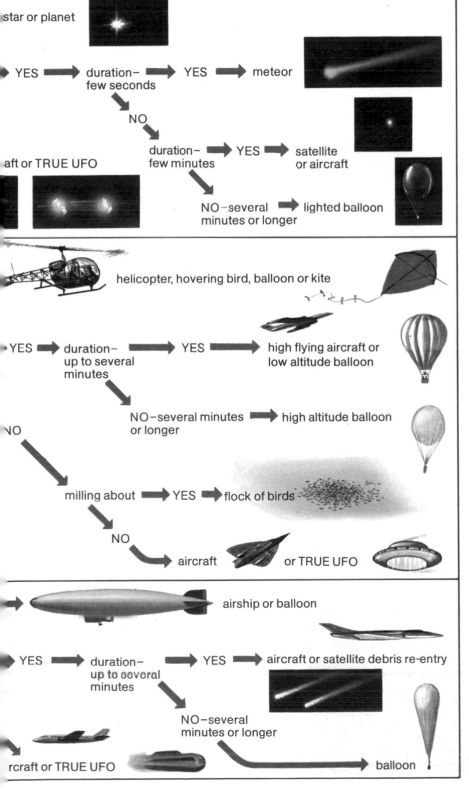

computer-programmed message. The aircraft is built to fly very slowly so that the message can be read. But if the lights are seen from an angle, very weird effects can result.

Aircraft are, of course, highly manoeuvrable, and helicopters even more so. Consequently, not only might they be seen as lights on a smooth flightpath, they can also be seen to alter direction, slow down, and even stop in mid-flight. The wind can carry away the sound of an aircraft's engines, leaving only a silent light in the sky.

Most of these effects would be seen only at night. But there is one object that is often seen and misidentified as a UFO during the day – the balloon. Weather centres release balloons at regular intervals, either to test wind direction or to carry instruments high into the sky from where they radio meteorological information back to Earth. At high altitude a balloon will reflect sunlight from its shiny surface while floating across the sky.

knows where to look. But often there are good reasons why stars and planets are not immediately recognised for what they are. Optical illusion, for example, and the phenomenon known as 'autokinesis', which causes a star apparently to dart about erratically in the sky, are common causes of misidentification. Since stars do not normally dart about, this effect instils the belief that the light comes not from a star but from a UFO.

If the light does appear to move, the next question is whether it follows a smooth flightpath or whether it hovers or seems to change direction dramatically. A smooth flightpath can indicate one of several things. Precisely what it is can usually be determined by the length of time the light is seen. If it is of very short duration, it could be a meteor – particles of dust or debris from space burning up as they enter the Earth's atmosphere. Meteors tend to glow for a second or two, leaving a trail of light as they streak silently through the night sky.

Occasionally, the debris is a little larger than usual and takes longer to burn up. This leads to the phenomenon known as a bolide or fireball, a brilliant light visible for up to 10 seconds and accompanied by a rumbling or whooshing sound. Fireballs have been seen in daylight too, although this is fairly rare. Usually, sightings of fireballs are so spectacular that they are witnessed by dozens of people over a wide area. They are very similar, in fact, to satellite re-entry, another common cause of UFO misidentification.

Circling the Earth are hundreds of man-made satellites. Many are too small to be seen from the ground, but others are visible at night as points of light that may take several minutes to cross the sky. As satellites re-enter the Earth's atmosphere, they can present a spectacular sight. As the pieces burn away, they glow in several colours, leaving a trail of lights through the upper atmosphere, which can take several minutes

Above left: an irregular, unearthly shape silhouetted against the sun can be very difficult to recognise as a flight of helicopters

Left: the spectacular comet Ikeya-Seki, which was seen in late 1965. A surprising number of heavenly bodies – including stars and planets – are reported as UFOS

to disappear. A few parts may even survive and reach the ground, as happened to the American Skylab, for example, which landed in Western Australia in July 1979.

But by far the most common cause of UFO misidentification is aircraft. Since aircraft possess many different types of lighting, there are plenty of opportunities for strange effects. Bright searchlights may be used in front of the plane, visible from miles away. Seen heading towards you, such a light can appear stationary for a long time before bursting into colour as the aircraft's navigation lights come into view. Strobe lights, brilliant pulsating blue-white flashes, can also be misconstrued. In many countries, aircraft are employed for advertising by using electronic lights that flash out a

Top: the rare lenticular cloud formation, which has the characteristic shape of a 'flying saucer'

Above: a high-flying kite, glinting in the sunlight with its control wires invisible, can take on the appearance of a typical UFO

Right: this research balloon was sent up 130,000 feet (40,000 metres) to investigate cosmic rays. Even experienced airmen have failed to recognise craft like this in flight

From the ground, the silvery dot drifting across the sky may be seen as a round or conical shape.

Medium-definition experiences are those that involve the clear perception of a shape. Though they have been seen at night, they are more commonly seen in daytime. They account for a further 35 per cent of all UFO cases and, as with low-definition experiences, the most important criterion is motion. A clearly defined shape that hovers for some time is unlikely to be an aircraft, although it could be a helicopter too distant to be heard.

Airships, tend also to be a common cause of misidentification. Under certain conditions their shape could be mistaken for a cigar-shaped UFO, hovering or slowly moving across the sky. Alternatively, as already mentioned, the object could be a balloon. Kites are another possible explanation. Seen at a distance, the controlling cord of a kite may not be visible and its irregular shape could easily be taken to be a UFO.

In most cases the object believed to be a UFO is seen moving in a constant direction at varying speeds. Again, this could well be an aircraft. In strong sunlight, for example, an aeroplane's wings and tailplane can be obscured leaving just a metallic body or cylinder visible. Though really the fuselage, it can look like a UFO. Even clouds have been mistaken for UFOs. A certain type of cloud, known as lenticular, looks like a structured disc. Though uncommon, its slow movement has fooled more than one observer.

Flocks of birds have also caused confusion. In daylight, the reflective underbellies of certain species can shine in sunlight and be seen as white ovals, obscuring all other detail. At night, it is even possible for street lighting to be reflected, creating different coloured oval shapes according to the type of lighting used.

Inevitably it has not been possible to list

every conceivable cause of misidentification. The figures issued by NUFON (the Northern UFO Network) contain 29 broad categories (see diagram) and there are known to be over 100 possible causes of misidentification that have occurred at some time or another.

Both case studies mentioned at the beginning of this article are quite typical of reported UFO sightings. Yet it is unlikely that the objects seen were UFOs. What Captain Mantell encountered was probably one of the 100-foot (30.5-metre) 'skyhook' balloons being secretly tested in the area at the time by the US Navy. These balloons were not known to Air Force officers, and although this was the probable identity of Mantell's UFO, the case has never been conclusively proven. Certainly the 'official' explanation that what observers on the ground saw was the planet Venus is not convincing.

As for the case of the Hertfordshire policemen, it was subsequently discovered that a

Russian booster-rocket re-entered the Earth's atmosphere that night. Its decay orbit took it over northern Europe and it was this that many witnesses mistook for a UFO. The New Zealand film was not connected to the Hertfordshire incident at all. And while there are still those who say that what the two policemen saw was a true UFO, most accept the 'official' explanation. This, of course, is not to say that all cases of UFO spotting turn out, after investigation, to be cases of Identified Flying Objects.

If none of the explanations outlined here seem to apply to the reported sighting then it is likely that the object you have seen is a true UFO.

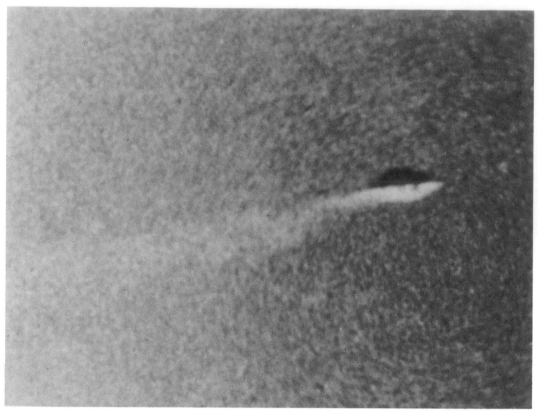

Left: a typical daylight disc. Note the unusual feature – an apparent trail of smoke streaming behind it

Below: the phenomenon known as an 'airglow' – luminescence of the sky at night. Odd enough to be taken for a UFO, it is actually caused by atoms in the upper atmosphere releasing energy that they have absorbed from solar radiation

Making a UFO report

If you saw an unidentified flying object, what would you do – and whom should you tell about your sighting? Official bodies often lack the resources to follow up UFO reports, but there are steps you can take yourself, and specialist organisations to contact in the event of a sighting

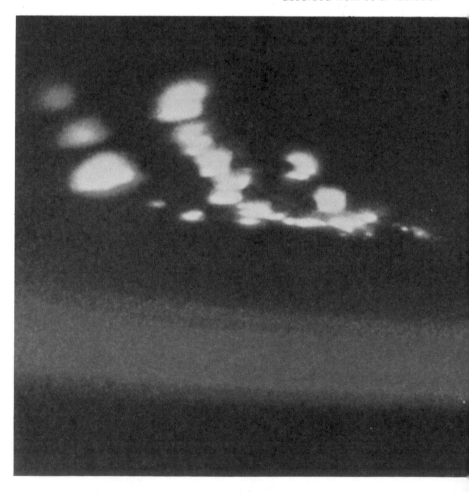

IN JULY 1978 a middle-aged couple in Manchester, England, saw a brilliant red cogwheel float across the sky. They thought they had seen a UFO. Not knowing anything about the subject they wrote to Patrick Moore, the astronomer, whose programmes they had watched on television. Perhaps they did not express themselves fully and Patrick Moore, who is neither a ufologist nor believes in UFOS, didn't ask them the right questions. He advised them that what they had seen was probably a meteor, albeit a spectacular one. The couple thought no more of the matter until, six months later, they happened to watch a programme in which a well-known UFO investigator appeared.

They contacted her and related their story. Whatever it was they had seen it was clear that it was not a meteor. It was too large to have been a meteor, and was seen in daylight for several minutes. (Meteors remain visible for only a few seconds.) What they had experienced, in fact, was an impressive close encounter of the first kind. It was only by chance that their valuable eyewitness report had not been lost forever.

Two years earlier, just a few miles from this sighting, Detective Sergeant Norman Collinson of the Manchester police force was returning from duty in the early hours of the morning when he saw a strange white disc in the sky. Naturally he reported his sighting to what he believed to be the 'proper authorities' and waited for a reply, if not an explanation. He was told by his superiors to whom he had reported the incident that his

phenomenon you have seen. It could, after all, be an IFO, an Identified Flying Object.

Another important step to take is to make notes about the environment and the area in which the sighting is made. Factors such as the barking of dogs or the sudden silence of birds may be significant. Of course, if you have a camera within reach, use it! It is surprising how many people who are perfectly equipped to take photographs are so overwhelmed by what they have seen that they fail to do so. If it is dark, and there is a controlled shutter speed on your camera, set it for a reasonably long exposure – probably

Right: many UFO reports describe craft that are much more complex than a simple, featureless 'flying saucer'. This drawing shows a number of details that crop up in sighting after sighting – but how many would you remember if this UFO flashed by at high speed? Try drawing it from memory in 24 hours' time and check how much you have recalled accurately

account would be passed on to the Ministry of Defence. But, despite several attempts to get an answer, Norman heard no more. Frustrated by the Ministry, he contacted his local university, but received only noncommittal replies to his questioning. When he asked for the address of the local UFO group, for example, he was told, 'Oh . . . you don't want to bother with them.'

But with persistence, Norman did contact such a group. Not only was his case a valuable addition to the evidence for UFOs, but Norman became a keen UFO investigator himself.

Both these cases illustrate the importance of what can happen after someone has sighted a true UFO. Whom to contact is very important. As both these cases show, it is not always easy to find out who is the right person to contact. If you have seen something strange in the sky that seems to pass all the tests outlined in the previous chapter, what should you do?

If you believe that what you have seen might be a true UFO, it is important to try to find corroborative witnesses. It is not, however, advisable to knock on people's front doors – some people may not take too kindly to your intrusion. This does not mean that you should not try to call the attention of anyone close by. Their presence will add weight to your sighting, or they may be able to provide some other explanation of the

about one second. This offers a much better chance of recording what may be a relatively dim phenomenon, even if it appears to the eye to be reasonably bright.

If you are in a car switch on the ignition and if you have one, the radio. There are enough stories to support the belief that some UFO phenomena can cause interference with electrical systems. Such evidence can be extremely important, so it is a point well worth remembering.

As you watch the thing in the sky try a couple of quick experiments. Move your head from side to side and watch what happens to the UFO. Very probably nothing will, but at least you will be able to eliminate one claim commonly made by disbelievers. This is that pieces of dead matter in the eye's optical system, known as floaters, are often taken to be UFOs. If a floater is the cause, the 'UFO' will move as your eyes move.

Secondly, try *willing* the UFO in a particular direction! This may sound ridiculous, but there is a school of thought that says UFOs are related to psychic phenomena. If this is so, then it should be possible for a witness to exert some degree of control over them. Interesting evidence may conceivably emerge from this exercise.

UFO encounters rarely last for a long time and there is unlikely to be the opportunity to telephone anyone while the object is still in view. Time is better spent taking in as much

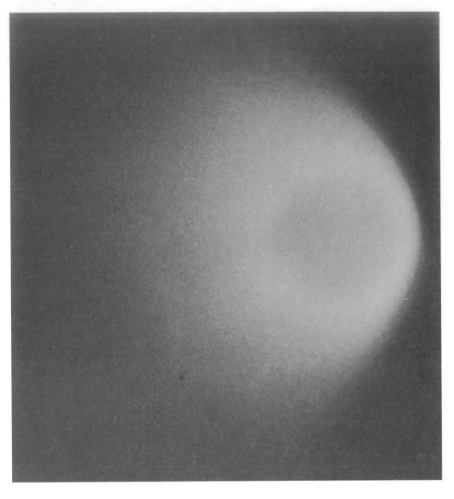

story, but in most countries, with the exception of France and the USA, where certain official procedures exist, there will be little they can do.

In some cases the police may refer the matter to the Defence Ministry. But as often as not the sighting will get no further than your local police station. Unfortunately, this is inevitable. The police force have many tasks to perform and experience has taught them that most UFO reports are not really very important. Consequently, they tend to be given a low priority. But the police should be contacted if you think that the object you have seen has landed. Their presence at the scene of the landing would provide very valuable corroboration. Otherwise, you are probably advised not to waste their time.

Another agency you may think of notifying is the local airfield, either civil or military. As with the police, there is little they can do or are prepared to do unless it seems to them that your report justifies calling in a defence establishment. Airport staff may be able to tell you if any aircraft were in the area at the time of your sighting, but it is not advisable to ask them if they read anything unusual on their radar. A denial might mean that they genuinely had not, or it could be that they had, but for some reason were not willing to tell you. The matter, for example, might already have been passed on to the Defence Ministry, who would want to make their own investigation.

Above: this weird light in the night is a barium cloud, launched into the upper atmosphere as part of an investigation of the Earth's electrical and magnetic fields conducted by NASA during the early 1970s. While bodies like NASA tend to deny the existence of UFOS, they can help identify unusual but explicable phenomena in the skies

Right: detailed forms like these are used by UFO organisations to record every aspect of a sighting

detail of the object as possible. This is a skill that improves with practice. Look at the picture of the UFO on the previous page for a minute. The next day, try drawing it from memory in as much detail as possible, without cheating by looking at the original. Try the same experiment with other UFO illustrations in The Age of the UFO, varying the length of time from as little as an hour to as long as a week between examining the picture and redrawing it. The importance of being able to recall in detail what you have seen will become apparent in the next step.

After the UFO has disappeared, do not discuss the details of what you have seen with anyone else who might be around. Simply exchange telephone numbers and addresses, just as you would if you were involved in a road accident. Agree with other witnesses on who is to report the sighting and to whom. Finally, advise all the witnesses that at the first possible opportunity they should draw the object you have all seen, and write out a statement describing the sighting. Each witness should do this independently, and not talk about it to anyone else until they have done so. It is surprising how easy it is to be unwittingly influenced by what others say .

To whom should you report your UFO sighting? There are several possibilities, and you should think carefully before acting. The most obvious choice is the police. They will probably regard it as their duty to check your

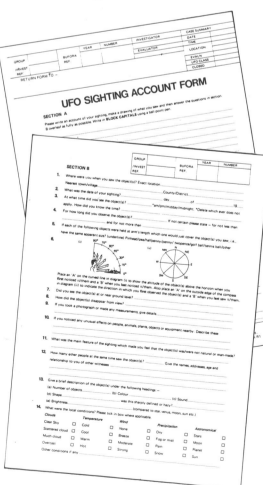

Test your powers of observation

When witnessing any strange or dramatic event, such as spotting a UFO, it is very important to be able to recall *exactly* what you saw. But try this experiment: look at the picture on the left for about 10 seconds. Stop reading this article while you try to remember what was in the picture. Draw it from memory. You will probably find that your attempt is far from being a perfect reproduction of the original.

You might think this experiment has little relevance to UFO spotting. Surely a UFO would present such an unusual sight that it would make an indelible impression on the memory? But experience with witnesses of accidents or crimes, which are not everyday observations for most people, does not bear this out. What we *see* is not always the same as what we are able to *recall* having seen.

After looking at the picture, men will probably be more likely to have a good recall of the young lady at the head of the bus queue. Women, on the other hand, are more likely to remember details of her clothing.

Our memories of what we have seen tend to be conditioned by what interests us personally. And what we remember also depends to some extent on past experiences – what we are used to seeing. People unfamiliar with London's black cabs or double-decker buses will probably have noticed them in the picture, but may not remember the time on the clock or the number of the bus – nor even have noticed them at all. Similarly there will be some who fail to spot the UFO on first glancing at the picture. How much did you take in?

As far as newspapers, radio and television are concerned, try to resist the temptation to approach them. The media will probably be interested only if they think they can use your story, and that may depend on whether it is quiet or busy in the newsroom, rather than on the credibility or intrinsic interest of your sighting.

The most sensible step to take if you have seen what you believe to be a UFO is to contact a UFO investigator as soon as possible. They are trained to help you and to record accurately the necessary information for scientific appraisal.

There are many kinds of UFO investigator and UFO investigation group. Some are motivated by an almost religious belief in UFOs and will be biased. Others may border on the eccentric, attracting cranks and frauds. Most, however, are serious-minded and are concerned with establishing the authenticity of your sighting. A list of reputable UFO organisations and their addresses is given at the end of this article. If your country is not included in the list, it does not necessarily mean that there is no serious UFO society there. Write to the British address. All the groups listed are associated with the international UFO magazine *Flying Saucer Review*, which is distributed in over 60 countries. Your letter will be forwarded to a local agency.

Each report is treated confidentially and almost all UFO groups use a standard report form. You will probably be asked to fill in one of these forms. You might also be asked if it is possible for a UFO investigator to come and see you at a time and place of your choosing.

Naturally, if you happen to come face to face with what you may think is a UFO, it is not always easy to remember exactly what to do. The oddness of the occasion may well lead you to panic. Yet it is always worth trying to remain calm and remembering the procedure outlined in this chapter. The more well-authenticated, well-documented, cases there are, the more will be discovered about these elusive intruders.

International UFO organisations
United Kingdom: UFO Investigators Network, 9 Whitethroat Walk, Birchwood, Warrington, Cheshire, England WA3 6PQ
North America: Center for UFO Studies, 1609 Sherman Avenue, Room 207, Evanston, Illinois, USA 60201
Australasia: Australian Centre for UFO Studies, PO Box 546, Gosford, New South Wales, Australia 2250

As round as saucers

Mysterious circles in isolated fields, with flattened surfaces that look as though something heavy had made the depression . . . can these really be UFO 'nests' – the traces of an alien landing – as many believe? Or is there an alternative explanation?

AS THE SPACE PROGRAMMES have revealed more and more about our Universe, hopes have faded that our neighbouring planets are inhabited. As a result, the theory that intelligent beings from other planets are visiting Earth in UFOs has been largely destroyed – and the very premise that UFOs have a physical existence is threatened. Is it any wonder, then, that supporters of the extra-terrestrial hypothesis for the origin of UFOs look up in interest when there is a discovery of a circle of flattened grass or crops in the middle of a field, with no easy or apparent explanation to hand?

Such physical ground traces of alleged UFOs have been reported all over the world. Called UFO 'nests', they take the form of a circular indentation or depression in the ground with a spiral effect left on the flattened surface. A typical 'nest' was discovered in 1966, in swampland at Tully, Queensland, Australia. The reeds, which had been swirled clockwise, looked 'as if they had been subjected to some terrific rotary force'. On a farm near Garrison, Iowa, USA, in 1969, an alleged UFO hovering over a soya bean field left a large circular area of seared plants. And in Pretoria, South Africa, in 1965 the traces took more dramatic form. After two police officers were involved in a close encounter

Top: the curious circle at Cley Hill, near Warminster in Wiltshire, which was discovered in the summer of 1982, and another ring in an adjacent field (above), found at about the same time. According to many UFO enthusiasts, such circles are evidence of UFO landings; meteorologists, however, offer a different, more earthly explanation

with a UFO that they said had landed on the road in front of them, they found a 6-foot (2-metre) circular area of the macadam road burned, with part of it caved in.

In the summer of 1980 three large circles of flattened corn were discovered by farmers at Westbury in Wiltshire, England. These rings were within a few hundred yards of each other, although they appeared at different times over a period of roughly 10 weeks. They were all found at the foot of the Westbury White Horse, a prehistoric hill figure cut into a very steep incline. It seemed signficant that Westbury is only a short distance from Warminster, which is one of Britain's most famous centres of UFO phenomena.

The British UFO investigation organisation PROBE decided to look into the Westbury circles and visited the site in August 1980. Unfortunately, according to the farm owner, the first of the three rings had been harvested and all traces of it were gone. But the other two yielded vital information.

Both rings were huge in diameter, one measuring about 60 feet (18 metres) across and the other slightly smaller. The corn in each ring was flattened in a clockwise spiral to a depth of 3 inches (7 centimetres), but the corn at the perimeters still stood 3½ feet (105 centimetres) high. The apparent centres of the circles – that is, where the spirals seemed to originate – were not at the true centres of the flattened areas.

The corn stalks themselves, although bent at ground level, were otherwise undamaged, giving the impression that they had somehow been bent by a great force of air pressure rather than by direct contact with a solid object. No scorch marks were present, and there were no odours, marks, stains or residue. The flattened corn was not discoloured and, except for being bent, was in the same condition as the untouched corn. No tracks led to or from the circles.

PROBE took samples of the soil and corn to Bristol University for testing, including spectroscopic analyses and radioactivity tests, but all of these proved negative. There

Below: one of the three circles at Westbury in Wiltshire, found in the summer of 1980. Members of the Bristol-based UFO research group PROBE were swiftly on the scene

Bottom: the three 'mystery' rings at Cheesefoot Head in Hampshire, which appeared in the summer of 1981

was no radiation present in the samples. They contained no deposits other than those expected in farmland soil treated chemically.

The investigators could find no immediate solution, but other people had ready answers. One hypothesis was that a helicopter had hovered over the fields so low that its downdraught had flattened the corn. This, however, had to be ruled out: a helicopter's downdraught would flatten the corn in a tapering effect, not a spiral. The favourite theory was that the circles were UFO 'nests'.

In the summer of 1981, while the mystery at Westbury Hill remained unsolved, more 'nests' appeared. The location this time was Cheesefoot Head, just east of Winchester in Hampshire. There were three circles in an approximate north-west to south-east direction. They seemed identical to those at Westbury, with features including a sharp cut-off at their perimeters and corn flattened

in clockwise spirals. They were also at the base of a hill. However, these circles were different in that there was one large one between two smaller ones, which were less than half its size. This large ring measured nearly 62 feet (19 metres) across, which put it in the same category as the Westbury circles.

During the year between the discovery of the Westbury and Cheesefoot Head circles, a theory was being worked on by the Tornado and Storm Research Organisation at Trowbridge in Wiltshire. Their idea was that the circles had been caused by fair-weather whirlwinds. Those who argued against this pointed out that, while it is known that whirlwinds have damaged large areas of crops on many occasions, such damage has always resulted in the crops being scattered about the fields in a random fashion. In the cases of Westbury and Cheesefoot Head, the damage was precise and restricted in area. It was thought inconceivable that a fair-weather whirlwind could cut a neat circle in the corn or that it would dissipate without wandering in the direction of the prevailing winds, as is its habit, which would scatter the crops.

Whirlwinds may start when a layer of fast-moving cool air traps a layer of moist, warm air beneath it, creating an imbalance. The warm air then rushes upwards at great speed, and air flowing in from the sides gives the updraughts a twist. This twist sets the vortex spinning and the whirlwind results. Whirlwinds are more likely to occur in a wind shear – that is, when there is a difference in wind speed over a small area with, for example, a light wind on the surface and a strong one higher up. This shear creates the turbulence that can sometimes trigger the spin in the vortex and produce the whirlwind. The wind shear itself is created at the boundary between advancing air masses and pre-existing air masses with different wind directions, humidity and temperature.

A whirlwind can last from a few seconds to a few minutes and can wreak havoc during this short span of time. Sizes vary greatly from about 3 feet (1 metre) to over 65 feet (20 metres). In open land, whirlwinds tend to travel either where the advancing wind takes them or along the boundary of the two air masses. The damage they do is characterised by trenches and untidy strewing of flattened crops, bearing no resemblance to a circle.

So how could the whirlwind theory apply to the 'mystery circles'?

Both sets of circles were located beneath steep hillsides with a concave shape, and this vital factor makes the theory plausible. Imagine that the retreating air mass is backed up against the hillside so that the advancing front is temporarily halted. Any whirlwind born at this moment will have to spend its force in this one place.

Triple whirlwinds

In the case of the Westbury circles, this theory would easily explain the appearance of three separate circles over the summer months of 1980, there having been many days that offered suitable weather conditions for whirlwinds. The Cheesefoot Head circles are more difficult to explain because they seemed so symmetrical: they were more or less equidistant from each other and their centres were aligned. But this can be accounted for if we infer that, after the first whirlwind died, the frontal boundary advanced further before another whirlwind was

born, and that this process was repeated once again, forming the three circles in a row.

It is not surprising that some have attacked this theory, pointing out that it takes coincidence too far. However, after the publication of the fair-weather whirlwind theory in *The PROBE Report* in late 1981, readers were asked to watch out for any mystery circles during the summer of 1982. And in August 1982 another one was discovered, at the base of Cley Hill 2 miles (4 kilometres) west of Warminster. Again PROBE investigators surveyed the area. The circle had been harvested, but was still clearly visible – and the investigators found another ring in an adjacent field. This second circle was sharply defined and measured approximately 50 feet (15 metres) in diameter. The close proximity of the circles to the steep face of Cley Hill gives strong support to the theory that the topography created the conditions for fixed whirlwinds, which made these new circles.

Discussions with the farmers engaged in harvesting at the time the circles appeared revealed that there had been four more circles carved out of the corn in the surrounding fields, although one of these was more oval in shape.

The fair-weather whirlwind hypothesis

Below right: how a stationary whirlwind might be born. In 1, a retreating air mass is displaced by an advancing one. A whirlwind may form if conditions of speed, temperature and humidity are right. Such a whirlwind would ordinarily be carried along by the advancing air. In 2, however, a stationary pocket of air is formed, trapped by the hillside. The newly produced whirlwind can be trapped here and, circling in one spot with great force, could easily form a circular depression in the ground – and this is the new explanation offered for the Westbury, Cheesefoot Head and Cley Hill 'mystery' circles

Below: a fair-weather whirlwind photographed in Essex in 1976

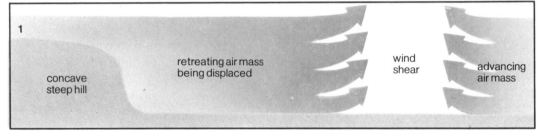

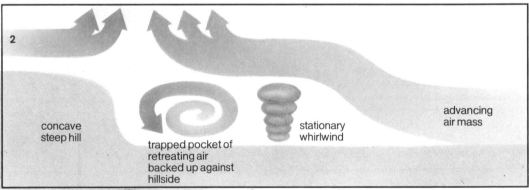

does not, of course, explain every alleged UFO 'nest' that has been reported, but it does serve to explain the 'mystery circles' that have so excited England's West Country. In Australia, too, many UFO 'nests' have been unearthed and it is interesting that the type of ring that has perplexed the Australian researchers the most is of the 'swirled and depressed crop' variety – like the Westbury, Cheesefoot Head and Cley Hill rings. Will investigators discover that fair-weather whirlwinds occur where alleged UFO 'nests' appear. Can it be that the whirlwind theory is the final answer to the UFO 'nest' enigma?

First catch your saucer

The study of UFOs is an increasingly complex business involving big money and sophisticated hardware. Modern investigators and the instruments they are using are fast turning science fiction into science fact

MOST UFO RESEARCH is carried out at second hand – following up what other people say they experienced. This means that ufologists often work with very nebulous material; it also means that sceptics, with a fair show of reason, can assert that the 'evidence' could be explained as either hallucination or mis-interpretation – or just plain lies.

So every ufologist hankers for a more direct contact with the subject of his research – something to dissect, measure or analyse. Best of all, of course, he would like a close encounter of his own; it frustrates him that the most exciting things seem always to happen to people who tend not to appreciate their good fortune. Why can't it be the chairman of the British UFO Research Association who has a close encounter? Why don't the aliens abduct famous ufologists such as Aimé Michel or Dr J. Allen Hynek, who are probably in the best position to evaluate such an experience? (Yet, if such eminent 'believers' were actually abducted, perhaps it would seem too good to be true.)

Failing such unlikely happenings, the ufologist would appreciate tangible evidence that could be analysed objectively: a crashed

A close encounter with a car's headlights? Probably not, though UFO sightings sometimes turn out to be the product of terrestrial rather than extra-terrestrial objects. This photograph taken in Montserrat, Spain, is only one of some 500 photographs, each recording similar aerial phenomena in the same region

'saucer' would be ideal, or even a few fragments of one. But, again, the phenomenon seems reluctant to oblige. So the ufologist has to lower his sights yet further and seek confirmation of human testimony through the use of monitoring instruments – such as radar – or photographs that contain easily recognisable points of reference and other useful data. This is one form of practical ufology.

The other form consists of testing hypotheses. If an analysis of UFO reports shows that strange objects are more likely to appear in one place rather than another, or at one time rather than another, or only under certain meteorological conditions, then these are things that can be tested. Similarly, if a witness reports that he has made contact with aliens who have provided information about themselves, this too can sometimes be tested. Some supposed alien entities give details of their planet of origin, as occurred in the case of the 'Ummites'. If astronomers were able to locate such a planet – where none had hitherto been known – this would be a significant verification, if not absolute proof, of the encounter.

Both approaches have been attempted, although to a very limited degree. The almost total lack of funding available means that most ufologists have to finance their own research; it is hardly surprising, therefore, that it is liable to be both on a small scale and intermittent compared with more orthodox scientific research.

Of course, it is far better to try to obtain evidence directly, rather than via witnesses. Not every ufologist is a reliable witness, but most will almost certainly be in a better position to judge what they see than the average man or woman in the street. In the early, optimistic days of ufology, simple skywatching was a favourite occupation, even among the most academic ufologists. In fact, in the 1950s there seemed to be so many UFOs about for it to make sense for those interested in the phenomenon to gather at a favourable location with cameras and any other monitoring equipment that could be mustered – and hope for the best.

In Britain one particular location has become associated with skywatching: the hills above Warminster in Wiltshire. Over the years, thousands of casual observers have spent nights on Cradle Hill. The results, however, have been ambiguous, to say the least. If there were ever any genuine phenomena, they rapidly became overshadowed by too many reports of malobserved helicopters, car headlights, even other observers' torches or cigarette lighters – to say nothing of deliberate hoaxes.

A welcoming committee

Even so, nothing at Warminster was ever quite as ridiculous as the *soirée d'observation* organised by the French Institut Mondial des Sciences Avancées in association with the noted science fiction author Jimmy Guieu in June 1982. The soirée was held in a ruined castle in Alsace where luminous phenomena had been reported. It was a curious affair. Over 50 people turned up despite pouring rain: the barbecue was a great success, a hypnotist on the staff of the institute performed spectacularly, and by midnight a good many bottles of wine had been drunk. And the phenomena? One of the participants said: 'The Ovnis [UFOs] did not come. And even if they had come, we would not have seen them for the early morning mist, nor heard them for the clink of bottles.'

Fortunately, not all skywatching is so puerile. Probably the most ambitious plan was Project Starlight International, set up by Ray Stanford in a rural area near Austin, Texas, USA. Starting in 1973 he and his team, who comprised a research facility of the Association for the Understanding of Man, gathered an impressive array of monitoring and communications equipment. This included a radar unit, perched on a tower from which it could scan the entire valley below, and a set of recording magnetometers that monitor and automatically record a wide range of anomalous events, including electrostatic effects, temperature changes, gravitational disturbances, barometric alterations, and even unusual sounds. There were also two devices for communicating with UFOs: one, the UFO Vector, employs a red laser

beam that can direct a signal containing up to $2\frac{1}{2}$ million bits – units of information – per second, in the form of voice or video signals, to any UFO in line of sight, and automatically records any response; the other is an array of 91 spotlights, arranged in a circle on the ground around a central light, that can be manipulated to form thousands of patterned signals. These are intended to communicate with UFOs in mathematical or other codes.

Then there is ARGUS – appropriately named after the watchman of classical myth – an acronym for 'automatic ring-up on geolocated UFO sightings', which means that when the monitors indicate that a UFO is in the area, they also alert the human observers, who then photograph the object. As the UFO moves out of the area, the monitors plot its course, alerting different observers on the ground. All the photographs are then computer-analysed to try to establish the UFO's distance, size and altitude.

Operation Starlight is a UFO observer's dream: equipment estimated as costing something like half a million dollars is clearly out of reach of most UFO organisations. But even so, what chance is there that UFOs will manifest in precisely the right place to be detected even by all this sophisticated instrumentation? Yet the project claims several impressive sightings. When Charles Hickson, one of the alleged abductees in the controversial and disputed Pascagoula case in October 1973, was visiting the facility, a large orange 'daylight disc' was reported. On 10 December 1975 another orange-golden object was sighted, and some 42

Two men whose mission is to identify the unidentifiable: Frenchman Jimmy Guieu (above) and American Ray Stanford (right), director of Project Starlight International. Stanford is shown with his latest gadget which, he says, will enable him to communicate with UFOs. The device is designed to transmit images to the spacecraft on a laser beam

Below: Arne Thomassen, one of the people involved with investigations in Hessdalen, Norway, sets up equipment preparatory to a long wait: UFOs do not always arrive on cue. One of Thomassen's colleagues on the UFO-Norge project thinks it fair to assume that 'they' are watching us watching them; perhaps this accounts for their shyness. But the long wait pays off when images like this (right) are captured on film. Taken by Thomassen in September 1982, the photograph shows an unidentified object suspended in the skies over Hessdalen – shortly before disappearing from sight

photographs taken, before it moved away. Some of the objects monitored have been shown to be natural in origin, but even negative results are an essential part of the operation – by providing data that can be analysed and, by a process of elimination, cases can be properly assessed. A case that might otherwise have been filed as a 'UFO' can, thanks to Project Starlight, be filmed and perhaps shown to be the planet Saturn (this actually occurred in 1974).

'This project is unique anywhere in the world,' claims Stanford. 'We are trying to gain evidence so that the scientific community will take this thing [ufology] seriously.' To judge by the project's files, Stanford has not had a very satisfactory return on his great investment in both time and equipment, but such an ambitious project at least calls for admiration and deserves to be successful if *any* practical approach is capable of elucidating the UFO riddle.

A totally different approach to skywatching has been adopted by Spanish ufologist Luis José Grifol of Barcelona. Since the mid

1970s, Grifol has been visiting the local mountain district of Montserrat, which he believes to be particularly favoured by UFOs because of its long cultural and religious tradition. Pious pilgrims and tourists alike are attracted to the spectacular region with its dramatically shaped rocks: perhaps, in the light of recent and well-informed speculation, it may be the geophysical character of Montserrat that attracts UFOs. But whatever the explanations, between 1977 and the end of 1982 Grifol had secured some 500 photographs of anomalous aerial phenomena in that region alone.

Grifol makes contact

Instead of relying on sophisticated instruments, Grifol believes that UFOs communicate telepathically with him. The crew members of the UFOs he has photographed are, he claims, 'space intelligences' who come from a planet located between the stars Bellatrix and Rigel, near Mintaka in the constellation of Orion. In August 1980, in the presence of 17 witnesses, Grifol asked his alien contacts for proof of their relationship, suggesting that they move their UFOs in response to his directions. They did so, he claims, over a period of 20 seconds.

Grifol alleges that to establish this kind of contact one has to be in a suitable mental and spiritual state, detached from mundane preoccupations and concerning oneself more with 'higher' matters. Unfortunately, such vague assertions are of little evidential value: most ufologists would have felt happier if Grifol's sightings had been confirmed on one of Starlight's instruments. Nonetheless, Grifol has his 500 remarkable photographs.

But Warminster and the hills of Spain are not the only areas noted for their UFOs. Inland from Trondheim in the central region

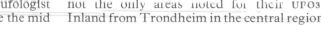

of Norway is the thinly populated district of Hessdalen. There is no obvious reason why it should be specially favoured by UFOs: yet since December 1981 there has been a continuous flow of reports from the area. This kind of concentration of 'visits' is rare enough in any case; that they were sustained over so long a period gave Norway's ufologists a unique opportunity for observation. However, it is difficult to see just why the UFOs chose Hessdalen, as Arne Thomassen comments:

Why they [UFOs] show such seemingly great interest in the unpopulated mountain valleys in central Norway is difficult to figure out. There is very little in this area to spy on, and our military capability is unlikely to be of any particular interest to such doubtless highly advanced entities. The possibility that they are visiting some selected people or programming their minds seems unlikely since Hessdalen is very thinly populated. The UFOs mostly move through valleys where no people live at all.

A celebrated UFO

This eyewitness account is typical of the reports received by UFO-Norge. Bjarne Lillevold, a miner, describes what he saw on 24 September 1982:

As I was on my way home from work, I and a colleague saw a light against the mountains near Hessdalen. We drove about 5 kilometres [3 miles], and then the object began to descend towards the forest, near Ålen. When we ourselves reached Ålen, the object was hovering close to the trees. My companion, who hadn't seen the celebrated UFO of Hessdalen before, was very excited by the sight. We drove to the centre of Ålen, and then saw a second object which came from the direction of Hessdalen and halted below the other. I then drove on my moped to Hessdalskjølen, where I saw an object near a cottage. At first I thought the cottage itself was on fire, but then I saw it was something else, which looked like an upside-down Christmas tree and bigger than the cottage beside it. It was about 4 metres [13 feet] above the hill, and had a red light on it which blinked: there also seemed to be a curious 'blanket' over the whole thing. The object was moving up and down like a yo-yo for about twenty minutes; when it was close to the ground the light faded, but at the height of the manoeuvre it was so bright that I could not look at it for long. When the light was near the ground I could see through it as though it was made of glass. . . .

It is interesting that in many respects Lillevold's experience resembles the famous Cash-Landrum sighting in Huffman, Texas,

One coloured blob may not be convincing enough proof of the existence of UFOs but when the image has been recorded hundreds of times by various witnesses using different equipment then the evidence becomes difficult to ignore. Here is one example of the many unidentified objects seen over Montserrat (right) and similar phenomena recorded over Hessdalen (below right)

Below: the Spanish ufologist Luis José Grifol on site in Montserrat. He eschews the use of sophisticated equipment

which also involved a large, bright object alternately rising and falling, with a light that varied in intensity.

The Norwegian investigators were determined to do more than passively record such accounts, and to make the most of the opportunity for practical research. As Leif Havik of UFO-Norge comments, 'We should have stayed for at least a month to get any results. However, with very few active members, with inadequate resources and with no support from anybody at all, we have done our best.' Armed with what they could raise in the way of magnetic detectors, spectrum analysers and field strength detectors, infrared cameras and so on, they made several expeditions into the rugged terrain of Hessdalen. But, although the instrumental results were disappointing, a great many photographs of anomalous phenomena were taken by seven different photographers, all of which present much the same kind of image. Most appear to be little more than vaguely shaped blobs of various colours, but there is

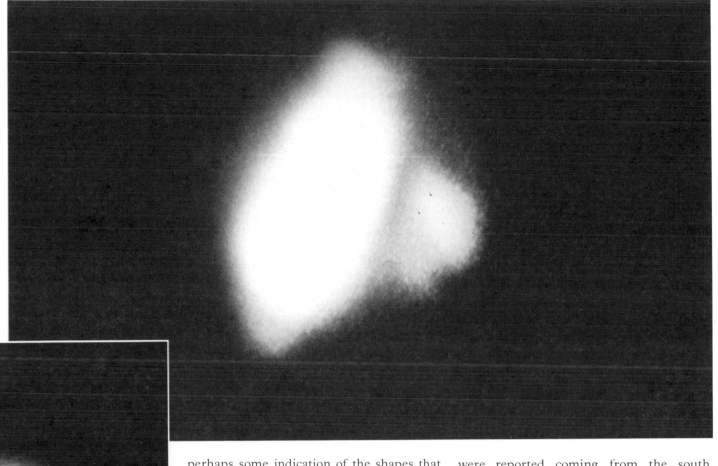

perhaps some indication of the shapes that witnesses have reported, ranging from simple rectangles to the classic disc shapes. Consistent patterns of movement have also been recorded – so this research may well prove to be of great significance.

The Norwegian investigators hope that they will at least secure sufficient evidence to convince others, who have more means at their disposal, that there is a phenomenon worth studying. Requests for help or information to the Norwegian Air Force have been of no avail; they claim that because nothing criminal has been reported, such matters are outside their jurisdiction. UFO-Norge has sought to establish that UFOs are, indeed, potentially criminal, in that they are violating Norwegian airspace, but the officials remain unconvinced.

Date, time and direction

Nevertheless, the evidence for the existence of UFOs is mounting, and with it the case for investigation. Analysis of UFO-Norge data is revealing some patterns in behaviour: the time of day affects the number of sightings and so, for no reason yet apparent, does the date – the majority of sightings seem to occur between the 15th and the 25th day of the month. Another curious fact is that twice as many UFOs have been reported travelling from south to north as vice versa. This was true also of the celebrated 'ghost rockets' that flew over Norway and other Scandinavian countries in 1946, when all but a handful

were reported coming from the south, prompting theorists to suppose that they were some kind of military device originating from the former Nazi missile sites at Peenemünde – although this was almost certainly not the case.

There is another aspect of the Hessdalen sightings that is even more disconcerting, although in this case Leif Havik can offer an explanation. He, like Grifol in Spain, believes that UFOs – or those who control them – are well aware of the fact that they are being watched and investigated. That UFOs seem to disappear just as Havik is about to record their presence may bear this out:

> The main reason why I think they are under some kind of control is this: five times I have seen a UFO just when I have arrived on the mountain, before I had time to get my camera. On all five occasions, I was less than 100 metres [325 feet] from the observation point I had selected.

In fact, anecdotes of such elusiveness are common – and not only in ufology: observers at Loch Ness claim a similar 'bloody-mindedness' on the part of their quarry. However, there is some persuasive evidence that UFOs are indeed acting in response to the activity of human observers. And on some occasions, this phenomenon is recorded by monitoring instruments.

Watching us, watching them

When Harley Rutledge set out on a routine UFO investigation he did not reckon on it taking seven years to complete. Nor was he to know that his final report would be a landmark in UFO research and his techniques were to influence other important projects

'PRACTICAL UFOLOGY' is, for many, a contradiction in terms. Faced with the elusive and often paradoxical nature of the evidence, they have concluded that there is no possible material explanation for the phenomenon and instead tend to regard the UFO as a psychological or psychic manifestation.

But French-born ufologist Jacques Vallée is just one of the more advanced thinkers among ufologists who thinks the subject is much more complex. In a paper delivered to the American Institute of Aeronautics and Astronautics in 1975, he declared: 'The UFO phenomenon is the product of a technology that integrates physical and psychic phenomena.' If this is so then, since orthodox science is better equipped to cope with physical than with psychic material, it might well be best to concentrate primarily on investigating the material aspect.

It was in just such a matter-of-fact frame of mind that Harley Rutledge embarked on what probably ranks as the most important piece of practical ufology yet carried out. It began in 1973 when, as professor of physics

at Southeast Missouri State University at Cape Girardeau, he was confronted with an intriguing challenge. Near the town of Piedmont, some 50 miles (80 kilometres) from Cape Girardeau, curious lights had been seen on many occasions by many witnesses, in circumstances that seemed to defy any conventional explanation. As a scientist, he accepted the challenge to explain the phenomena – and he collected a team of specialists in various fields, gathered whatever monitoring and recording instruments he could find, and set off for the site in the expectation that two or three weekends of expert observation should suffice.

But it was not until seven years later that the report on the investigation was published: and it was the result of nearly 2000 man-hours of observation by himself and his team of colleagues. During that period they observed 178 UFOs, 157 of which were recorded on their monitoring instruments. They combined visual observation and photographic records with radar and other forms of detection that were set up in separate locations for simultaneous monitoring.

The great majority of the phenomena observed by Rutledge's team were lights in the sky, generally at night, with little or no discernible shape. There has been an increasing tendency among ufologists to disregard this type of sighting unless there is very good circumstantial evidence surrounding it, because there is very little one can deduce from a blob of light. Besides, lights

The sky at night over Piedmont (below) and Cape Girardeau (bottom). It was phenomena such as these that in 1973 started Harley Rutledge on his studies. Until then researchers were beginning to grow disenchanted with lights in the sky as evidence of UFO activity, since such sightings were open to many interpretations. But Project Investigation was to use monitoring techniques that proved that images, like the two shown here, were very definitely not the product of natural phenomena

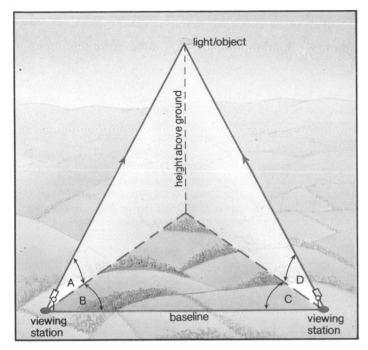

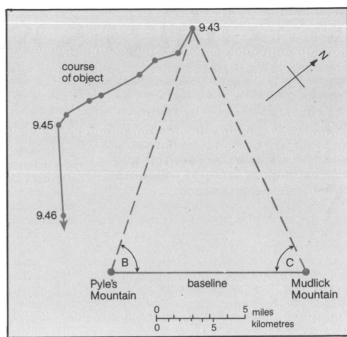

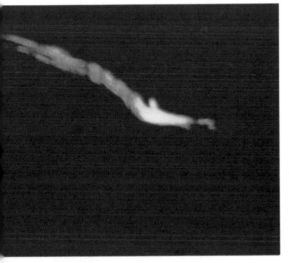

are the most easily misinterpreted of all visual phenomena: whereas a domed disc with portholes must be either a 'nuts and bolts' craft or an illusion of some kind, a light-blob can be anything from a car headlamp to a meteorite, a satellite or even light reflected off a flock of birds. Rutledge's highly practical approach, concerned only with the *facts* of the sightings, quickly eliminated any such obvious causes of misidentification. Using the surveyors' technique of triangulation, the precise location and course of the objects could be established and plotted, which meant that their size, altitude and speed could also be accurately calculated.

Here is a typical example of the observations made by Rutledge's team, a sighting recorded on 25 May 1973. That evening, two field units had been set up, one on Pyle's Mountain ('P') and the other on a fire tower on Mudlick Mountain ('M') some 11 miles (18 kilometres) distant; these two observation points were equipped with monitoring

Above left: the principles of triangulation, which can be used to plot an object's height and distance from the ground. To make the calculation the vertical angles (A and D) and the horizontal angles (B and C) must be measured simultaneously from two points on the ground a known distance apart (baseline)

Above right: a plan view of the course of a UFO seen on 25 May 1973, as it was plotted by Project Investigation. At 9.43 p.m. researchers in the observation posts at Pyle's Mountain and Mudlick Mountain, 11 miles (18 kilometres) apart, had the object in view. Using triangulation, they were able to measure the height and the distance of the UFO and so pinpoint its position. Between 9.43 and 9.46, nine such points were located at 15-second intervals

instruments, and were in radio contact with each other.

At 9.37 p.m. the four observers at P reported a light towards the west. The observers at M immediately confirmed it, and at once initiated the measuring of bearings and altitudes, which were transmitted every 15 seconds, at the same time being recorded on video tape.

At 9.42 P reported the object as 'moving across the sky rather slowly; it is fairly bright, say a first-magnitude star. It is yellowish-orange in colour.' M reported, 'We have it in full view now.'

By 9.43, with both posts obtaining a clear view of the object, its precise location was calculated by triangulation. Between 9.43 and 9.46, nine such points were located at 15-second intervals; one point was missed because of radio interference, but P confirmed that the object was still on its apparent course.

Lost and found

At 9.46 M lost sight of the object; at 9.48 and 9.50 P had two further observations, but in the absence of simultaneous observations from M these could be considered accurate only as regards direction.

The result of this series of matched observations was that the object was plotted precisely over an erratic course of more than 15 miles (25 kilometres) and less precisely over a considerably greater distance. Analysis of this data showed that the object was travelling initially at about 310 miles per hour (500 km/h), accelerating after changing its course to about 325 miles per hour (523 km/h). While this gives little positive information about the nature of the phenomenon, it eliminates many possible explanations. No car could be at such an altitude; no bird could fly that fast; no satellite could fly so low; no meteorite could change its course in such a way, and so on.

By such means, Project Investigation has established beyond question the reality of the phenomenon and invalidates most, if not all, naturalistic explanations. Its instrumental record provides a solid basis for future research. But Rutledge's observations also established that the objects seemed to respond specifically to the actions of the observers. On at least 80 occasions, he registered an apparent synchronicity between something connected with the observers, and the objects. But it was not a consistent pattern of behaviour – sometimes the objects would respond in one way, sometimes in another. At the same time, however, such synchronicity occurred too often to be easily dismissed as coincidence.

Watching – or being watched?
The events in themselves were trivial. For example, on 21 June 1973 Rutledge pointed his flashlight up at a stationary light; at once it began to move, seemingly careful to avoid the observation post by veering away. On 20 June 1976, he was pointing at what seemed to be a new star and it immediately 'went out'. On several occasions 'stars' halted, or began to move, or changed course when observation began, a camera was aimed, or car headlights came on or off. There were even cases in which the object seemed to be responding to the voices of the observers – at a distance of 2 miles (3 kilometres) or more – to radio messages between observation posts, and even to the thoughts of the observers (although this, of course, cannot be established scientifically, and so could be dismissed as unacceptably subjective). But such behaviour at least justifies the hypothesis that the objects are possessed of a certain degree of intelligence, or are controlled by intelligent beings. It also seems to indicate that they possess very sophisticated means of registering the actions of observers who were, of course, at ground level – mostly in the darkness – and not easily detectable from the air.

Perhaps it would be inadvisable to draw premature conclusions from the results of Rutledge's project, but no one has done more to establish the physical reality of the UFO phenomenon.

Once hard facts have been established, they can be used as a basis for hypotheses that can be tested; and this is the second form that practical ufology can usefully take. But because the facts of ufology are themselves so much in dispute, the opportunities for testing hypotheses are much more limited: yet it is surprising how often ufologists fail even to take the most obvious practical steps. In *The Welsh triangle* (1979), investigator Peter Paget claimed that Stack Rock, in Dyfed, was the site of a secret UFO base. Yet, even though he was researching in the area, he

Below: Harley Rutledge with his portable battery-operated oscilloscope and spectrum analyser

Bottom: workers on Project Investigation set up their equipment in a gesture equivalent to putting out the 'welcome' mat. Despite the preparations, UFOs or those who control them still seem to play hard to get. Harley Rutledge and his team noted that on occasions the objects appeared deliberately to move out of the line of vision when the monitoring devices were switched on

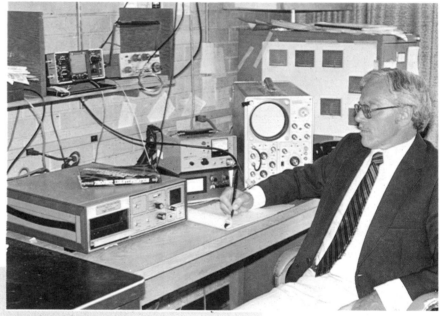

never took the step of visiting the island itself to establish the truth. If his claim had been correct, he would, of course, have made one of the most sensational discoveries in the history of the world – and would have been able to live in comfort for the rest of his days on the proceeds. Instead it was a BBC television reporter, Brynmor Williams, who chartered a boat to visit Stack Rock and see if he could find a UFO base there. He found none.

Those who put forward sensational claims should be able to back them with some kind of evidence. Circular areas of flattened crops, and other curious physical traces, have often been claimed as evidence of saucer landings: the PROBE group of Bristol took a cold look at such claims (see page 20) with fascinating results. The same group, in 1981, decided to test their theories about a 'UFO' sighting at Warminster – that, they felt, sounded suspiciously as though it might have been a balloon. They did not doubt the sincerity of the witness, feeling that she had, indeed, seen an unidentified object flying across her field

Below: Alvin Lawson with Judy Kendall – one of the people who claim to have been taken on board a UFO. She is one of the few abductees who has not become a guru to the movement and claimed other sightings

Bottom: is it an alien spacecraft? Is it a UFO? No, it's a balloon floating in the skies over Warminster. The photograph was taken by the PROBE group during an experiment to prove that a witness's UFO sighting had in fact been a balloon

they play an important part in eliminating false data from the files, enabling the 'true' phenomenon to be seen more clearly.

But the most dramatic experiment in practical ufology was almost certainly that conducted by the psychologist Professor Alvin Lawson of California. His comparison of 'imaginary abductees' with persons who claim to have been abducted on board UFOs relates only to a limited part of the UFO phenomenon, of course, but he and his colleagues have established that ordinary people, with little knowledge of the UFO phenomenon, are capable – in the hypnotic state – of fabricating an imaginary abduction event that matches, in extraordinary detail, the stories told by people who claim actually to have been abducted. Certainly at first sight this tends to support the supposition that the 'real' abductees are simply fantasising; but this is by no means an obvious conclusion.

Supporting the view that the 'real' accounts are what they claim to be is, Lawson noted, the fact that there were marked differences in the ways the two classes of subject told their stories. The descriptions of their alleged abductions were very similar, but the 'real' witnesses seemed to have a greater emotional stake in their story. Of course this, too, may be accounted for in psychological terms; clearly, the way lies open for much further research, such as Lawson's later exploration of the possibility that abduction stories reflect memories of birth traumas.

The evidence Lawson has gathered for this hypothesis is very persuasive but, as he himself is the first to insist, it remains nothing but a hypothesis, inviting other ufologists to seek to establish or refute its validity. Lawson's great achievement has been to demonstrate that some, at least, of the mass of ufological data can be put to the test. And it is this approach that will almost certainly solve the UFO riddle – one day.

of vision, as she described. But the speed, direction and flight characteristics were such that a natural explanation seemed possible.

So a balloon was obtained, and 'flown' – on a thread – along a course similar to that of the alleged UFO: the witness was invited to watch, and photographs were taken. The witness agreed that what she could now see was probably what she had originally seen. A futher test in which the balloon was released – and duly lost – confirmed this opinion, and the conclusion was that 'the investigation and resultant tests showed that the UFO as reported resembled, behaved like – and most probably was – a silver/red plastic/aluminium laminate balloon, released some time before the sighting from a location west of Warminster.'

Such debunking operations may not be the most gratifying aspect of ufology, but

UFOs: the case for a cover up

The US government has long denied any interest in UFOs, yet keeps thousands of UFO documents on the secret list. When UFO researchers unmasked this secrecy, they revealed a bizarre CIA plot to mislead the public

UFO RESEARCHERS HAVE long maintained that their governments know more about the UFO phenomenon than they officially admit. One reason for thinking this has been the unfailingly sceptical attitude taken by government officials when questioned about any particular sighting – even the best-documented reports are greeted with cries of 'weather balloons' or 'the planet Venus seen under unusual conditions'. Another cause for suspicion has been the peculiar interest that UFOs take in military establishments from time to time. Some, at least, of the malevolent and infamous men in black may have been genuine government agents, and the thought may linger in many ufologists' minds that the MIB's elusive nature is only the smoke of folklore behind which lurks the sinister fire of clandestine operations. In the

An unidentified flying object skims over the desert outside Phoenix, Arizona, on 12 September 1972. Checked by computerised enhancement techniques, the photograph has been declared genuine by Ground Saucer Watch. Despite evidence like this, secret government agencies like the CIA (inset: the agency's official seal) deny the existence of UFOs

United States the idea of a deliberate government attack on ufology was confirmed for many by the publication in 1969 of the Condon Report, widely regarded as at best complacent or at worst wilfully ignorant.

Documents obtained by Ground Saucer Watch (GSW) from the United States government under the Freedom of Information Act now confirm that there has indeed been a cover up – right from the start of the modern UFO era in the late 1940s. But what is revealed by the documents is not that there is a worldwide plot to hide the true nature of UFOs – involving secret contact with extraterrestrials or some gruesome conspiracy against humanity, or some other outlandish suggestion. What is indicated, rather, is that the US government wishes to maintain a certain public *attitude* toward UFOs.

This atmosphere of doubt and derision has been created in a number of ways. Anyone can offer more or less plausible explanations for a UFO sighting: bright planets, unusual atmospheric conditions, meteorites, aircraft and so on. This approach

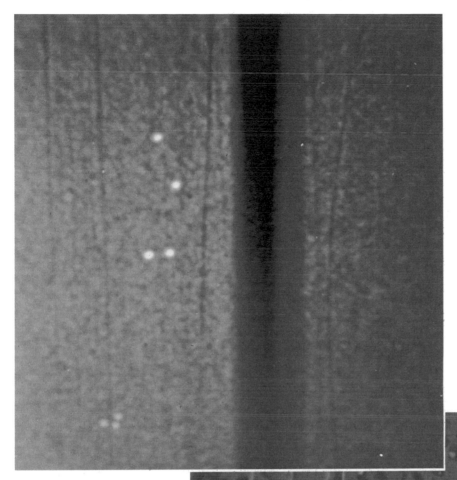

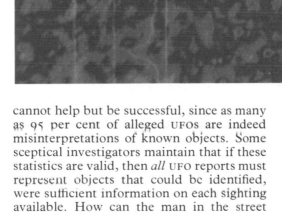

Above: a still from the film shot by Delbert C. Newhouse on 2 July 1952, 7 miles (11 kilometres) north of Tremonton, Utah, USA. Newhouse saw 'gunmetal-coloured objects shaped like two saucers, one inverted on top of the other' near the eastern horizon. Mystified, he shot some 16-millimetre film. A few frames have been released, but many more remain in CIA hands. Ground Saucer Watch analysed the available frames with a range of techniques that included colour contrasting (right) – which demonstrated that the objects were indeed solid. Sceptics have claimed the UFOs were birds or planes but computerised images of these at comparable distances (overleaf centre: a bird; overleaf bottom: a plane) show different characteristics of shape, reflectivity and density. GSW concluded that the images represented craft about 50 feet (15 metres) in diameter and 5 to 7 miles (8 to 11 kilometres) distant

are easily accepted. The few researchers who believed that they saw through the screen of official denials were easily dismissed as mavericks or cranks. There was, according to the official line, nothing to research. The government knew about everything there was to be seen in the sky.

But perhaps the cover up was so successful because no one could prove it was going on. There was no hard evidence to back the claim that the government was not being completely honest with the public.

And if the government knows so much, why haven't ex-employees come forward with their stories – revelations far more explosive, potentially, than any political scandal. Yet fewer than a dozen such individuals have come forward.

Despite all this, one's suspicions remain. Over the years GSW has encountered numerous incidents that showed every sign of direct or indirect government interference. Photographs went missing. Ground markings were ploughed under. Occasional witnesses talked about visits from military or intelligence officers who wanted to suppress the story of their UFO encounter. Too many cases came to an abrupt halt because some of the evidence

cannot help but be successful, since as many as 95 per cent of alleged UFOs are indeed misinterpretations of known objects. Some sceptical investigators maintain that if these statistics are valid, then *all* UFO reports must represent objects that could be identified, were sufficient information on each sighting available. How can the man in the street argue with logic like that?

The debunking campaign has been successful too because well-known military or government figures have weighed in against the UFO. Most people have an automatic respect for public figures, whose statements

was missing, making it impossible to reach a firm conclusion.

Largely at the insistence of Todd Zechel, GSW's director of research (and himself an ex-member of the intelligence community), it was decided to attack the issue head on – and approach the government directly. In the first place, GSW questioned the US Air Force – with predictable results. Typical replies were that 'the phenomenon does not represent any advanced technology beyond our present capability and . . . poses no direct threat to the United States.' And that 'there is no evidence indicating that sightings categorized as "unidentified" are extra-terrestrial vehicles.' This was no more than expected; the next step was to confront the CIA – the agency most likely to be involved in suppressing UFO material. The CIA's reply – in a letter to GSW dated 26 March 1976 – is intriguing in the light of later events:

In order that you may be aware of the true facts concerning the involvement of the CIA in the investigation of UFO phenomena, let me give you the following brief history. Late in 1952, the National Security Council levied upon the CIA the requirement to determine if the existence of UFOs would create a danger to the security of the United States. The Office of Scientific Intelligence established the Intelligence Advisory Committee to study the matter. That committee made the recommendations [in] the *Robertson Panel Report*. At no time prior to the formation of the Robertson Panel and subsequent to this issuance of the panel's report [in January 1953], has the CIA engaged in the study of UFO phenomena. The *Robertson Panel Report* is the summation of the Agency's interest and

Above: research director Todd Zechel (left) and director William H. Spaulding (right) of Ground Saucer Watch, discussing the UFO problem

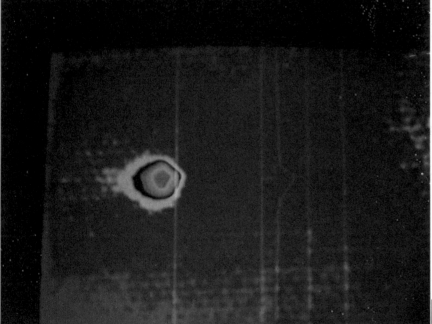

involvement in this matter.

The Robertson Panel's conclusions – after an intensive briefing by top airmen, astronomers and several CIA men – were simple. There was no cause for alarm militarily or scientifically, but – significantly for our case – the panel concluded that 'the continued emphasis on the reporting of these phenomena does, in these perilous times, result in a threat to the orderly functioning of the protective organs of the body politic.' Their recommendations were framed accordingly – debunk UFOs and educate people to recognise aerial phenomena.

In fact, the CIA did not let the matter drop there and then in 1953. Searches through the National Archives had shown that many reports were missing from the files. Dozens more letters to other agencies and even to the White House simply elicited the same official response – essentially, that UFOs did not exist. Why, then, the missing documents? When GSW made specific requests under the Freedom of Information Act a few papers were released – and so highly 'sanitised' that only a mind reader could have made sense of some of them. GSW then decided to attack in the courts. After 14 months of gruelling legal action the government released, on 15 December 1978, close to 1000 pages of documents. It was a major victory for GSW and ufology in general. What do the papers show?

First, that CIA involvement in UFOs actually pre-dates the National Security Council directive to set up what became the Robertson Panel – indeed it was the CIA that urged an investigation on the Council! Second, the implications for psychological warfare attract considerable attention. As one memo puts it, 'a fair proportion of our population is mentally conditioned to the acceptance of the incredible. In this fact lies the potential for the touching-off of mass hysteria and panic.' The third concern is with the vulnerability of US air defences: 'At any moment of attack . . . we cannot . . . distinguish hardware from phantom. . . .' The use of the word 'phantom' is interesting here. For another memo, from the Deputy Director for Intelligence, CIA, dated November 1952, says bluntly:

Sightings of unexplained objects at great altitudes and traveling at high speeds in the vicinity of major US defense installations are of such a nature that they are not attributable to natural phenomena or known types of aerial vehicles.

In the light of that it is not surprising that when Edward Tauss, then Acting Chief of the Weapons and Equipment Division of the Office of Scientific Intelligence, recommended that the CIA 'continue' (*not* 'begin') coverage of the subject in August 1952, he should add:

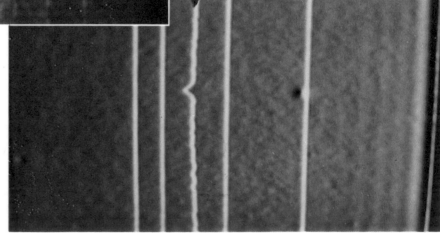

It is strongly urged, however, that no indication of CIA interest or concern reach the press or public, in view of their probably alarmist tendencies to accept such interest as 'confirmatory' of the soundness of 'unpublished facts in the hands of the US government'.

It is clear then that the government – or the CIA at least – believed in the reality of the UFO phenomenon. It was also alarmed by it. And it was determined to keep what it did know to itself.

Nor was the report of the Robertson Panel the last word, though the CIA pretended to accept its findings. The US Air Force, after all, maintained Project Blue Book until 1969, after the Condon Committee published its findings – though whether Blue Book was ever told the whole truth either by the USAF itself or by other defence agencies remains in

Right: the last members of Project Blue Book, the US Air Force's full-time UFO investigation unit, disbanded in 1969 while under the leadership of Major Hector Quintanilla (seated). The project's tiny staff was unable to deal in any depth with the thousands of UFO reports it received every year, suggesting that the USAF was dragging its feet over the UFO question. But the more likely explanation is that the real research was being done in secret by the CIA, leaving Blue Book as a public relations front

The marine, the CIA and the UFO

One of the oddest UFO cases on record is the 1952 sighting by US Marine Ralph Mayher (top). It is odd not because of the sighting itself, which was as 'normal' as any UFO event, but because of what happened afterward to Mayher and the film he managed to take.

Ralph Mayher had heard that on the night of 28 July 1952 a couple named Goldstein had seen a flying saucer near their home. He was an experienced movie photographer and was interested

in UFOs, so he arranged to meet the Goldsteins the next day and rented a camera – he had a theory that saucers sometimes appear on consecutive nights. At 9.30 p.m. on 29 July Mayher heard a woman across the street shout that a UFO was in view. The Goldsteins and another neighbour, Herman Stern, also saw the object, which remained visible over the ocean for about three minutes. Mayher managed to shoot only some 40 frames of film because his view was obscured by

trees and buildings. The object was travelling horizontally toward the witnesses then 'turned' and shot away.

Mayher had his film processed at once and, as his unit commander had no objections, released some frames to the Miami press (centre) and even recorded a radio interview. But within 48 hours, USAF investigators were on the scene and threw a security blanket over the case. Mayher was visited by a number of men with CIA credentials, who apparently told him to keep quiet about the event. On enquiry Mayher was also told that the USAF thought the 'pinpoints of light' (sic) too small to analyse properly. But the film was never returned.

Perhaps the strangest part of the story is that while well-informed UFO investigators like Major Donald Keyhoe heard nothing of the film, ace debunker Dr Donald Menzel soon became familiar with it. With surreal inventiveness, Menzel said it showed a cobweb. GSW's computer analysis (bottom) indicates that the object is solid, 50 feet (15 metres) in diameter, and travelling at 2500 miles per hour (4000 km/h).

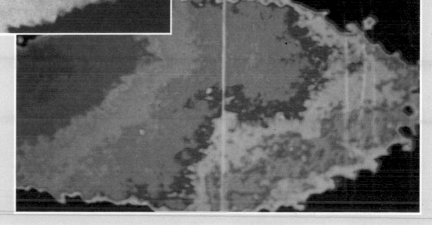

some doubt. The probable fate of the film taken by US Navy Warrant Officer Delbert C. Newhouse in 1952 – the 'Tremonton movie' that was shown to the Robertson Panel – is one indication of the CIA's true reaction to the evidence.

This film has been subject to several attempts at debunking. According to the witness, it shows a number of unusual craft travelling at enormous speed some 10 miles (16 kilometres) from the camera. Newhouse's report of the incident (he was a trained Navy photographer) is confirmed by GSW's computerised tests on the film – as it was by the USAF photo laboratory at Wright-Patterson AFB, who first analysed it. The film was then handed to the Naval Photographic Interpretation Center (NavPIC) at Anacostia, Maryland, and subjected to over 1000 man-hours of study. The Navy had no explanation for the objects but said they appeared to be 'self-luminous' spheres travelling at up to 7560 miles per hour (12,096 km/h). The Robertson Panel argued over the film for about two hours. They were also shown film of seagulls giving intense reflections of light in bright sunshine. The panel duly reported that 'the objects were considered strongly to represent birds.'

Who laid on that film of seagulls? Was it the CIA, experienced hands as they were at manipulation and suggestion? What they did not do was stop studying films of UFOs. As soon as the Robertson Panel had reported, NavPIC was dissolved. Some of its members, however, were moved to the CIA to form the National Photographic Interpretation Center (NPIC). Material dating from at least 1950 is kept there. Says GSW's Todd Zechel: 'There is a direct link between NavPIC's work on the Tremonton analysis and the decision of the CIA to place the analysis programme under its direct authority. In other words, rather than thinking the Tremonton analysis was in error, as has been purported, the CIA was impressed enough to immediately transfer the project to its headquarters.'

A cover for the CIA

Small wonder, then, that the USAF's Project Blue Book got such short shrift. According to Todd Zechel, Blue Book was 'in reality . . . no more than a PR front, primarily covering for the secret research being conducted by the CIA. . . . to give Blue Book full support would have been a waste, since it would have been duplicating research already being conducted by the CIA. Therefore, and for the most part unwittingly, Blue Book's façade enabled the CIA to pull off the greatest propaganda fraud in history.'

The documents obtained by GSW support the view that the CIA has persisted in UFO research. Among them are numerous reports, dutifully filed by US embassies abroad, of UFO sightings: 25 cases from Spain alone in one nine-month period between 1973 and 1974, a case from Portugal, multiple events

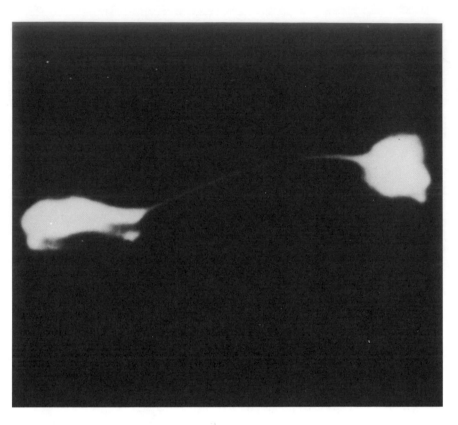

An unexplained mass of light seen over Ibiza in May 1974, which remained stationary for a brief period before rapidly climbing to a high altitude and vanishing. Reports such as this have been collected by the CIA from all over the world. Despite official claims that the agency ceased to have an interest in UFOs in 1953, documents have been obtained from CIA archives detailing sightings as late as 1976

in Tunisia in 1976 with many witnesses, radar tracking and police reports. 'A very concerned Chief of Military Security, General Balma' wanted to know if the US Sixth Fleet could 'shed any light on who or what they might be'. Not only was this – and innumerable other cases – being reported in 1976, seven years after the US government had supposedly given up its interest in UFOs in the wake of the Condon Report, but all UFO reports from the embassies are sent to the CIA – and the even more shadowy Defense Intelligence Agency, the National Security Council, the Secretary of Defense and the Secretary of State.

Of course it is in the government's interests to pretend that it can identify everything in the sky: the security of the Western Alliance depends on that assumption. But the evidence indicates that the cover up does not stop at a desire to prevent alarm and despondency from spreading among the people. Just the opposite, if you happen to be a witness to a UFO: agents from the CIA Directorate of Operations (Clandestine Services) and Domestic Operations Division (sometimes called the 'Contact Division') have been known to harass, intimidate and silence people.

Further to this, a more sinister game is perhaps being played out. For while the intelligence services attempt to deflate the UFO controversy, it would seem that they are also helping to feed it. It is to this aspect of the cover up, and the possible reasons for it, that we turn next.

For decades ufology has been in a state of confusion and disarray, struggling to research a phenomenon for which there is only slender evidence, say investigators. And the reason? Secret government agencies have been manipulating the evidence and the witnesses

WHAT CONCLUSIONS can we draw from the documents that GSW has drawn from the CIA and the State Department? To answer that question, we first have to look objectively at some salient facts about the state of ufology. For that is the raw material that the CIA has used to its advantage over the years in its campaign of debunking, disinformation and calculated manipulation.

In the first place, most information about UFOS is based on the (usually unsupported) word of the witnesses. In many instances, this type of report is labelled 'authentic' by the pro-UFO community after an investigation that usually amounts to little more than a conversation with the participants. The

The Goodyear blimp broadcasts its message to the world. But at some angles, could it be taken for a UFO? On 29 April 1978, Mr and Mrs S of Aurora, Illinois, reported a brilliantly lit, saucer-shaped craft 'as big as a football field' that was also seen by numerous other witnesses. With lights 'twirling round it', it followed the couple's car and allegedly caused power failures in the locality. But Allan Hendry, then investigator for the Center for UFO Studies, identified the 'saucer' as an aircraft owned by Ad Airlines of Chicago. This 'classic' UFO – and its mundane explanation – is a perfect example of the suggestibility of people. Anyone wishing to exploit such credulousness would have an easy task

ability of witnesses to 'identify' unusual aerial phenomena is notoriously unreliable: take for example the numerous cases of dome-shaped, spinning, saucer-like craft that perform extraordinary manoeuvres and display unusual lighting configurations reported by numerous reliable individuals – and then turn out to be aircraft towing advertising material. Lack of time, money and effective research techniques all contribute to the large element of foul-up in ufology.

On the other hand not all UFO events can be categorised as 'identifiable'. There is a small residue of events that seem to be caused by real objects (or what appear to be real objects). Blue Book estimated these at some 3 per cent of the total; civilian investigators put the figure at about 8 per cent. Probably the true figure is somewhere in between. But relatively little can be done to investigate these cases scientifically: there are few physical traces to take into the laboratory. What does seem certain is that no event represents a visitation from outer space. The mathematical odds are simply too remote for the extra-terrestrial hypothesis to be taken seriously. Whatever true UFOS are, they would appear

Agents of confusion

to have a distinctly earthly origin.

Even so, the transparent ineffectiveness of the official investigations, the ineptitude of the special commissions, and the constant stonewalling of the government led many civilian researchers to believe that a massive conspiracy was at work to cover up the government's knowledge of contact from outer space. In the 1940s, rumours of crashed saucers and dead aliens were rife. In the 1970s there were contactee and abduction stories galore. Not only that, but odd leaks and whispers of information came the way of the research groups from seemingly well-placed military and intelligence sources. What other conclusion was there to draw? Who else but aliens could be behind these tantalising stories?

Undoubtedly the government – as embodied in the CIA – has been involved in a cover up, as we have seen in the previous article. But what we are about to suggest is that while the CIA was collecting UFO information from around the globe (though claiming to be doing nothing of the kind), it was also manufacturing the rumour that the government knew more than it was prepared to admit. This tactic was employed partly to

Top: artist's impression of the 'spacecraft' seen by Joe Simonton in 1961, one of whose occupants gave him a pancake (above). Was he hoaxed by a secret government agency such as the DIA or NSA (below: their official seals)? And to what extent has the US government connived at rumours of 'captured aliens'? This picture (right) almost certainly shows a monkey used in rocket tests, not (as alleged) a space visitor

distract ufologists' attention from what the government was actually up to, and partly to add to the disarray of ufology.

Behind the smokescreen of confusion and ignorance that it created, the CIA could proceed with its own outlandish experiments, whose real nature would be further disguised by the fact that they seemed no weirder than the rest of the whole bizarre phenomenon. And such activity would be just as intractable to scientific investigation, whether by the USAF or by civilians. In this it was fundamental that the USAF's investigations, for example, should be kept secret.

Clues to what really came to fascinate the CIA about the UFO question are scattered throughout the documents obtained by GSW. Of course, the government's conspirators of silence may not be from the CIA: they may be from the Defense Intelligence Agency, the National Security Agency, or the super-secret National Reconnaissance Organisation, or some clandestine group within any of these. Though the evidence to hand points to the CIA, the precise identity of the culprits is unimportant as long as the principles on which they seem to be working remain obscure.

From the first the CIA was intrigued by the psychological implications of the flying saucer mystery. Says part of one memorandum from 1952:

With world-wide sightings reported, it was found that, up to the time of this investigation, there had been in the Soviet press no report or comment on flying saucers. With a state-controlled press, this could only result from an official policy decision. The question, therefore, arises as to whether or not these sightings: 1) could be controlled, 2) could be predicted, and 3) could be used from a psychological warfare

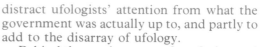

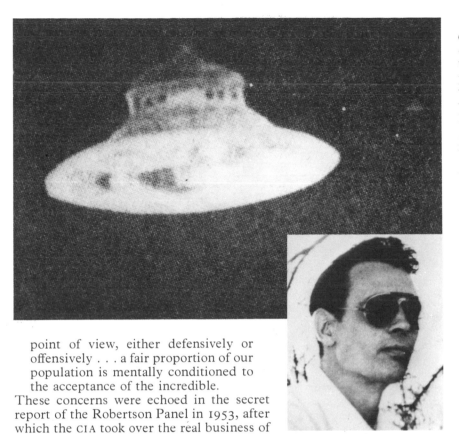

point of view, either defensively or offensively . . . a fair proportion of our population is mentally conditioned to the acceptance of the incredible.

These concerns were echoed in the secret report of the Robertson Panel in 1953, after which the CIA took over the real business of UFO investigation. At this time, the documents show, the CIA's Office of Scientific Intelligence was privately convinced that UFOs were extra-terrestrial craft. While awaiting proof of this, a debunking campaign was designed to defuse any potential public hysteria. Everyone expected that UFOs, like any other fad, would thus be helped to evaporate from the public consciousness.

The 'spaceship' (top) that was photographed by Howard Menger (above). The ship is suspiciously similar to that seen by Adamski, and its occupants imparted a similar, banal, wisdom. Who hoaxed whom?

But at some point – perhaps when the extra-terrestrial hypothesis was discarded, or perhaps when it became indisputable that UFOs were not simply a passing craze, or perhaps with the growth of secret high-technology research – the Agency realised that it could conduct experiments in psychological warfare of its own. If the Soviets were not behind the sightings in an attempt to manipulate the populace, there was no reason why the CIA should not get behind them instead. The benefits would be manifold: the military could get on with its secret aerial projects in comfort, since anyone coming unwittingly in contact with them would fall foul of the CIA's disinformation service and public debunking routine; and the CIA would discover just how far public attitudes could be manipulated, how individuals reacted to bizarre and unprecedented events, and how the information was disseminated and what reactions it generated.

This paradoxical programme of simultaneous encouragement and discouragement of the UFO controversy would work on several fronts. The idea of a cover up would be nurtured through leaks of classified information to civilian investigators, while a number of events could, quite simply, be staged. A number of agents infiltrating the research organisations would then be able to feed disinformation to the UFO groups and at the same time monitor their awareness of secret military hardware. Friends in the press would dutifully play up UFO material whether it were hoax, misidentification or staged event.

This programme is what GSW calls the

Anonymity guaranteed

At a UFO conference held at Fort Smith, Arkansas, in 1974 the research group APRO announced that henceforth it was intending to concentrate solely on contactee and abduction cases. Whether this was out of boredom with run-of-the-mill UFO sightings or because APRO hoped to gain publicity is not known. Some of the cases APRO has espoused are highly questionable – the alleged Walton abduction case being but one instance. Here is another.

In February 1981 Ground Saucer Watch received from APRO an anonymous letter purporting to come from a US airman. It described a UFO landing near Kirtland Air Force Base, New Mexico. An individual in a metallic suit got out, got in again, and the craft flew away. A Civil Air Patrol Cadet, one Craig R. Weitzel, apparently took photographs of the landing. Later, he was (the letter said) visited by men in black, which

Coral Lorenzen, founder of APRO which concentrates on UFO contacts and abductions. Mrs Lorenzen has said that such cases show 'a careful, methodical and in-depth study of Earth and its inhabitants is underway'

Weitzel reported to the USAF security police, who in turn notified the Kirtland AFB Office of Special Investigations. A Mr Dody then looked into the matter, though the letter-writer claimed that Dody later disavowed all knowledge of the incident. The letter-writer also claimed that his commanding officer, one Colonel Bruce Purvine, had admitted to him that OSI was investigating UFO sightings – in the greatest secrecy. Mention was also made of crashed saucers, some of which are supposedly kept in the Sandia area of Kirtland AFB.

Ground Saucer Watch did what it could to check this report, which confirmed the existence of the Sandia area and of Mr Dody of the OSI. Colonel Purvine expressed some astonishment that he should be reported as discussing classified information with enlisted men, and denied discussing UFOs at all with anyone. He also pointed out that the 'airman' had got the name of Col. Purvine's command quite wrong.

Who led APRO up the garden path?

'Federal hypothesis'. It would not require especially large resources to be effective, since only a small number – no more than the unexplained 5 per cent – of events need to be created. The network of enthusiasts would do the rest. As the ripples spread out from ufologists a segment of the public would respond with psychic experiences, fantasies a smattering of hoaxes and numerous 'induced' misinterpretations of aircraft, birds and planets. Another flap would be under way. And a similar pattern of manipulation could be used to cover up mishaps with military equipment or explain away occasional instances of its illegal testing. Once the technique was established there would be no reason not to use it to distract public attention from political embarrassment at home or abroad.

How far can we prove the Federal hypothesis? The documents obtained under the Freedom of Information Act reveal the CIA's persistent interest in psychological warfare. Is it coincidence that several members of the board of Governors of the National Investigations Committee on Aerial Phenomena (NICAP) are former members of the CIA? One, Colonel Joseph Bryan III, USAF (Ret.), is actually reputed to have been the founder of the CIA's psychological warfare section;

Above: a ground marking allegedly left by a UFO near Tully in Queensland, Australia, in 1966. Hard evidence like this is rare – and is rarely investigated by qualified scientists

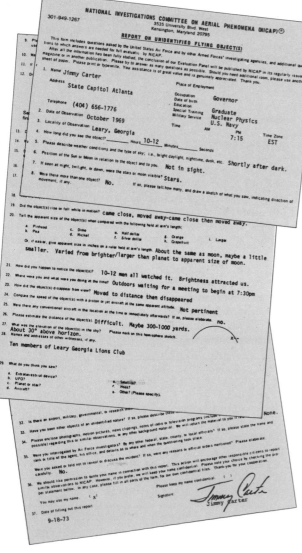

In its attempts to get to the truth about the UFO phenomenon, GSW made an approach to President Jimmy Carter (above), who, while campaigning for the presidency, had announced his intention to pursue the mystery and had himself filed a UFO report (left). But NASA denied Carter's request to review UFO data, and the President himself was unable to further GSW's suit against the CIA. Said GSW: 'The guests in the White House come and go every four to eight years, but the CIA goes on for ever'

another NICAP officer, Nicholas de Rochefort, had come to the CIA through its predecessor, the Office of Strategic Services – and was also an expert in psychological warfare. No less telling in GSW's view is the decision by the Aerial Phenomena Research Organisation in 1974 to concentrate solely on contact and abduction cases, which may have led them straight into the hands of the manipulators (see box). How many other UFO organisations have been infiltrated? How many other publications have been fed stories?

There is evidence that Generso Pope, owner of the *National Enquirer*, is an ex-CIA member and is still an associate of the Covert Action Staff (Disinformation and Propaganda) of the CIA's Operations Directorate (Clandestine Services). And who has paid the highest sums for the most exotic and sensational UFO stories – and so helped shape American popular opinion – but the *National Enquirer*? Such a technique is standard with the CIA: in December 1977 the *New York Times* reported that in the mid 1960s the CIA 'owned, subsidised or otherwise influenced . . . more than 800 news and public information organisations and individuals'.

It is also significant that UFO stories undergo reincarnation: the crashed saucer tales of the 1940s are emerging once again in the 1980s, while the fashion for contactee experiences of the early 1950s recurred in the 1970s. In a more sinister vein, what kind of psychological manipulation may be involved in close encounter cases? How many times have we all heard a baffled researcher say in all honesty that the event was 'real in the mind of the witness', despite a total lack of supporting evidence? It is at such specific instances of the UFO phenomenon, and its manipulation, that we must look next.

UFOs: a Federal case

Is a government conspiracy really at the root of the UFO mystery? A study of the documents obtained by Ground Saucer Watch, suggests several reasons why the CIA and the US military might indeed embark on such a programme of deception

'I SUGGEST THAT we discuss at an early board meeting the possible offensive or defensive utilization of these phenomena for psychological warfare purposes.'

The subject of the secret memorandum in which this sentence appeared was 'Flying Saucers'. It was written in the early 1950s by Walter B. Smith, Director of the CIA, to the Director of the Psychological Strategy Board. And it would appear that in the intervening years the CIA – or possibly some other clandestine agency – has indeed been using the UFO phenomenon in a form of psychological warfare. And the objects of the CIA's attention have been the citizens of the United States.

This is, to say the least, a disturbing proposition, but there are several reasons why the US government might want to encourage a belief in UFOs, and then manipulate that belief among the populace at large. By looking at specific aspects of the UFO phenomenon as we now understand it, these reasons become clear.

In the first place the United States has a

Above: a Teledyne Ryan 262 remotely controlled drone on a test flight. The craft is designed to be virtually invisible to radar and infra-red detection, and is nearly soundless. Its purpose: surveillance and electronic warfare. Pilotless craft are a new growth area for military technology and perhaps for ufology too

Right: Boeing's version of a Stealth aircraft prototype

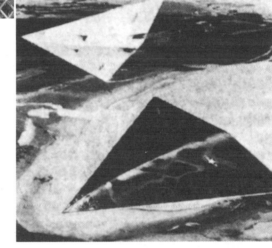

Roswell and after

'The many rumours regarding the flying disc became a reality yesterday when the intelligence office of the 509th Bomb Group of the Eighth Air Force, Roswell Army Air Field, was fortunate enough to gain possession of a disc through the co-operation of one of the local ranchers and the sheriff's office of Chaves County.'

Thus began the press release issued by Lieutenant Walter Haut of the US Army Air Force on 8 July 1947 – and so the legend of the Roswell Incident was born. In fact, what was found was wreckage of a rather unusual type – so unusual, according to Major (later Lieutenant Colonel) Jesse A. Marcel, that it was rapidly substituted with the remains of a weather balloon, which he then presented to the press (left) as the material he had found in the New Mexico desert.

The case for a flying disc or some extra-terrestrial craft being involved is flimsy to say the least, and based largely on second-hand accounts to boot, while members of a University of Pennsylvania archaeology team who helped gather the wreckage have apparently not been contacted by researchers.

So what did crash? On 3 July 1947, the approximate date of the crash, the White Sands Missile Range launched both a V-2 rocket and (for the US Army Air Force) the first polyethylene balloons. Either of these, impacting off the range, may have been responsible for the wreckage found in the desert – and would have caused the embarrassed 'cover up' that followed the ill-advised press notice issued by Lieutenant Haut. Likewise, the accounts of the material as light but very tough and distinctly unfamiliar would be explained.

The significance of the incident for ufologists may lie in White Sands' own admission that some 7 per cent of their firings go awry, including heavyweight tactical missiles like the Pershing (right): one crashed in 1967 in Van Horn, Texas, 250 miles (400 kilometres) away.

massive investment in military technology, especially in the field of airborne weapons. And while the armed services have literally thousands of square miles of desert and scrub in which to test craft such as the radar-defeating 'Stealth' aeroplane, remotely piloted vehicles, unusual aerofoil configurations and even biochemical weapons, there are occasions when these need to be tested in unrestricted areas. The advantage of a general willingness to 'believe in UFOs' is inestimable in such a case.

Take the Stealth aircraft, for instance. Development work on an aeroplane that can make itself virtually invisible to radar has been going on since at least 1966. The project was classified in 1977, but pictures released by Boeing show a small, oddly shaped bomber resembling nothing so much as a paper dart, unusual enough, perhaps, to be taken for a UFO even in daylight.

But in 1975 a mobile radar unit of the United States Air Force in California picked up a target flying at 460 miles per hour (740 km/h) from Edwards Air Force Base. Then it turned – and in one sweep of the radar had vanished. This was taken to mean that it had accelerated instantly to over 2000 miles per hour (3200 km/h) – typical UFO behaviour! In fact, the target was a Stealth aircraft on test, and had switched to its 'invisible' mode just after it came on screen. Officially it was logged as 'unidentified' – one part of the USAF seeing no need for another part to know what it was doing. The foundations of the UFO myth were made a little stronger – and the secret aircraft remained secret.

The presence of 'moles' from the intelligence community within UFO organisations will further ensure that no really vital information can leak to the outside world without being first carefully distorted. In much the same way, what looks like an over-enthusiastic and ill-informed reaction on the part of a press officer in the US Army Air Force has been kept alive as 'evidence' of an alien saucer that supposedly crashed in New Mexico in July 1947 – just days after the first polyethylene research balloons were launched from the nearby White Sands proving ground (see box).

More sinister are the unexplained cases of cattle mutilation associated with UFO sightings, reported from the USA. The 'operations' on these animals are always said to have been done with unnerving neatness. It is possible – and if one accepts the notion of a government UFO conspiracy it is probable – that this 'surgery' is performed on animals that have been exposed to biochemical weapons. On this theory the government is deliberately reinforcing the belief in the incredible or paranormal origin of the mutilations. It may be doing this to camouflage its tests of biochemical weapons and of the extent to which their use is detectable by experienced farmers and veterinary surgeons. Or it may be using the UFO mythology to disguise

Snippy the horse, owned by Mrs Berle Lewis (centre) of Alamosa, Colorado, USA, is tested for radiation after dying 'in mysterious circumstances'. Radiation was indeed detected – so was the damage to the animal caused by predators, or was there some more human agency at work? Those who prefer a paranormal explanation or who offer ufonauts as the culprits may be unwittingly aiding a cover up of tests of biochemical weapons

gruesome incompetence by the military – the unintentional injury of cattle by its toxic materials.

A more direct form of experiment in aggressive psychology may lie behind the murky history of the 'men in black'. It is altogether likely that the CIA has actually staged a number of UFO events, especially contact and abduction cases. The recurrent claim of MIB victims that no one but they knew of the sighting would then be a delusion, 'MIBs' having in fact set it up.

It would serve the interests of psychological warfare to know how people react to empty threats: the MIBs, after all, never seem to follow through their promises to maim or silence their unwilling hosts.

Similarly, the MIB technique could be used to evaluate responses to bizarre (not to say unearthly) behaviour. Hence the stream of surreal comments, inane questions and asocial activity that MIBs like to indulge in. Techniques of surveillance are now so subtle that agents would not have to follow through the visit, which could simply be recorded remotely. And any leakage only adds to the mass of incoherent absurdities that make up most of ufology.

This absurdity is deliberate. A phenomenon with no logic, yet that undeniably exists, serves to keep investigators occupied in the hopeless attempt to *create* a logic, a theory, that will tie all the loose ends together. In turn a very large public will apply its energies to ufology, energies that cannot reach a conclusion. This serves government purposes – *any* government's purposes. It was apparent very early on that the public was not going to get tired of the UFO question (even the sceptical Robertson Panel gloomily predicted an increase in sightings). The clever solution was then to direct this interest and control it – and hope that a large number of otherwise troublesome people would be kept occupied with an insoluble problem,

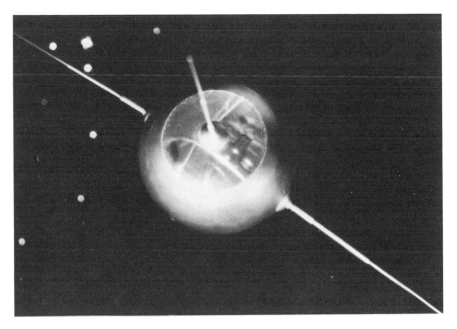

enthusiasts in their belief that sceptics are ignoring the issue of the century while government and scientists are covering up the truth. As they are, but not quite in the way that ufologists first thought.

This conspiracy theory will probably be offensive to many ufologists. But one further fact supports it: and that is the total lack of progress that has been made on the question of what true UFOs really are. If researchers could answer that question, the concern with abductions and contact cases (which consumes so much more energy among researchers) would have some purpose.

The present state of publicly available knowledge is ably summarised by William H. Spaulding, who first raised the 'Federal hypothesis' to account for the elusiveness of the phenomenon:

What new, startling breakthroughs have emerged from the pro-saucer movement? The past 30 years have

thus removing some sources of political challenge. A persistent harping on the (actually untenable) extra-terrestrial hypothesis has undoubtedly led to the creation of several pseudo-religions. The adherents of these saucer cults will certainly not berate the government for its mishandling of the economy or foreign policy, since the Galactic Brotherhood will see us right in the end.

Public dissatisfaction with the US government's performance was certainly diverted by a UFO event in 1957 – an indication of both how quickly and how soon the operation was mounted. At that time the United States suffered several humiliations as attempt after attempt to launch its first space vehicle, the Vanguard rocket, ended in disaster. Then in November 1957 the USSR succeeded in putting a *second* satellite into orbit, a mere 30 days after the epoch-making *Sputnik*. Within hours UFOs appeared over Texas and New Mexico – and elbowed the Soviet achievement out of the headlines. With so much interest in space, the extra-terrestrial obsession was given another nudge forward, and national embarrassment was temporarily forgotten.

Even abduction cases can serve a dual – or even triple – purpose. It is not difficult to stage a UFO encounter or abduction that is 'real in the mind of the witness', provided one can get at the victim with drugs, hypnosis – or both. Other special effects would scarcely stretch the resources or ingenuity of a banana republic, let alone the US government. And so the experimenters could add to the UFO myth; test their psychological or hallucinogenic techniques; note whether the victim succumbs entirely; observe how the information is treated by the media, by ufologists and by the public; and, having generated another outrageous story, keep serious scientists away from the UFO scene. The subjective reality of the experience for the witness will also strengthen 'saucer'

Above: *Sputnik I*, whose launch in October 1957 shocked Americans by its demonstration of Soviet technological superiority. It may be no accident that when the USSR launched a second satellite only a month later, a sudden wave of UFO reports from Texas and New Mexico flooded the press to divert the public's attention

Right: the ufonaut, drawn by Betty Hill (below), that allegedly abducted her and her husband Barney. Were they the victims of a bizarre experiment in mind-bending by CIA psychologists?

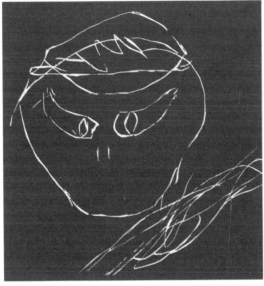

been wasted attempting to research something that wasn't there in the first place. . . . The fact that the saucer belief system has survived so long with so little logical and evidential support is a testimony to the tenacity of human credulity. The audacity and creativity of the CIA and other researchers in this subject have created three generations of enthusiasts and have captured the imagination of the public. . . . What makes the saucer saga so interesting and significant is that it is a genuine psycho-social movement that has been born and is still growing in our own time.

A world-famous authority on UFOs once expressed his private belief that the phenomenon was controlled by some kind of intelligence – though whose it was he was not prepared to say.

The answer seems to be that UFOs, in the USA at least, are controlled not so much by an intelligence as by an intelligence *agency*.

Have UFOs crashed on Earth?

Ever since the term 'flying saucer' was coined in 1947, there have been rumours that the US government has one or more crashed UFOs – complete with alien pilots – in its custody. There is some compelling evidence to support this extraordinary idea

ALMOST AS SOON as the first 'flying saucers' were reported in 1947, rumours began to circulate that one of them had crashed and was under examination by American scientists. It was logical enough: given the great number that seemed to be around, it seemed statistically certain that sooner or later one of them would suffer an accident or breakdown, or be shot down by some earthly power.

Such reasoning assumed that the UFOS were solid, material objects, liable to physical accident or mechanical malfunction. In those early days there was little question in anyone's mind that the UFOS were as solid as terrestrial aircraft: the only question was, where did they originate?

What threw the crashed saucer legend into disrepute was, paradoxically, a book that set out to establish it as fact. In 1950 an American writer named Frank Scully brought out *Behind the flying saucers*, which became a sensational bestseller in both the USA and Europe. Something of the contemporary climate of opinion comes over in the dust-cover blurb: 'It is typical of the whole extraordinary and delightful business of the flying saucers that the first person to attempt a serious book about them should be the show business magazine *Variety's* ace columnist.' The point could have been made even more strongly by mentioning that Scully was also the author of *Fun in bed* (not a sex manual, but a collection of diversions for the bedridden), which was sufficiently successful to be followed by *More fun in bed* and *Junior fun in bed*. True, there were few serious ufologists around in 1950; but Scully's credentials did nothing to enhance the credibility of his story.

The story Scully had to tell needed all the support it could get. In the course of his professional writing, he claimed, he had come across a Texas oilman named Silas Newton who, in turn, told Scully of his colleague 'Dr Gee' – who, he alleged, had first-hand knowledge of three UFOs that were held in the custody of the United States military, along with 16 dead occupants, about 3 feet (1 metre) tall. No supportive evidence was produced: all depended on the word of 'Dr Gee', who claimed to have been one of the scientists called in by the authorities to examine the UFOs.

This drawback did not prevent Scully's book selling more than 60,000 copies; but it did mean that, when, two years later, a journalist named J.P. Kahn wrote an article pointing out the weaknesses of Scully's story, he found it easy enough to persuade the world that it was a total fabrication. The fact that Kahn's exposé was itself full of exaggerations and inaccuracies was overlooked: it made its point, which was that Scully had taken his story on trust and done virtually no independent research. Newton and 'Dr Gee' were labelled frauds.

The disrepute into which the crash-and-capture story subsequently fell was not, of course, entirely due to Scully's shortcomings. Quite independently, public opinion was swinging round to the idea that UFOs, whatever else they might be, were not man-made; and if they were the products of an extra-terrestrial technology, the technology that had brought them to Earth might also save them from the breakdowns and accidents to which earthly machines are liable.

It was not until some 25 years later that the crashed saucer legend surfaced again. In April 1976 there appeared in the pages of *Official UFO* (at that time a fairly serious journal) an article entitled 'What about crashed UFOs?', by the widely respected investigator Raymond Fowler. Instead of serving up the vague rumours of the past, he produced dramatic new evidence in the form of a technician's sworn statement that he had personally examined a crashed UFO at Kingman, Arizona, on 21 May 1953.

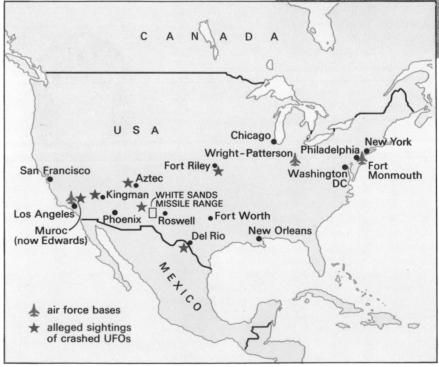

air force bases
★ alleged sightings of crashed UFOs

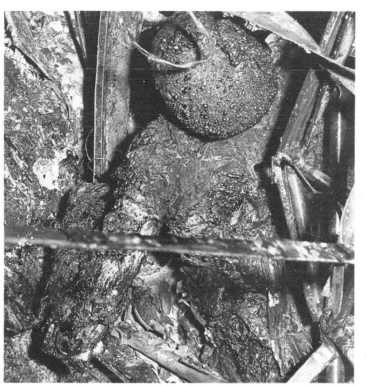

Left: a photograph of an alleged dead alien retrieved from a UFO that crashed in New Mexico on 7 July 1948. In evaluating the photograph, it is perhaps worth noting the distinctly terrestrial spectacle frames beneath the shoulder of the 'humanoid'

Below: a flying saucer collides with the Washington Monument in this still from the 1956 movie *Earth vs flying saucers*. However advanced the technology of UFOs, the argument goes, there is no reason why they should not sometimes crash – and if they do, then surely it is natural for the military to take an interest?

Above: the cover of the August 1979 issue of the American *UFO Review* – with a 'special "Would you believe" supplement' – shows a US soldier standing guard over a captured UFO. Despite such sensationalism, there is evidence to support the suspicion that the US military is holding crashed UFOs – and their alien occupants – for examination

Left: the sites of some of the alleged sightings between 1947 and 1953 of UFO wreckage in the hands of the military – and the airfields then used for weapons testing

From then on, interest in the subject became both more serious and more intense. Another investigator of repute, Leonard Stringfield, dedicated himself to the search for further evidence; and while he ranged far and wide in his quest, William Moore and Stanton Friedman, in conjunction with Charles Berlitz, concentrated on a single case that was to become famous – the Roswell incident – dealt with in the next chapter.

Strange corpses

The story, in outline, is as follows. Sitting outside their home on the night of 2 July 1947, a couple at Roswell, New Mexico, saw a glowing object streak across the sky. About 75 miles (120 kilometres) further on in the direction of its path, a rancher next morning found extraordinary debris scattered over his ground. A further 150 miles (240 kilometres) or so away, an engineer and some archaeologists came across the remains of an unidentifiable flying vehicle, together with several very strange bodies. The authorities took control, announced that the object was simply a weather balloon, and nothing more was heard of the matter – until Moore, Friedman and Berlitz took it up.

Other cases, uncannily similar in some respects, abound. On 7 July 1948, near Del Rio, Texas, USA, unusual radar sightings led to the suspicion that an unidentified flying object had crashed some 30 miles (50 kilometres) across the Mexican border. With permission from the Mexican government, US troops went to investigate, and found a metallic disc, with the burned bodies of the crew, more or less human-like beings about 5 feet (1.5 metres) tall. The object, which had been clocked at 2000 miles per hour (3200

km/h) by radar, had been simultaneously seen on radar by USAF Colonel Whitcomb in an F94. He landed at his home base and immediately took off for the scene in a borrowed light aircraft; he found Mexican troops in control, and the object hidden from sight. A naval intelligence officer arrived in time to see the crash area roped off and some object being loaded onto trucks.

The troops taking part were apparently warned that if they spoke of the matter they would be 'the sorriest people around'. Some photographs, allegedly of the bodies of the

Right: in 1953 a metallurgist named Daly, who worked at the Wright-Patterson Air Force Base in Ohio, was sent on a secret mission to examine what appeared to be a flying saucer. After carrying out tests on it for two days, he concluded it must be of extra-terrestrial origin

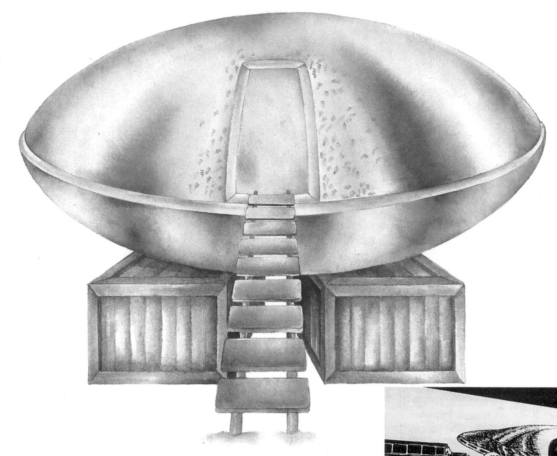

Far right: a crashed UFO in the Arizona desert is illuminated by the glare of spotlights. A civilian engineer, known by the pseudonym of 'Fritz Werner', brought in to calculate the object's speed of impact, notices the body of a small humanoid figure in a metallic suit. In 1973, Werner signed an affidavit testifying that this incident had occurred to him 20 years before

occupants, were circulating clandestinely some years later; they continue to be the subject of controversial debate.

Sometime in 1952, at the Muroc Air Force Base in California, a USAF radar operator tracked an object descending towards Earth at great speed. After a crash had been confirmed, he was instructed 'You didn't see anything.' Later he learned that a UFO, more than 17 yards (16 metres) in diameter, had crashed in a desert area not far away. It was metallic, and badly burned: it contained bodies of beings about 5 feet (1.5 metres) tall. The debris was kept for a while at the base, then allegedly shipped to the Wright-Patterson Air Force Base at Dayton in Ohio. There is strong evidence that at this time some object was indeed secretly shipped to the Wright-Patterson base.

Possibly relating to the same incident is a film that was shown the following spring, apparently by the military authorities, to a select group, including a radar specialist, a Mr T.E., who was working for the army and air force, stationed at Fort Monmouth, New Jersey, and who had secret security clearance. The five-minute movie showed a silver disc-shaped object embedded in the sand in a remote desert area; it had a dome on top, and an open hatch or door. Some 10 to 15 military personnel could be seen standing near the craft, and its diameter, based on a comparison of its size with that of the human figures, appeared to be 6 to 8 yards (5 to 7 metres). The film also showed the bodies of three dead occupants: they were small and human-like, with over-large heads. The viewers were told to think about the film but not to tell anyone about it; two weeks later they were told it was a hoax. This seems strange, for there is a certain amount of evidence that the film was shown to officers at a number of military bases; clearly someone, somewhere, felt that it was important for them to see it. It seems all the more unlikely because, quite apart from the poor quality of the film, which – paradoxically – tends to suggest it is genuine, the cost in time and effort of setting up so elaborate a fake would have been formidable.

Fragmentary evidence

In June 1952 six Norwegian army jets on summer manoeuvres over the bleakly inhospitable islands of Spitzbergen (right) spotted wreckage in a mountain area near the Hinlopen Straits. Within hours, using ski-planes, Norwegian investigators were on the site, including an expert on rocketry. No doubt a Soviet vehicle or missile was suspected, but instead they found the wreckage of a disc-shaped object, with 46 jet-like orifices on the rim; and the object seemed to be made of an unknown metal. There was no trace of occupants.

But what is perhaps the most remarkable aspect of this incident is the

The most explicit item of evidence in the entire crashed UFO saga is an affidavit signed in 1973 by a certain Fritz Werner – a pseudonym, although his true identity is known – who swore that he had assisted at the investigation into a crashed unknown object. While serving as project engineer on an air force contract near Kingman, Arizona, in 1953, he was given an assignment: along with some 15 others, he was taken early one morning under strict security conditions in a blacked-out bus on a five-hour journey. He and his companions were told that a super-secret air force craft had crashed, and that each of them was to investigate the crash in terms of his specific field of expertise.

Werner described the object as like two deep saucers, one inverted on the other, about 11 yards (10 metres) in diameter, made of dull silver metal, with an open hatch to the interior. His particular task was to calculate the object's impact velocity from the traces. He found no landing gear, also no dents or scratches. In a tent nearby he saw a dead humanoid on a table, about 4 feet 3 inches (1.3 metres) in height. Not only were the investigators instructed to tell nobody of the incident, they were not even allowed to discuss it among themselves.

Another incident from 1953 that may confirm the Fritz Werner report is the case of a metallurgist named Daly who worked for the air force at the Wright-Patterson AFB, Ohio. He described being taken to a location, unidentified but abounding in hot sand; for the last part of his journey he was blind-folded. For two days he was required to examine the structure of a silvery metallic craft lying undamaged in the sand. He concluded it was not of earthly origin; he saw no sign of occupants.

Despite the evident discrepancies, these two reports may relate to the same incident. Relevant, too, may be the evidence given by the wife of a guard at Wright-Patterson; she alleged that, at about this time, her husband

witnessed scientists examining the bodies of large-headed humanoids, about 3 feet (1 metre) in height.

Another incident, two years later, at the Wright-Patterson base, may confirm that pilots of crashed spacecraft were taken there for examination. A woman whose duty was to catalogue all incoming material relating to UFOs stated that she saw the bodies of two dead humanoids, about 5 feet (1.5 metres) tall, with large heads, being transferred from one location to another.

In March 1964 it was reported that a round, flat UFO, giving off a bright blue and orange light, had crashed high on Mount Chitpec, Mexico. Officials wanted to take it to the nearest town, San Cristobal de las Casas – but the local tribe, the Chalulas, insisted it was a gift from God and the Virgin, and refused to allow its removal.

Bolivian mystery

In Tarija, in the most remote and inaccessible part of Bolivia, many people saw a glowing object cross the afternoon sky on 6 May 1978. It was generally described as a metallic cylinder, some 8 or 9 yards (7 or 8 metres) in length, and artificial, though without windows or structural details. It was closely followed by another, smaller object. A few seconds later there was the sound of a great explosion, accompanied by an 'earthquake' that was registered on seismic equipment over some 77,000 square miles (200,000 square kilometres); after the crash, the smaller object was seen to fly away.

The object's rate of travel was far too slow for it to have been a meteor, and investigation ruled out a satellite returning to Earth. But while speculation bubbled in the press, a security blackout was officially imposed. Reporters saw the object removed by technicians, and asserted that it had been taken by the United States Air Force back to the USA. NASA denied being involved – as it would, of course, have done even if it had been.

The foregoing cases have been presented with a minimum of comment. They have been put together from accounts that often contain contradictory statements; they represent, however, the most coherent version available. At the same time, they represent less than half the alleged incidents. The evidence is very far from being convincing; at the same time, it is very hard to discount it altogether. To assert that every one of these allegations is a lie, or a misinterpretation of some simple event, is to call in question a great number of witnesses, unknown to one another yet many of them wholeheartedly trusted by experienced investigators. Their accounts, while often hazy and contradictory, nevertheless all point in the same direction.

comment of a high-ranking army officer, Colonel Gernod Darnbyl of the Norwegian general staff, who in 1955 said: 'The crashing of the Spitzbergen disc was highly important. Although our present scientific knowledge does not permit us to solve all the riddles, I am confident that these remains from Spitzbergen will be of utmost importance. Some time ago a misunderstanding was caused by saying that this disc probably was of Soviet origin. We wish to state categorically that it was not built by any country on Earth. The materials used in its construction are completely unknown to the experts who took part in the investigation.' He added that American and British experts were being consulted; since then – nothing. . . .

The best-documented case of a crashed saucer occurred near Roswell, deep in the New Mexican desert, in July 1947. The military first claimed to have it in custody, then denied its existence. What was the reason for this sudden change of mind?

THE BELIEF THAT A FLYING SAUCER has crashed and been confiscated by the authorities has proved very difficult either to prove or to disprove. 'Believers' point to a rich assortment of isolated facts, rumours, hints and unsupported testimonies and insist that together they make up a case that demands serious investigation. The sceptics reply that no single item of evidence is conclusive and that there exists no solid case at all, only a myth created by those who wish to believe in it. A hoax or a misidentification, the sceptics claim, started the story and gave the lead to all kinds of rumour-mongers and hoaxers, sensationalist journalists and genuine out-and-out paranoids.

To evaluate this accusation, it is necessary to identify the earliest known form of the story, and see how much truth can be found in it. If it can be shown to be spurious, then perhaps the subsequent versions are no better. If, on the other hand, there seems to be some substance to it, then it may be worth investigating the story further.

The first occurrence of the story seems to relate to a cluster of events that occurred near the town of Roswell, New Mexico, commencing on 2 July 1947. The date is very significant: this was only a few days after Kenneth Arnold had his noted sighting over the Cascade Mountains in Washington state, a sighting that can be said to mark the beginning of the modern UFO epoch.

At about 9.50 on the night of 2 July 1947, Mr and Mrs Wilmot, of Roswell, New Mexico, were sitting out on their front porch when all of a sudden 'a big glowing object' zoomed out of the sky from the south-east, and headed north-east towards the smaller town of Corona. It was travelling at high speed, and was in sight for only 40 to 50 seconds; they were able, however, to describe it as oval in shape, like 'two inverted saucers faced mouth to mouth'. Dan Wilmot thought it was completely silent; his wife thought she heard a slight swishing sound.

The following morning Barney Barnett, a civil engineer from Socorro, New Mexico, was working in a desert area, the plains of San Agustin, some 250 miles (400 kilometres) west of Roswell, and just west of Socorro. He saw sunlight reflecting off some kind of metallic object in what should have been empty desert; so, thinking it might be a crashed aircraft, he went towards it. What he found was 'some sort of metallic, disc-shaped object', 25 to 30 feet (8 to 10 metres) in diameter.

While inspecting it, he was joined by some archaeology students from the University of Pennsylvania. Together they contemplated an astonishing sight: beside the machine itself, which seemed to have been split open by explosion or impact, there were dead bodies scattered over the ground, and others still inside the machine. They were human-like, but small-eyed and hairless, and with heads over-large in proportion to their size. They were wearing grey, one-piece clothing, without belts or zips.

What happened at Roswell?

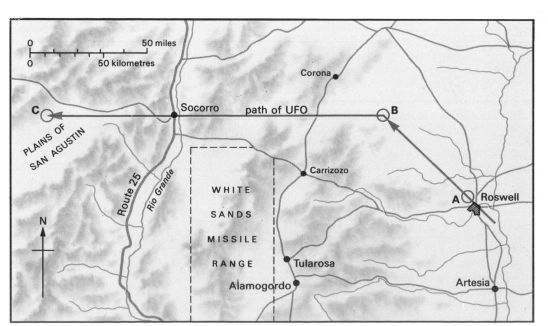

Left: map showing the estimated course of the alleged spacecraft first seen by Mr and Mrs Wilmot in Roswell (A) at about 9.50 p.m. on 2 July 1947. Evidence of the craft's passage in the form of some strange metallic debris was found by 'Mac' Brazel on his ranch near Corona, New Mexico (B). And on the morning of 3 July a civil engineer working at San Agustin (C) found what appeared to be a crashed UFO, complete with dead humanoids

Flying Saucer
swell Region

Ex-King Carol Weds Mme. Lupescu

Former King Carol of Romania and Mme. Dena Lupescu relax aboard the S. S America bound for Cuba and Mexico in May, 1941. A member of Carol's household in Rio de Janeiro said the ex-king and his companion for 23 years in reign and exile were recently married at their hotel Copacabana Palace suite. (AP Wirephoto)

Miners and Operators Sign Highest Wage Pact in History

Air Force General Says Army Not Doing Experiments

Above: the front page of the *Roswell Daily Record* for Tuesday, 8 July 1947. The headline was
followed by a press statement from the Army Air Force saying that the 'flying disk' had been examined at Roswell Army Air Field and was now in the hands of 'higher headquarters'. The military subsequently denied that the craft had been anything but a weather balloon

Right: 'Mac' Brazel, who discovered what was apparently UFO wreckage on his ranch near Corona, New Mexico. Two years later, his son Bill happened to mention in a tavern that he still had some of the wreckage. The very next day, it was confiscated by the military

Shortly after, a jeep containing an army officer drove up, and declared that the army was taking over control. The area was cordoned off: the civilians were told to leave the area, and warned that it was their patriotic duty to keep silent about what they had seen. Barnett heard later that the army brought in a large truck and took the object away.

Though Barnett is now dead – he is one of the principal witnesses, whom investigators, of course, were unable to interview – he told his story to some friends. The investigators found no reason to doubt their word; nor, from what they learned of Barnett himself, did they find any reason to disbelieve what he told his friends in private. However, all attempts to check his story by tracking down the archaeological students have so far been unsuccessful.

On or close to the same date, 'Mac' Brazel, a rancher, made a strange find on his ranch near Corona, New Mexico, about 75 miles (120 kilometres) north-west of Roswell, and 150 miles (240 kilometres) east of the site of Barnett's discovery. Brazel's was a small, rough ranch in isolated country, nearly 30 miles (50 kilometres) from the nearest town. His wife and family normally lived in town so that his children could attend school, but they were with him at the time of these events. Brazel died in 1963; this account is based on an interview with his son Bill.

The previous night there had been a severe thunder storm – a not infrequent occurrence in this region – and Brazel had heard a loud explosion quite distinct from the thunder. Next morning, he rode out to check on his sheep, and found a collection of unidentifiable wreckage strewn over an area of ground some quarter of a mile (400

metres) in length, in a narrow strip running in the direction of Socorro. Having more important concerns, he didn't at the time take much interest in the wreckage; but a day or two later he thought he would go back and take another look.

What he found was fragments of a metallic, foil-like substance, very thin and pliable, but immensely tough – he could neither crease nor permanently bend it. There seemed to be some markings resembling writing, and attached to some of the fragments was a tape-like material which, when held to the light, seemed to have a design on it, vaguely floral in appearance.

The following night he happened to visit Corona, the nearest town, and there he told friends of his find: in return he learned that several people had seen flying saucers lately in the neighbourhood – more than a dozen in all, and not apparently attributable to rocket tests from the nearby White Sands Missile Range. He wondered if his find was in some way connected with these sightings, and next day, while visiting the larger town of Roswell on farming business, he informed the sheriff. The sheriff advised him to go to the military with his story: there was an Army Air Force base just outside Roswell.

Silenced by the authorities

A reporter from the local radio station heard of Brazel's discovery, and recorded an interview with him before he went to see the military. But when the local radio station started to put the story out, it was immediately silenced by the authorities, who claimed to be speaking in the national interest and threatened the station with removal of its licence. And when Brazel got to the military, he found they were very definitely interested: they held him for questioning while troops descended on his ranch and combed the area to gather every scrap of the strange material. A number of local residents had heard enough about the matter to go out to the Brazel ranch to see for themselves, but they found the road blocked by troops and the area cordoned off. It was several days before the army allowed Brazel to return home; he was discouraged and upset at the way he had been treated – 'Gosh, I just tried to do a good deed and they put me in jail for it.' He said he had been told to keep quiet about his find, and told his children there was no need for them to know more than what they would read in the papers.

But the papers and the radio had conflicting, fragmented accounts to give their publics. Among those who had been alerted by the news to visit the Brazel ranch was reporter Johnny McBoyle, part owner of Radio KSWS of Roswell. On 7 July Radio KOAT in nearby Albuquerque, which possessed more extensive transmission facilities, received a telephone message from McBoyle, for relay: 'A flying saucer has crashed. . . . No, I'm not joking . . . . near Roswell. I've been there

and seen it. It's like a big crumpled dishpan. Some rancher has hauled it under a cattle shelter with his tractor. The army is there and they are going to pick it up. The whole area is now closed off. And get this – they're saying something about little men being on board. . . . Start getting this on the teletype right away while I'm on the phone. . . .'

The operator began to comply, but the teleprinter suddenly stopped transmitting and instead printed an incoming message: 'ATTENTION ALBUQUERQUE: DO NOT TRANSMIT THIS MESSAGE. STOP COMMUNICATION IMMEDIATELY.' The caller was unidentified.

When the operator got in touch with McBoyle again, the reporter said: 'Forget about it. You never heard it. Look, you're not supposed to know.'

Discrepancies between these accounts are at once apparent. McBoyle claimed to have

actually seen an object 'like a crumpled dishpan' on a ranch near Roswell, which seems to imply the Brazel ranch: yet Brazel is supposed to have found only fragments, a matter on which his surviving children today are quite clear. Curiously, too, the headlines of the *Roswell Daily Record* for 8 July read 'RAAF captures flying saucer on ranch in Roswell region'.

The story accompanying that headline was in the form of a press statement from the Army Air Force, and was printed as a quotation from the Public Relations Officer at Roswell Army Air Field, First Lieutenant Haut. The press release stated:

The many rumours regarding the flying disc became a reality yesterday when the intelligence office of the 509th Bomb Group of the Eighth Air Force, Roswell Army Air Field, was fortunate enough to gain possession of a disc through the co-operation of one of the local ranchers and the sheriff's office of Chaves county.

The flying object landed on a ranch near Roswell some time last week. Not having phone facilities, the rancher stored the disc until such time as he was

able to contact the sheriff's office, who in turn notified Major Jesse A. Marcel, of the 509th Bomb Group Intelligence Office.

Action was immediately taken and the disc was picked up at the rancher's home. It was inspected at the Roswell Army Air Field and subsequently loaned by Major Marcel to higher headquarters.

Was Lieutenant Haut acting under instructions from his base commander? According to his own recollections, he was: Colonel Blanchard asked him to write and distribute a news release to the effect that the Army Air Force had recovered the remains of a crashed flying saucer. Haut asked if it was possible for him to see the object, but Colonel Blanchard told him this would be impossible. If Haut *was* acting under instructions, his press report takes on the status of an official statement. And if so, it deserves to be taken very seriously, for the army unit that put it out was not a group likely to act irresponsibly. The 509th Bomb Group was something of an élite force, made up of hand-picked personnel, and Colonel Blanchard went on to reach the rank of general. If the

Above: General Ramey (left) with his adjutant, Colonel Dubose. Only a few hours after its release, General Ramey squashed the army announcement that it was examining a 'flying disk'. This picture was intended to substantiate the claim that the alleged UFO was merely a weather balloon; but it was widely alleged that the debris was fake

Left: a view of the New Mexican desert at White Sands Proving Ground, where a V-2 rocket-testing programme was in progress at the time of the Roswell incident

Below left: a guided missile takes off from White Sands in a test undertaken during the 1960s. The path of the alleged Roswell UFO passed very close to White Sands – perhaps a reason for concern on the part of the military

Top: Major Jesse Marcel, who was initially put in charge of the alleged UFO wreckage. The original debris was apparently made up of fragments of a foil-like, metallic substance, pliable but immensely tough: it could be neither creased nor permanently bent. Marcel did not believe that the object was a wrecked weather balloon

statement was official, it is certain that the Army Air Force would not have issued it unless they considered they had good grounds for doing so. However, it all rests on Lieutenant Haut's own recollection of events, so this interpretation must remain provisional.

Whatever the truth is, the report displeased the army at a higher level. Within hours of the press announcement, General Ramey, from Fort Worth in the adjoining state of Texas, went on the radio to tell the public that the entire affair was a case of mistaken identification. As for flying saucers, he declared, 'there is no such gadget known to the Army, at least not at this level.'

The radio disclaimer was followed by a press conference: photographers were allowed to photograph the fragments from a distance. In a second press conference they were allowed to get closer, but it was widely suspected that the material they were shown on the second occasion was not the same as the first, nor was it what had been found on the Brazel ranch. It was extremely fragile and flimsy, as was to be expected if it came from the stray weather balloon that the army claimed it to be. Brazel himself, while keeping quiet as instructed, insisted 'I am sure what I found was not any weather observation balloon.'

Brazel's son Bill collected some of the fragments, and kept them. Two years later, however, he happened to mention them in a tavern in Corona. The very next day he received a visit from the military, who told him it was important for national security and confiscated his collection. That, two years after the event, the army should be so concerned about some stray fragments of a weather balloon is, at the very least, improbable.

We must also note as particularly strange

the fact that Brazel was kept in military custody even after the authorities had identified the fragments as being from a harmless balloon. By any standards, if they were telling the truth, they seem to have over-reacted to an astonishing degree.

The Roswell incident cannot be dismissed as hysteria. Brazel had not acted hysterically, but calmly, indeed casually, out of a simple patriotic wish to do what was right. He had no political, religious or personal axe to grind, he was seeking neither fame nor fortune. Again, hysteria does not account for the army's press statement: military intelligence officers are not apt to jeopardise their careers, to say nothing of the national interest, by issuing sensational rumours as fact. In this instance it is their later actions, rather than the initial statement, that give the impression of hasty action, intended to defuse the explosive character of the original announcement.

Fragmentary evidence?

We should not disregard the contradictions and inconsistencies in the knowledge we have of what may have happened at Roswell during those July days; but neither should we exaggerate their significance, as we piece together fragments of largely hearsay testimony gathered many years after the event. We do seem justified in concluding that together they point to some such sequence of events as this: that the Wilmots saw a large, glowing object hurtle through the sky in the direction of Brazel's ranch; that Brazel heard an explosion that night and next morning found debris from some kind of accident; and that, after changing direction in consequence of that accident, the object proceeded in a westwards direction, passing over Socorro to crash finally at San Agustin, where it was seen by Barnett.

That this chain of events may have occurred is borne out by the reports published in the local papers at the time, and by first- and second-hand testimony obtained directly from many of those who saw and heard things, It seems equally clear that there was a rapid and urgent move by the authorities to clamp down on the release of information: the interrupted broadcast and radio transmission, the intervention by General Ramey from Fort Worth, the two press conferences with their unsatisfactory alternative explanation – all this gives good cause to believe that the army was concerned about something more important than a weather balloon that had lost its way.

And the Roswell story doesn't end there, nor was it the only incident of its kind. What of the object itself, alleged to have been taken away by the army? What about those alien bodies strewn across the desert? What did the military do with the remains?

To most ordinary people the idea that the US government holds secret details of crashed UFOs sounds like paranoid nonsense. Many researchers point to a disturbing amount of evidence that something *is* being officially covered up – but what?

'SOMEWHERE in the US there is a locked warehouse, guarded as no other place has ever been, accessible only to men of the highest security clearance possible in the government and the Pentagon. Because in that warehouse stronghold lies irrefutable evidence that UFOS exist.'

So, in 1974, American ufologist Otto Binder, author of one of the most objective books on the subject, *What we really know about flying saucers*, expressed the belief that the US government has captured, and holds, a spacecraft from beyond this Earth. It is a belief that is for many an article of faith, but for many others no more than a deliciously

Picking up the pieces

spine-tingling myth; while there is undoubtedly insufficient substance to the story to justify the former in their total commitment, there is quite enough to make even the most sceptical pause to ask whether, just possibly, there might be a little fire at the source of so much smoke.

In a field of enquiry in which, as we have seen, the evidence is so sparse, so contradictory and so lacking in support, and often emanating from anonymous witnesses or nothing more than hearsay, it is tempting to dismiss the crash-and-capture myth as either the concoction of sensationalist journalists or the projection of individual paranoias. For many years, alternating between these hypotheses, serious ufology managed to avoid challenging the myth.

But things changed when, among other things, the Watergate affair and revelations about the war in South-east Asia showed just how secretive the US government was capable of being, how deviously it could act, how far it was prepared to lie to the American public. For years it had been claimed that the CIA had not the slightest interest in UFOS; but the Freedom of Information Act, which became law in 1976, enabled investigators to obtain documentary proof that, on the contrary, the CIA had long taken a very serious interest (see page 32). This information was obtained from the tiny portion of official documentation that the US government had been

Above: Washington DC at night – and in the centre of the picture is the Watergate Hotel, a name now universally synonymous with skullduggery at high levels. Ufologists are concerned that there may be a 'cosmic Watergate' in operation, a cover up centred on rumours and counter-rumours of crashed saucers. Perhaps these stories – and others connected with UFOS – are meant to divert our attention from something quite different . . .

Right: the NASA Flight Research Center at Edwards AFB, California. In 1947 (when it was known as Muroc AFB) it was believed to be the secret destination of the heavily guarded wreckage of a crashed saucer

forced to disclose: there still remains an incalculable quantity that it is able to withhold from the public on grounds of national security – what secrets may be contained in it can only be guessed at.

But sufficient has been learned to justify ufologists in taking a closer, harder look at some of the more extreme claims. By the 1970s a new generation of ufologists had appeared on the scene, men and women who were no longer willing to accept reports at their face value, whether it was a question of witness testimony on the one hand or official explanations on the other.

For this, much of the credit must go to

Home on the range

White Sands Missile Range (WSMR) in New Mexico is not far, by American standards, from Roswell: some 300 miles (480 kilometres) down US Route 70. Since 1945, WSMR has launched no less than 30,000 assorted pieces of military hardware into the sky – among them the Lance missile (right). Are there any grounds for thinking that the 1947 Roswell saucer – or any other – came from White Sands?

Ufologist William H. Spaulding, of Ground Saucer Watch (GSW), believes so. Research by GSW shows a disproportionately high number of 'unexplained' high-strangeness UFO sightings in New Mexico and its adjoining states. It is worth remembering, too, the enormous range of items – from early USAF Snark cruise missiles to radar balloons and

modified German V-2 rockets – that WSMR handled even in the early days.

Not all of these behaved like conventional rockets and could easily be mistaken for 'alien craft', especially as most firings were made at night until 1964. And as early as December 1946 a V-2 engaged in 'biological research' was blasted 116 miles (185 kilometres) into space: one such test, carrying animals, going awry, could form the single seed for all the pickled-alien myths in ufology. And should such a crash result from an illegal test across state lines, there would be all the more reason to silence civilian witnesses.

White Sands admits that some 7 per cent of its tests are aborted – giving an average of more than one possible crash a week since the Second World War. Small wonder, then, that tales of UFOs and downed saucers abound in the south-western United States.

Left: President Dwight D. Eisenhower, whose golfing vacation may have been interrupted to visit Muroc – to have a look at the wreckage of a crashed saucer (and maybe the bodies of its crew) on 20 February 1954. Someone's eye is on a US president at all hours, but official accounts of Eisenhower's movements during that day seem curiously garbled. Real or imagined, his visit to Muroc is now part of ufological myth

veteran ufologist Leonard Stringfield, who has almost single-handedly put together evidence that the American government has UFOs and UFO entities in its possession. The result of his efforts is a dossier of testimony that, while largely emanating from individuals who prefer to remain anonymous, nevertheless is coherent and consistent to an impressive degree. Meanwhile, operating on a narrower front but in greater depth, William Moore and Stanton Friedman, along with Charles Berlitz, uncovered the intricacies of the Roswell incident discussed earlier, which established beyond any reasonable doubt that an unidentified object – not necessarily of alien origin – got into trouble over New Mexico in 1947, and that

the US government was both very concerned about the incident and extremely embarrassed by it.

There is strong, consistent and clear-cut evidence that an exceptionally large load – the wreckage of the crashed object, perhaps – was carried across country by the military at that time, under conditions of maximum secrecy: a series of reports have been brought to light, each of them trivial in itself, but adding up to a convincing picture. The destination of some of the material was widely alleged to be Muroc Air Force Base, California – and this was the location for one of the most incredible, yet at the same time one of the most enduring, components of the myth. It is claimed that on 20 February 1954 the President of the United States, General Eisenhower, went to Muroc to see the saucers for himself.

In principle, it is perfectly possible. Eisenhower was at that time enjoying a golfing vacation on a friend's ranch at Palm Springs, only 90 miles (150 kilometres) away from Muroc; yet only a week previously he had returned from a quail-shooting holiday in Georgia. Would even the most sporting president, it has been asked, take two such vacations in such close succession?

The movements of the president are, of course, followed closely by the press, who expect to know where he is, and more or less what he is doing, at any hour of the day. Yet on 20 February, for several hours, the press had no idea of his whereabouts. It was even rumoured that he was dead. A press conference was hastily called to explain that he had had to have emergency dental treatment. Some years later the dentist's family was questioned; they had a vague notion that something of the sort might have happened – a surprisingly casual attitude to what should

have been a very memorable event!

In May 1954 a certain Gerald Light, in company with some distinguished visitors, went to Muroc, and wrote a letter after his visit describing how he had seen five separate and distinct extra-terrestrial craft being studied by the air force, and confirming Eisenhower's visit. Unfortunately, virtually nothing is known about Light, though the letter he wrote undoubtedly exists. British UFO author Desmond Leslie also claimed to have spoken to USAF personnel who confirmed the Eisenhower visit, and Frank Scully's widow, in support of her husband's maligned book *Behind the flying saucers* (see page 40), stated that they once employed a carpenter who had at one time worked at the nearby Muroc base, and he too spoke of the presidential visit. An author who collaborated with UFO hoaxer George Adamski and an anonymous workman may not be the most convincing witnesses, yet their testimony is both independent and consistent.

Faced with evidence that is at the same time so specific and so inconclusive, several theorists have suggested that the entire UFO phenomenon is a deliberate smokescreen put out by governments to conceal a more sinister truth. There was ironic confirmation of this in 1977, when on 20 September the inhabitants of the Soviet city of Petrozavodsk saw a 'jellyfish-like' object in the pre-dawn sky. The immediate reaction of the witnesses was that it was a UFO, and the incident aroused great interest throughout the country and even abroad. The Soviet government, like other governments round the world, denied the existence of UFOs – yet here was a sighting it could not deny.

And indeed it could not – but for quite a different reason than the public supposed. For what witnesses had seen was the launching of the Kosmos-955 spy satellite from the secret base at Plesetsk – but this was, of course, an explanation the Soviet authorities could not reveal. Rather than break security,

The impenetrable depths of a Canadian forest where, some ufologists suggest, secret terrestrial organisations are busy manufacturing UFOs. But if this is so, why are so many different kinds of UFO seen in widely different places, including densely populated areas such as New York and London?

they had no choice but to allow the Russian public to go on believing they had seen a UFO; politically, it was better that it should be thought a UFO than one of their own secret devices!

'The CIA has proof that UFOs exist' was the headline to an article in *UFO Report* in 1977, in which a former US intelligence agent confessed that the CIA had deliberately suppressed evidence about UFOs. But suppose these leaks were themselves a part of the CIA's continuing campaign to distract attention from their own research projects?

What on Earth?

Such hypotheses are discounted by many people on the grounds that UFOs apparently display a technology so far ahead of any that we have achieved as to make it unlikely that such advances have been made in secret by any Earth government. But if the UFOs are indeed of earthly origin, where is their base? In the Canadian forests, as one investigator has suggested? It seems improbable. Why are they seen in so many different forms and in so many different places? Why are there so many reports of occupants who are noticeably different from humans? There are countless objections to the 'home-made' hypothesis.

But there is also much supporting evidence. In a case of December 1980 three people, two middle-aged women and a child, driving in Texas, saw a huge glowing object from their car, and stopped to look at it. They suffered burns severe enough to keep one of them in hospital for a week: whatever the object was, it was capable of emitting dangerous radiation at a considerable distance. Surely the US government would not be experimenting with so dangerous a device in a public place? But if it was not operated by or with the co-operation of the US military, why was it accompanied – as all three witnesses firmly testify – by some 23 helicopters, of a type used by the USAF?

This case – the Cash-Landrum case – is under active investigation by the Mutual UFO Investigation Network (MUFON); if that investigation reaches a clear conclusion, it could settle the question of UFO origins, for some cases if not for every one, once and for all. A detailed study of the incident appears in chapter 4.

But such stories, however improbable, are plentiful; there are far more than have been mentioned in these articles. While each one of them is at best a plausible anecdote, together they make up a coherent body of evidence that suggests that the US government, and possibly other governments elsewhere, have in their possession devices that, whether they are extra-terrestrial UFOs or super-secret military devices, these powers do not wish the public to know about. We cannot say for certain what is being covered up; but that a cover up exists seems to be established beyond reasonable doubt.

Are UFOs illusions, delusions – or alien craft? The US government set up several research projects to find the answer – but the attitude of the investigators was often far from objective

DR JACQUES VALLÉE, pioneer UFO researcher, once remarked that he had been 'struck by the fact that in the *Encyclopaedia Britannica* the entry for "unidentified flying object" falls between "unicorn" and "unified field theory".' This seemed, he added, an apt location for the UFO phenomenon. It also sums up the dilemma that has faced United States governments and scientists since the 'flying saucer' mystery first came to the notice of the public in June 1947. Is it something magical, like the unicorn, or a scientific problem?

When UFO reports first began to flood in the responsibility for their investigation was handed over to the US Air Force: apparently technological devices were roaming the skies, and the origin of such devices was naturally suspect. Nobody asked: what are

A UFO looms menacingly over the Capitol building in Washington DC, in a scene from the 1950s movie *Earth versus the flying saucers*. This was based on several magazine articles by Major Donald Keyhoe claiming that the US Air Force had deliberately misled the public by explaining away all reports of UFOs as misidentified mundane objects, such as weather balloons. But UFOs, said Keyhoe, were real – and possibly deadly

these phenomena? Everyone assumed they were machines, and the only question worth asking was, where did they come from?

Although reports of 'flying saucers' started coming in 1947, few people realised that reports of bizarre objects in the sky were not new. There had been the airship sightings in the US midwest in 1896 and 1897 and later in Europe, the 'Foo' fighters seen during the Second World War, and the ghost rockets in Scandinavia immediately after it. Dr C. C. Wylie, of the University of Iowa, was quick to condemn the flying saucer phenomenon as 'mass hysteria'. Columbia University's astronomer Jan Schilt said the objects were caused by 'a speeding aircraft churning up the atmosphere and disturbing the light rays'. And one of the first theories tested by the USAF was that the 'saucers' were gliding hailstones!

The public joined in a UFO jamboree, buying 'UFO' souvenirs and hoax discs to place in neighbours' gardens. But an opinion poll in August 1947 showed that most people believed that UFOs were simply misidentified everyday objects; virtually nobody thought they came from outer space. One psychologist summed up the mood of the day by saying that the only question remaining was: 'Is it an illusion (based on something objective) or a delusion (based on nothing tangible at all)?'

Fearing UFOs to be secret weapons, the technical intelligence division of the Air Material Command was asked to collect

'UFOs are bunk'

reports at Wright Field (later Wright-Patterson Air Force Base) in Dayton, Ohio.

On 23 September 1947 (just three months into the UFO 'craze') Lieutenant-General Nathan F. Twining, the AMC Commander, wrote to the commanding officer of the US Army Air Force saying: 'The phenomenon reported is something real and not visionary or fictitious. . . .' He recommended a full-scale investigation. So, as the world laughed, the USAF issued its orders, and Project Sign came into being during January 1948.

It is worth noting that for many years the USAF denied the existence of Twining's letter with its unequivocal stance – just one of many instances in which they suppressed sensitive documents that went against the official line that UFOs did not exist.

Sign of the times?

By mid 1948 Sign had rejected the secret weapons hypothesis. Yet UFOs continued to display unquestionable evidence of being physical craft. This created two schools of thought. One said that all UFOs were real, but only in the sense that they were misidentified. The other argued that the objects were alien in origin. The alien hypothesis was undoubtedly the most popular, and Sign's 'estimate of situation' report favoured the alien theory. Chief of Staff General Hoyt S. Vandenberg responded by classifying the report as 'top secret'. It was rejected by the USAF and shortly afterwards it was destroyed.

The rebuff had a demoralising effect on the staff of Project Sign. However, they continued to check out UFO reports, using advanced techniques and employing scientific consultants. Their final report in February 1949 recorded that 20 per cent of the cases reported to them remained unexplained; and they recommended an intensified full-time USAF study into the UFO question.

Project Grudge (Sign's aptly named successor) aimed to eliminate the troublesome problem of UFOs. Positive support was offered to any journalist willing to write an article proclaiming UFOs as nonsense.

This was an extraordinary change in policy. Scarcely a year separated the Sign report – which had promoted the alien theory – and the final report of Project Grudge (August 1949), which recommended that UFO study should be greatly downgraded. In fact Grudge had actually received 23 per cent more reports than Sign – but had dismissed them all as being 'psychological'.

But was the Sign report really ignored at high level? Or was it secretly acted upon? There are many who regard the events of the year between Sign's report and the closure of Grudge as inexplicable, except that the possibility of the UFOs' alien origin was taken so seriously that responsibility for UFO study was given top level rating – with Grudge and its successors merely acting as puppets, or public relation fronts.

When Grudge was shut down in 1950 a highly secret study called Project Twinkle began. This set out to investigate reports of curious green fireballs seen in New Mexico. Scientific observation posts were set up where most fireballs had been seen. But the phenomenon moved elsewhere. When the investigators followed, the UFOs moved again. One or two scientists asked for funds to investigate this odd behaviour, but they were turned down, and Twinkle ceased operations. However, green fireballs of the same type continue to be seen throughout the world. In May 1978 a former Royal Air Force pilot reported seeing three of them whizz past his car at Lymm, Cheshire.

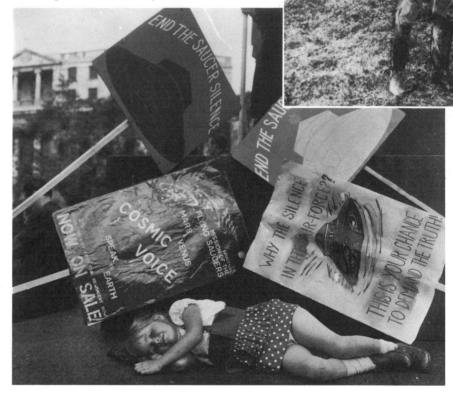

The era of allegations of 'cover ups' dawned. The USAF pursued a policy of explaining away the phenomenon at all costs. Later the purpose was said to be the ultimate eradication of the UFO problem by gradually playing down its significance. And this may make sense. For if UFOs were seen not to be a defence threat then why should the USAF worry about them – whatever they were? But even so, this behaviour fanned the fires of suspicion.

Donald Keyhoe, a retired Marine Corps Major, was the principal motivator of public belief in the cover up. He cited instances such as the death of Captain Thomas Mantell, killed in his aircraft while climbing to chase a UFO above Godman Air Force Base in Kentucky. It seems that Mantell was in pursuit of a secret US Navy weather balloon that had strayed into the area, but nobody told the Air Force about this until the balloon was declassified years later. Desperate for an answer – any answer – to squash the idea that

The 1950s saw various manifestations of public interest in flying saucers – not all of them serious. Strange discs were discovered in gardens or on farms (top) all over the United States, although they originated in workshops and garden sheds rather than some far-distant planet. And voicing the growing suspicions of many, the London Aetherius Society held a rally (above) in 1958 to draw attention to the government's alleged UFO cover up

The curious phenomenon of green fireballs (below) has been reported all over the world. Three emerald-green objects were seen by Mr Gerry Mitchell, a former RAF pilot, in May 1978, moving over the Shell Chemicals plant (bottom) near Lymm, Cheshire, England. When the USAF's Project Twinkle investigated a similar phenomenon in New Mexico in 1950 they noticed that wherever they set up their equipment, the UFOs moved to another location, suggesting that they possessed – or were guided by – some form of intelligence

Grudge, may also have been ignorant of the truth.

The first chief of Project Blue Book was intelligence officer Captain Edward J. Ruppelt. He was the only Air Force officer who openly admitted that he took UFOs very seriously. In his brief time at the helm he adopted new techniques and appointed proper scientific staff, including Dr J. Allen Hynek as chief scientific adviser. He proposed cost-effective scientific experiments intended to discover the truth once and for all, and often paid his own expenses to investigate interesting cases.

And most of them were very interesting: those he studied during 1952 and 1953 were frankly astonishing. In 1956 he published a book called *The report on unidentified flying objects*, which is packed with tales of radar contacts, military jet chases, movie films of UFOs, and so on. It is hard to read the text and not conclude that UFOs are real, solid phenomena.

This was a very strange state of affairs. In

Mantell had been shot down by an alien 'death-ray', the USAF claimed that Mantell had been chasing Venus – an explanation so inadequate that Keyhoe had no difficulty in persuading the press that the Air Force was covering up the truth.

Keyhoe launched his attack on the USAF's official UFO policy in the January 1950 issue of *True* magazine, with a story that rapidly became a sensation and stimulated a string of books, one of which was turned into a classic science-fiction movie, *Earth versus the flying saucers*. In 1957 he formed the National Investigations Committee on Aerial Phenomena (NICAP) to continue the fight against what he considered to be an obvious cover up by the Air Force. But if there was a cover up, it was probably at a much higher level. Project Blue Book, the last USAF project after

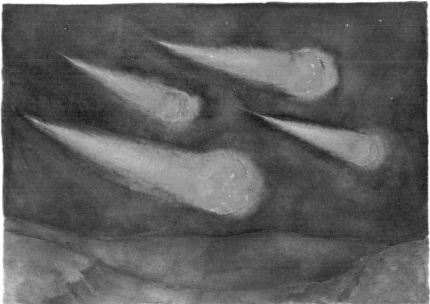

Left: an artist's impression of Captain Thomas Mantell's fatal encounter with a UFO above the Godman Air Force Base in Kentucky in 1948. Mantell's aircraft crashed when he climbed to chase the UFO – which the USAF claimed was the planet Venus. Major Keyhoe used this incident to persuade the public that there was an official cover up, and such was the prevailing mood that he had little difficulty in doing so. Mantell's 'UFO', however, seems to have been a US Navy weather balloon, which in some light and from some angles looks like a classic disc-shaped UFO (below)

1953 the official USAF line was still that UFOs were not of interest. But here was Ruppelt, the head of their own study group, publishing a book that not only stated otherwise but emphasised their significance.

Given what occurred after the Project Sign report, it is hardly surprising to learn that Ruppelt left the Air Force in 1953, very disillusioned at the official line on UFOs that his superiors expected him to convey to the public. In fact, he modified some of his more extreme statements in later editions of his book, possibly under official pressure. He died in 1960.

Until it was closed down in 1969 Project Blue Book continued to 'explain away' the UFO phenomenon.

The turning point in UFO history may well have come in January 1953 when the CIA ordered the convening of the Robertson Panel, an élite team of scientists who were to carry out yet another secret study of UFOs. They spent a mere four days looking at the best available evidence and gave their report on the basis of CIA fears that a hostile country might use UFO panics as cover for an invasion. Some of the panel's recommendations (declassified much later) included surveillance of civilian UFO groups to watch for enemy infiltration, enlisting psychologists – and perhaps even cartoonists – to make UFOs

appear ludicrous, and a wholesale, cold-blooded, debunking of cases. The USAF complied with some of these ideas enthusiastically. And later in 1953 it was even made an offence under the Espionage Act to release official UFO reports. This clamp-down did not apply only to military personnel but to anyone who knew about the anti-UFO propaganda campaign.

Another CIA denial

We can only guess at what effect the Robertson Panel had on serious UFO research. For although the CIA continued to deny that they had ever been interested in UFOs, we now know that they were extremely interested in them even before 1953.

The decade that followed this epic meeting of the Robertson Panel saw the rise of independent UFO research groups, most of which firmly believed that the USAF were deliberately withholding the truth. But the staff of Blue Book seem, in retrospect, to have been merely pawns. Several times they made efforts to pass on their UFO files to a more scientific body such as NASA, having recognised that UFOs were not a defence threat, but if anything worthy of proper scientific investigation. However, ironically, their own debunking methods had been so successful that no scientific group would

Right: Frank Ryman, a US Coast Guard, who took a photograph of a UFO (below) flying over Seattle, Washington, in May 1947, at the height of the first modern UFO craze. In September of that year Project Sign – the USAF's official UFO research project – came into being and rapidly favoured the alien hypothesis. Yet only two years later its successor, Project Grudge, was set up with the aim of discrediting the very idea of UFOs

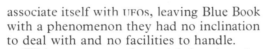

This led to one of the strangest and saddest tales in the history of UFO study: that of the Scientific Study of Unidentified Flying Objects undertaken by Colorado University for the USAF Office of Aerospace Research. The famous physicist Dr Edward U. Condon was asked to lead its two-year study. How those years – and the $500,000 grant – were spent created an undying controversy. From the outset Condon and his chief administrator Robert J. Low openly declared their disbelief in UFOs. When Low was asked to visit European ufologists – during a scheduled visit to attend a conference – he refused to do so and went to Loch Ness instead. As he put it, neither UFOs nor the monster existed, but it was interesting to compare the two phenomena.

A thousand times 'No'!

The negative findings of the 1000-page Condon Report, published in 1969, gave the USAF the opportunity to wash their hands of the whole UFO business – in public at least.

Fortunately, most readers of the report realised that Condon's negative conclusions simply did not tie in with the fact that one third of the cases his team investigated defied explanation. The report had some indirect results: several scientists became interested in the UFO phenomenon, and Dr Hynek, free of his Air Force commitments, went on to form the first science-based UFO group, the Center for UFO Studies, in 1973.

Pressure on the USAF to make their files public continued. Members of the American Association for the Advancement of Science, including Carl Sagan, Thornton Page and other scientists who were not convinced of the reality of UFOs, signed a petition requesting that the files be made open to scientists. Despite the impressive list of signatories it was turned down. Only when the new Freedom of Information Act became law in 1976 did the USAF finally give way.

Certainly these files reveal the incompetence of the USAF work. The standards of investigation of many civilian UFO groups were much higher. But the USAF's brief was only to investigate the threat to defence posed by UFOs – not to enquire into their essential nature. The release of previously classified information also brought to light many documents whose existence had previously been denied.

This fact, plus the lever of the new act, led to a decision by some ufologists to find out what else had gone on under cover. What part had the CIA – and other state security agencies – played?

As for the Condon Report files, they never were released. Dr Condon went to his grave insisting that UFOs were 'bunk' and calling all those who believed in them 'kooks'. He burnt all the records.

associate itself with UFOs, leaving Blue Book with a phenomenon they had no inclination to deal with and no facilities to handle.

With a new wave of UFO sightings in 1965, the USAF seized upon a suggestion by J. Allen Hynek that a scientific panel be convened to study the phenomenon; the panel first met in February 1966 under the directorship of Dr Brian O'Brien.

The O'Brien commission did not find any evidence of a defence threat but did recommend that selected universities examine 100 UFO cases each year, devoting 10 working days to each case. Each team, it was suggested, should include a psychologist, a physical scientist and an astronomer. They also urged Blue Book to make its files available to Congress and other 'public persons' to remove all suspicion of a cover up.

Within two months Congressman Gerald Ford, later US president, succeeded in establishing open Congress hearings at which the O'Brien recommendations were publicly urged onto the Air Force. This time there was no fight. They were adopted – all but for the release of the files.

When the US government finally opened its top secret UFO files to the public it was obvious that there had been a deliberate cover up. Other governments had, apparently, covered up too – but why? The implications of such a policy require careful assessment

ONE MIGHT THINK that the story of official UFO investigation in the United States ended with the eventual release of the Blue Book files in 1977. In fact, in one sense, it had only begun at this point. For it became evident that the CIA had played a dominant part in the UFO business – and not only, as many first suspected, by changing the United States Air Force's UFO policy through manipulating the Robertson Panel. In an attempt to find out what other clandestine operations had taken place, a civilian group, Ground Saucer Watch, and then later a specially formed 'action' campaign called Citizens Against UFO Secrecy, set up lawsuits to weedle out 'classified' information from the various intelligence agencies.

Using the new Freedom of Information Act as a lever, they succeeded – after a fight –

UFOs: the right to know

The British Ministry of Defence (MOD) has been collecting UFO reports since the 1960s and continues to do so. Its Whitehall offices (right) house files that would, if ever released, prove extremely interesting to ufologists. The number of UFO reports for 1981 alone – as quoted in the House of Lords UFO debate in March 1982 – show that the MOD collected over five times as many cases during that year as Britain's leading civilian UFO society, the British UFO Research Association (BUFORA).

The MOD says that UFO reports are the province of a department that has responsibility for low-flying aircraft. Renowned UFO researcher Jenny Randles has engaged in a lengthy battle with the department concerned, suggesting that it would be in everyone's best interest for it to release its UFO files to a scientific establishment, since the MOD has repeatedly claimed that whatever UFOs are, they represent no threat to national security. But she has been refused access to the files on the basis that they contain 'classified information'.

When, in 1983, she asked the MOD for a statement regarding its present policy on UFOs, she received the following:

'The sole interest of the Ministry of

No aliens in Whitehall

Defence in UFO reports is to establish whether they reveal anything of defence interest. . . . There is no unit within the Ministry appointed solely for the study of UFOs, and no staff are employed upon the subject on a full-time basis.

'The Ministry of Defence does not deny that there are strange things to see in the sky. It believes, however, that

in obtaining some reports. Although fragmentary, they reveal evidence of military involvement previously unknown. There was much that post-dated the closure of Project Blue Book, which had allegedly ended the US government's interest in UFOs. Dr J. Allen Hynek said in summarising these documents, 'In case after case in these military dispatches, the reliability and technical competence of the witness is attested to. In case after case, the UFO remains a UFO . . . that is, completely unidentified.'

Among the papers are radar-visual cases, jet plane chases and a very disturbing wave of sightings between 27 October and 10 November 1975 when low-level aerial objects that were not identified repeatedly 'buzzed' sensitive missile launch facilities and military weapons stores. There is also mention of the classic 1976 radar-visual report when an Iranian jet had apparently been inspected by a 'probe' from a UFO (see page 103). These accounts were often of such great interest that, as the circulation lists appended showed, copies were sent to the US Secretary of State, the Pentagon, the White House and several security agencies.

Under the direction of lawyer Peter Gersten, and several American UFO experts, the legal battle has continued. The existence of hundreds of pertinent documents has been admitted to by the authorities, but most of them have not been released. A lawsuit against the National Security Agency for the

Left: a flock of whooper swans. In certain atmospheric conditions or in twilight, a mass of white birds can look uncannily like luminous UFOs flying in formation. During the US government's cover up period *all* UFO reports were explained away as misidentified natural or everyday objects, such as birds, weather balloons – or even planets. Obviously some of these explanations were correct, but there still remained many genuine UFOs on file. And the British Ministry of Defence, while admitting that there are many strange things in the skies, takes a similar line

Above: Claude Poher (on the right), the director of the French group GEPAN, the only known government-funded UFO research team, which folded early in 1983. During its time, however, various members of the group made highly provocative public statements: for example, in 1979 Dr Pierre Guérin wrote in *Flying Saucer Review*, 'An intelligence controls the UFOs. And it is not ours'

release of 131 admitted UFO documents reached the Supreme Court of Appeals in 1982 after being rejected at all other levels. The following official statement illustrates the reason given for non-release of this material: 'Public interest in the disclosure is far outweighed by the sensitive nature of the materials and the obvious effect on national security their release may well entail.' Certain sceptics suggest that this simply implies that UFO investigations may also turn up top-secret defence data. But surely such information could be censored? Yet it remains highly probable that not even 'sanitised' versions of these papers will be accessible.

Sense and sensibilities

Even the ruling judges in these cases have been officially 'cleared' only to see lengthy affidavits explaining why the documents must not be released. Just what is it about UFOs that causes documents concerning them to be of such a sensitive nature? It is hardly surprising that some ufologists in the United States are more convinced than ever that their government has not told all it knows. And so the battle in the courts goes on – despite a desperate shortage of funds.

The American UFO scene being so confused, it is almost inevitable that the situation in Europe is in a similar state. Many European nations rely on the USA for defence aid – so it seems logical to direct the question of unidentified aerial objects in Europe at the US military.

It is possible, for example, that countries such as Britain have looked to the USA for a lead about UFOs and, noting the inconclusive nature of the USAF research projects and the negative Condon Report, concluded that UFOs represent no defence threat, in which case further research would be a waste of time. Then again, if secret, high-level investigation has been conducted into the UFO phenomenon – for whatever reason – the whole of NATO might conceivably have been made aware of this fact and, perhaps, its conclusions.

In Britain the Ministry of Defence says UFOs are not of 'defence interest' (see box). It

---

there are adequate material explanations for these. . . . It certainly has no evidence that alien spacecraft have landed on this planet.

'In response to demands for publication of UFO reports Viscount Long [of the MOD] said that he saw no objection to these reports being made public. We are therefore studying the best means of publishing this material.'

On the surface this seems a reasonable enough attitude, but still UFOs are not treated as a scientific issue by British government institutions.

A decision to release the British files was taken during 1982 but was severely delayed by the Falklands war. The decision was a direct result of a long battle waged by Lord Clancarty and his House of Lords All Party UFO Study Group, who finally forced the 1982 debate on the subject. The study group includes former Admiral of the Fleet, Lord Hill-Norton who – even while holding a top-level position in the MOD – knew nothing of the sheer scale of the UFO problem. He now believes that he was deliberately kept in ignorance of a cover up campaign – but on whose orders? And if someone at his level was not considered fit to be told of a cover up, then who was?

Spain's official line on UFOs has become increasingly open. In 1976 ufologist Juan José Benitez was astonished to be offered access to certain government UFO files; since then various detailed accounts of close encounters have been available for public scrutiny. One such was the 1979 case in which a Caravelle airliner (below) was 'buzzed' by a UFO (right) near Madrid. The pilot, Comandante Tejada (bottom), made a full report to the authorities, which was then passed on to ufologists

also says that is the only aspect of the problem that is of interest. Yet it continues to collect UFO reports, and when asked to hand the information over to a scientific institute it refuses to do so, using (as in the United States) the excuse that national security might be compromised. While this could, of course, be a wholly reasonable proposition, it could very easily be misconstrued as an attempt to hide unpalatable facts.

Other European governments have, in the past, behaved rather like that of Britain, but have gradually modified their approach to UFOs. Spain is typical of this new liberal attitude. In October 1976 the journalist and UFO investigator Juan José Benitez was rather astonished to be offered access to some government documents concerning UFOs. A whole batch of reports was 'cleared' for him, and others followed. These turned out to be detailed accounts of sightings of puzzling aerial phenomena, nearly always involving military personnel. Reports containing accounts of radar trackings and military jet

scramblings formed the basis of the documents that were released later.

Benitez has published the contents of several of these files in *Flying Saucer Review*, and there seems every indication that this new, open approach will continue. In November 1980, for example, the Spanish Minister of Transport said that, in his view, there was now no doubt that UFOs are 'real'. This followed an incident in 1974 in which a UFO, tracked on radar, made a close approach to a civil airliner, causing it to make a forced landing.

In June 1976, General Carlos Cabero was quoted as saying: 'I have for some time held the view that UFOs are extra-terrestrial craft.' He added that many countries were collaborating on research and that the world would soon be 'told the truth'.

But the first European nation to respond with a new initiative to the UFO phenomenon was France. Indeed the French stance on the subject remains unique throughout the world. (Yet, oddly, the British MOD stated some time ago that its position did not differ significantly from that of France.)

Between 28 January and 22 March 1974 the radio station France-Inter ran a nightly series of interviews with various world experts on UFOs. This included a most significant session with the then French Minister of Defence, M. Robert Galley. He talked freely about UFOs, saying:

I will indeed go so far as to say that it is irrefutable that there are things today that are inexplicable, or poorly explained. . . . I must say that if your listeners could see for themselves the mass of reports coming in from the airborne gendarmerie, from the mobile gendarmerie, and from the gendarmerie charged with the job of conducting investigations . . . then they would see that it is all pretty disturbing. . . .

Such a categorical statement is undeniably of the greatest importance. France is one of the most technologically advanced countries in the world. If its defence minister makes comments such as these then presumably they ought to be treated very seriously. Perhaps significantly, no British newspaper made any comment about this remarkable disclosure.

The police had indeed handled the official investigation of UFO reports in France; in 1970 they began to pass them to Dr Claude Poher at the Space Centre in Toulouse. Poher, a leading UFO researcher, worked on these in a private capacity and often reported his findings in *Flying Saucer Review*.

Not long after Galley's speech the French government gave Poher a grant to head a new team of scientists based at the Space Centre: the *Groupe d'Etude des Phénomènes Aerospatiaux Non-Identifiés* (GEPAN) – the group for the study of unidentified aerial phenomena. On the basis of its early results funds

In the early 1980s the French government seems to have become less enthusiastic about UFOs. It is said that, on his deathbed, President Georges Pompidou turned to his old friend the Defence Minister Robert Galley (below centre) saying: '. . . we have enough muck on our hands without bringing in the saucers.' And Dr Alain Esterle (bottom), then head of GEPAN, became noticeably withdrawn on the subject of UFOs – and shortly afterwards GEPAN was disbanded. Was this merely an economy measure – or was there something more sinister behind it?

According to Guérin, this unknown intelligence deliberately sets out to make scientists doubt its existence and also to persuade us that we are masters of the world – when the chilling truth is that we are not; it is. As he put it, when discussing the intelligence's motives, 'The ox will never know that he will be chopped up into beefsteaks.' However Guérin did not think we were destined for some larder in the sky. On the contrary, he believes this intelligence has continually guided our progress.

This was a member of a full-time official UFO project speaking. And he added that 'in our [presumably GEPAN's] opinion they [the governments of the world] do know the truth about the reality of UFOs but have no idea of how to go about tackling the problem.'

But Guérin made no more public statements. And Claude Poher left GEPAN to sail round the world in a home-made boat. He has not been heard from since. The next head of GEPAN, Dr Alain Esterle, remained much more tight-lipped than his predecessors, although he continued to receive support from civilian UFO societies.

In the circumstances, some people see this sudden change of attitude of the official French team as highly suspicious. And it is alleged, on good authority, that the French president Georges Pompidou, on his deathbed, said to his good friend the Defence Minister Galley: 'Don't you think we have enough muck on our hands without bringing in the saucers.' Some might read into such a statement Pompidou's belief in the existence of UFOs – and their nuisance value.

In late 1982 a number of French UFO groups began to express their frustrations at the sudden about-face of GEPAN's attitudes – but then the French government suddenly removed its financial backing. The group was disbanded.

were increased. It was the only known government-backed UFO research team in the world; and it seems that (to that French government at least) the output was well worth the investment. GEPAN published several reports in its first three years, but these stopped after about 1981.

A key member of the GEPAN team was the astrophysicist Dr Pierre Guérin. In 1979 he summarised its latest position in a lengthy paper published in *Flying Saucer Review*. Guérin's article can be described only as astonishing. For he thoroughly and logically eliminated all the stock explanations for UFOs and particularly those then in vogue (such as their psychic origin), concluding emphatically: 'An intelligence controls the UFOs. And it is not ours.'

As UFOs continue to be reported all over the world, governments can no longer deny that such things exist – but official attitudes tend to be characterised by alarming inconsistencies

THE GOVERNMENTS of the world seem, despite their protestations to the contrary, to take the subject of UFOs very seriously. The US government certainly does, and refuses to release key documents because, it claims, they would compromise national security. Britain maintains a 'stiff upper lip' on the subject as we have seen, but all the evidence points to an active interest in UFOs at a high level. Several European nations admit openly to the reality of UFOs; a leading scientist working with GEPAN, France's former government-funded UFO research

Above: UFO enthusiasts at the United Nations, including Dr Jacques Vallée (centre), the President of Grenada, Sir Eric Gairy (centre back) and Dr J. Allen Hynek (top left), discuss the global significance of UFOs

UFOs: an open secret

project, went further and proclaimed that the phenomenon is produced by an intelligence that is actually the dominant form of life on this planet. Such widespread interest seems inconsistent with the commonly held opinion that ufology is, at best, a 'pseudo-science' – and should stay that way.

Several of the smaller nations – such as those in South America – have issued bold statements concerning the reality and nature of UFOs. The media coverage of UFO reports in these countries is fairly extensive and rarely critical, so it is hardly surprising that they should offer their view that UFOs are representatives of a higher intelligence.

In 1978 the President of Grenada, Sir Eric Gairy, tried to force a United Nations debate on UFOs. Eventually he succeeded; several impressive depositions were made including contributions by Dr J. Allen Hynek and Dr Jacques Vallée. But nothing beyond a resolution calling for further action emerged, and Sir Eric was unable to push for the resolution to be implemented.

The situation in the Soviet Union is

characteristically complicated and obscured by officialdom. We know that parapsychology has always been treated with respect in the USSR but very little was known about the official Soviet attitude to UFOs until 1967, when Dr Jacques Vallée paid a visit there. As it happened, his trip coincided with the foundation of a scientific UFO research group, whose head was Dr Felix Zigel, professor of cosmology at Moscow's Institute of Aviation and the man responsible – under government direction – for the training of cosmonauts. Working with him in UFO research was an air force major called Stolyarov. They claimed that the authorities promised them, when their group was properly established, that they would be given the 1500 UFO reports in their possession. However this promise was never kept, the group eventually being told: 'You are too small, and the UFO problem is too big.'

Stolyarov and Zigel were, however, given permission to appear on national television, which they did on 10 November 1967, telling the Soviet citizens: 'UFOs are a very serious

Above: Hollywood's extra-terrestrial (E.T.) proves that he loves mankind. And despite his unpromising appearance, this creature has become a world-wide symbol of Man's longing to find – and understand – another race from somewhere 'over the rainbow'. Some ufologists, however, feel that this sympathetic portrayal of aliens is merely a form of propaganda – preparing us to meet our planet's 'true rulers'

Right: Dr Felix Zigel, one of the few officially approved ufologists of the USSR – yet even he seemed compelled to take part in blatant UFO cover ups

subject, which we must study fully.' They also launched an appeal for UFO reports.

Shortly after this, however, Zigel suddenly adopted a low profile. When US journalists Sheila Ostrander and Lynn Schroeder visited the USSR in the late 1960s to collect material for their *Psychic discoveries behind the Iron Curtain* the only scientist concerned they were not allowed to meet was Felix Zigel.

On 14 June 1980 at 11.50 p.m. an orange horseshoe-shaped UFO appeared in the sky to the north-west of Moscow: it was seen by thousands of people. The giant object actually cruised over the streets of the capital, causing great panic. Some people fled into fall-out shelters believing that the Third World War had started – but the object moved away without harming anyone. And next day the Soviet media made no mention of this event. However – somewhat oddly, in view of his strange reticence on the subject of UFOs – Zigel suddenly spoke of craft detaching themselves from the horseshoe-shaped 'mother ship' and disgorging aliens onto the streets of Moscow. Yet Zigel must have known that the 'UFO' was very probably the satellite Cosmos 1188 shortly after its launch from a site at Plesetsk, just north of Moscow. Western scientists were well aware of this and – although ordinary Soviet citizens are generally kept in the dark about their own government's activities – Zigel, as a trainer of cosmonauts, must have known about it. His extraordinary claims may, in fact, be proof that he had been finally let into the secrets contained in the 1500 official UFO reports – on

condition, presumably, that he became a pawn of the Soviet government. And this may have involved using unlikely UFO stories to act as a cover for some kind of secret government activities.

Although Zigel has published many articles about UFOs in the USSR, he seems to be very reluctant to share his data with ufologists elsewhere. Perhaps it is simply too problematic to smuggle information out of the country, but others have managed to do so – albeit with some difficulty. Nikita Schnee is one Soviet ufologist who regularly sends UFO reports to the West; commenting on Zigel's cases he says: 'We checked them out and not a single one was found to be true!'

Schnee works at a scientific research establishment and, together with fellow scientist Vladimir Azhazha, attempted to set up a private UFO research institute between 1978 and 1979. But they were continually blocked by the Communist Party who, announcing that the study of UFOs was 'anti-state', broke up their meetings. Zigel is alleged to have telephoned Schnee and said, 'Well, they dispersed you, eh! I fixed that for you!'

Closely guarded secrets?

Juri Lina is another Soviet ufologist who has sent UFO reports to the West that mirror the characteristics of typical cases elsewhere, including close encounters. However, Lina has suffered too. He claims he was persecuted because of his activities and eventually managed to escape by entering into an arranged marriage with a Finnish ufologist. Although he now lives in Finland, Lina returns to the USSR to lecture about UFOs – and, he says, the KGB still watches him closely. The only realistic conclusion about ufology in the USSR is that it is seen as dangerous – and therefore must be of great interest to the government.

The Australian authorities, on the other hand, seem only too eager to give researchers unlimited access to their UFO files. In late 1981 ufologist Bill Chalker was suddenly given the opportunity to see the UFO reports then in the possession of the Royal Australian Air Force (RAAF). During 1982 Chalker took up the offer with enthusiasm; he was even allowed to copy whatever he wanted – although, reasonably enough, he was required to sign a waiver to guarantee the confidentiality of the witnesses involved. No other restrictions were imposed on him.

The cases reported in the RAAF files apparently gave rise to the official pronouncement that 'nothing that has arisen from the three or four per cent of unexplained cases gives any firm support for the belief that interlopers from other places in the world, or outside it, have been visiting us.' However, according to Bill Chalker, many of the cases are extremely provocative.

Typical of these is the series of amazing events that took place around Brisbane airport on 4 November 1976. Ground staff saw

"...QUEST TO DISCOVER MORE ABOUT U.F.O.'S AND RELATED PHENOMENA..."

GRENADA

SIR ERIC GARY

$2

RESEARCH INTO U.F.O.'S

7 OCTOBER 1977

32ND REGULAR SESSION OF THE GENERAL ASSEMBLY OF THE UNITED NATIONS

a pulsing light in the sky, and the crew of an Elektra transport aircraft observed the same object keeping pace with them before moving off southwards at one and a half times their speed. A commercial jet was also 'paced' and a nearby light aircraft reported a close encounter. Both local weather radar and the airport radar tracked an unidentified object that seemed to match the sightings. The conclusion of the report in the RAAF files is that the light was 'most probably the planet Venus' and the radar returns 'ships at sea' – although the pilots all refuted the suggestion that they had been 'paced' by a planet, and the highly experienced radar operators said that they had never before picked up echoes from ships.

The RAAF had pursued the usual official line of enquiry, based entirely on concern over a possible threat to national defence. No scientific study was undertaken. Significantly, the files contain memoranda that suggest that some RAAF personnel were aware that a cover up would be suspected. One of them says: 'We only foster the incorrect (but nevertheless widely held) belief that we have much vital information to hide.'

Bill Chalker concludes that the openness of the assistance he was offered and the contents of the files themselves militate against the idea of an official cover up. In fact, the files indicate that the RAAF was as puzzled as anyone else about the UFO phenomenon – and there are many other cases, Chalker points out, that do not appear in the RAAF files – some of which 'are at the very least highly provocative'.

In 1981 Australia passed its own Freedom of Information Act – the consequences of which opened the official files to Bill Chalker. But perhaps such apparent openness is merely an attempt to discourage ufologists to investigate further.

Above: a postage stamp from Grenada, clearly showing its government's interest in UFOs

Below: Bill Chalker, an Australian ufologist who was actually offered top secret UFO documents by his government – but why?

If one looks at the official changes of attitude to UFOs since the 1970s a clear pattern seems to emerge. Spain released its files to interested parties in 1976; the Blue Book documents were made accessible to the US public in 1977; France set up an official UFO study group – which made some interesting – even astonishing – statements in the late 1970s; and in 1981 Australia opened its files. In 1982 Britain announced that its UFO files would be made public. In every case, the country concerned has maintained for years that UFOs do not exist, or that no such files have been kept.

The real E.T.

All of this may, of course, simply be a coincidence. And perhaps such movies as *Close encounters of the third kind* (1977) have created such a sense of unease in the public mind that governments have felt compelled to reassure people that there is, in fact, no sinister cover up – and so have released their files for public scrutiny. That may not be the whole story, however.

The fact that governments all over the world have kept records of UFO cases – and some of them spent vast sums of money on official studies of them – attests to the mystery surrounding the phenomenon. And the fact that no government has claimed to solve the enigma must be significant.

One apparently extraordinary explanation of the official attitude to UFOs has been put forward by the Earl of Clancarty – otherwise known as the UFO writer Brinsley le Poer Trench – who believes that there has, indeed, been a world-wide UFO cover up, but that it is gradually being replaced by a subtle 'UFO education' programme of which few people are aware. Lord Clancarty asserts that we are being conditioned to accept the truth; perhaps even enormously popular movies such as *E.T. – the extra-terrestrial*, where the alien is presented as extremely lovable, are part of this education campaign. Nobody will fear UFOs any more.

But if this is true, what are we being prepared for? Lord Clancarty – together with an increasing number of other ufologists – suspects that UFOs represent the real rulers of this planet. And such a revelation could not be sprung on the world without the most appalling panic; hence the need for the re-education programme.

If this is the real reason for the curiously inconsistent behaviour of the world governments over the UFO issue, then they have an unenviable task ahead of them – to ensure that the millions of people on Earth, of widely different cultures, are prepared to receive the greatest news story ever. Yet the world has a right to know the truth about UFOs, be it disappointingly mundane or as astoundingly significant as Lord Clancarty's theory suggests. The evidence seems to point to a move towards discovering the truth. Are the days of the cover up nearly over?

UFOs
and science

*Advanced technology is now being used
in the investigation of UFO sighting
reports; such techniques as photo
analysis by computer, sophisticated
radar scanning and advanced
aeronautics are invaluable in separating
hoaxes and red herrings from genuine
UFO mysteries.*

A force to be reckoned with

Many UFO sightings are heralded by the erratic behaviour of electrical equipment and the failure of car engines. What forces could create these disturbances? Are they deliberately produced, or mere side effects of the UFOs passing? Several notable cases and the proposed explanations provide fascinating material for speculation

THE EVENING OF 2 NOVEMBER 1957 was an eventful one for Patrolman A. J. Fowler, on duty at police headquarters in the American town of Levelland, in Texas. At about 11 p.m. he received the first of several puzzling telephone calls. It was from one Pedro Saucedo, who had been driving 4 miles (6 kilometres) west of Levelland with a companion when a torpedo-shaped, brilliantly lit, yellow and white object approached the truck at high speed. As the object passed close overhead the truck's headlights went out and its engine died. The object gave off considerable heat and when Saucedo got out of the truck to look at it he had to drop to the ground. As the UFO moved into the distance the headlights came on again and the engine was easily restarted. The two men drove for

Right: a luminous sphere hangs over the Spanish island of Gran Canaria on a June night in 1976. This photograph is one of a series of 36 of this UFO. During other sightings made that night, presumably of the same object, a radio and a television set cut out

Below: the UFO that was seen by Pedro Saucedo near Levelland, Texas. While it was nearby the engine and headlights of Saucedo's truck failed

some distance before telephoning the police. However, Officer Fowler attached no importance to the call.

An hour later, a man telephoned from 4 miles (6 kilometres) east of Levelland (in the direction in which the first object had been travelling) and told Patrolman Fowler that he had come upon a brilliant egg-shaped object about 200 feet (60 metres) long, sitting in the middle of the road. As the car approached, its engine failed and the headlights went out. The witness said that the object was lit up like a large neon light and threw a bright glare over the whole area. When he got out of his car the UFO took off and rose some distance. Then its light went out. The car's engine could then be restarted.

A short time later Officer Fowler received another call. Another motorist had been stopped by a glowing object sitting in the road. His engine and lights had failed.

Soon after midnight Newell Wright was driving towards Levelland when his car ammeter began fluctuating, the engine died, and the lights went out. He got out to look at the engine, but found nothing apparently wrong with battery or wiring. He then noticed an oval object on the road ahead, similar to those of the previous sightings.

During the next hour at least four more similar reports came in. A fire marshal spoke of a red light that he saw in the sky as his

Above: a Curtiss C-46 of Brazil's Varig Airlines. An aircraft of this type suffered severe electrical disturbance during a UFO sighting in 1957

Below: east of Levelland, in the second incident of 2 November 1957, a UFO straddling the road caused a vehicle to stall

UFO-related we have to establish that the report is not a hoax, and that the UFO was not really a man-made or natural object. It is believed by many researchers that a few cases of damage may have been caused by ball lightning. But the value of this explanation is questionable since scientists are as baffled by ball lightning as they are by UFOs.

Aircrew have noticed disturbances to electrical systems during UFO sightings. On 4 November 1957 a Varig Airlines C-46 on a flight between Porto Alegre and São Paulo,

vehicle lost power and its lights went out. A similar red light was reported by a sheriff and his deputy.

That November night in Levelland was exceptional. But people in all parts of the world have reported similar puzzling events at various times. The vehicle faults that have sometimes been described as occurring when a UFO has been observed have included static on the radio, rough running or complete failure of the engine, wildly fluctuating instruments, headlight failure and even severe damage to the wiring of a vehicle. In most cases the driver has been able to restart the engine when the object has left the area. In a few cases the drivers or passengers have been very shocked and have referred to strange sensations of heat or static electricity, or to unusual odours.

Vehicle interference cases are examples of close encounters; generally they are of the second kind, in which there are effects on the environment, but no alien beings are reported. However, in one listing of 400 cases, over 60 included reports of humanoids, and are thus classed as close encounters of the third kind.

Sometimes a vehicle is permanently damaged; scientists then have a physical change to study, and not merely the observer's account of what he thought happened. However, before the vehicle damage is accepted as

is a very precisely controlled field.

We see very specific interference in a report from Iran. On 18 September 1976 an unidentified object was spotted by officials in the control tower at Mehrabad Airport, Tehran, and two Phantom jets of the Iranian Air Force were sent up to investigate. The pilots described the object as round; as they approached, it accelerated to many times the speed of sound and then turned to chase the jets for a short time. When the pilots rashly tried to open fire the electronically operated gun controls failed to respond. The aircraft's electronic systems, including radio, would not operate within 3 miles (5 kilometres) of the object.

To summarise: there have been many cases since the Second World War of disturbance to vehicles when UFOs are nearby. In addition to apparently electrical and magnetic effects, drivers and passengers have reported air pressure changes, temperature changes, temporary paralysis, 'sunburn', and other mental and bodily changes.

There is much loose talk about the causes

Brazil, encountered an unusual object. The pilot and co-pilot saw a red light moving quickly towards them. Suddenly the object seemed to jump through an arc of 45° and grow larger. There was a smell of burning rubber in the aircraft and the direction finder, a generator and the radio transmitter burned out. The object then disappeared almost instantaneously.

Boats have been involved, too. At about 3 p.m. on 15 December 1968 at Hawk Inlet, Alaska, two men on board the cargo boat *Teel* observed a round, white light moving slowly towards them. At 7 p.m. the object was still visible, apparently floating on the water. Then it rose and flew away over a nearby mountain ridge.

On the following evening the same strange light was seen again. It moved slowly until it was directly above the *Teel*'s mast, at a height of about 70 feet (21 metres). There was no sound. The *Teel*'s crew contacted Elmendorf Air Force Base and the coastguard by radio. After about five minutes the boat's power and radio went dead. An auxiliary diesel power generator hesitated and showed signs of failing; then the object moved away and the generator began to function normally. The object disappeared from view after 15 minutes. An American scientist, Dr James Harder, suggested that the UFO may have been short-circuiting the electric generator in some way, giving the diesel engine so much work to do that it nearly stalled.

Many people call these 'electromagnetic' effects. However, this does not help to explain them and begs the question of their causes. In fact, modern physics cannot explain many of the effects that are reported. For example, it has been argued that UFOs must emit a powerful magnetic field, which affects vehicle instruments. But if this is so, it

Top: an unidentified floating object. At Hawk Inlet, Alaska, the crew of the cargo boat *Teel* observed a white light for two successive nights. It apparently affected the boat's electrical systems and diesel generator

Above: a Phantom of the former Imperial Iranian Air Force. The sophisticated electronic gun control systems of one of these supersonic fighters failed at the moment when its pilot was trying to fire on a UFO, and other electronic systems were disturbed

Mind over motor

The links between UFOs and traditional 'psychic' phenomena have been explored extensively in recent years. Among the disturbances produced by poltergeists – disturbances that may originate in the minds of victims – electromagnetic effects are relatively rare, but not unknown. One young woman who had been adopted as a baby had the traumatic experience, only a week before her marriage, of meeting her real mother. On her return home that evening she switched on all the lights. One by one all of them 'blew' – some literally

of these apparent disturbances. Ufologists speak of 'intense electromagnetic fields' as being responsible. A small amount of research has been carried out, and is still proceeding, to put some substance into these speculations.

One official investigation that is widely known was carried out for the Condon Committee (see page 178). A team studied the effects of strong magnetic fields on the patterns of magnetism in car bodies. They found that during manufacture, cars acquire magnetic fields that are a record of the Earth's magnetic field at that time and place. In normal conditions, this pattern of magnetism does not change, and will be identical for all cars of a given model and year.

When the investigators subjected a car body to a changing magnetic field, by passing magnets over it, they found that the pattern of its magnetisation was changed. They concluded that any car that was subjected to a magnetic field intense enough to cause it to malfunction would carry an altered pattern of magnetisation as a consequence.

Two cars that allegedly malfunctioned during UFO sightings were studied: in both cases it was found that their magnetisation patterns had not changed since their manufacture. The cause of the disturbance could not have been an intense magnetic field.

Duplicating the effects

This is not to say that magnetic fields could not be important in other cases. Very few cars involved in UFO sightings receive the thorough study that is needed to establish how and why the effects are produced.

A team set up by the British UFO Research Association has made some small-scale experiments on the effects of magnetic fields. One interesting finding is that the current-voltage regulator of many cars can be disturbed by comparatively low-strength fields. However, with the bonnet down, the body of a car is an effective magnetic shield: extremely high field strengths outside the car would be needed to produce even weak fields

exploding. This event, resembling poltergeist phenomena, may have been related to her distraught state.

Electromagnetic effects are among the psychokinetic (PK) phenomena that have been induced in the laboratory. At Aston University, Birmingham, in England, the parapsychologist Julian Isaacs has found that such effects are more likely to occur when his subjects are exposed to a picture of a baby, or to the word 'baby' – for reasons not yet apparent.

If UFOs are productions of the minds of those who witness them – though none the less real for that – then the same must be true of associated effects, such as vehicle breakdowns.

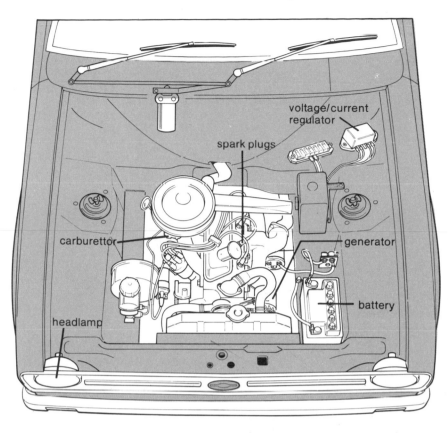

Above: the parts of a car engine that have been tested to discover their susceptibility to disturbances from external sources include: the battery; the generator, which recharges the battery; the spark plugs, which ignite the fuel; and the voltage-current regulator. Power can be drained from the battery through the headlights by microwave radiation, according to one ufologist, while reduced air pressure would disturb the engine by impairing the carburettor's functioning

inside the engine compartment.

Other causes of vehicle disturbance that have been suggested include microwaves, which could cause heating of car components, and intense ultraviolet light, which could release electrons in the metal of the car body and give rise to stray voltages and currents (and could perhaps be associated with the skin burns reported in some cases).

One of the oddest suggestions, though one that has been carefully worked out, is that microwave radiation could affect tungsten headlamp filaments in such a way that large amounts of current could be drained from the battery, causing the engine to stall.

However, a drained battery will not function again until it has been recharged, whereas in many cases, such as those described above, the car engine has restarted immediately upon the departure of the UFO.

UFO research organisations, underfinanced and dependent on their members' voluntary efforts, cannot mount the major investigations that would be required to discover physical effects capable of bringing a vehicle to a stop and dousing its headlights. But we may be sure that official circles with more ample resources take an intense interest in this question. The military could not fail to be interested in the possibility of a 'vehicle-stopping' ray – especially if it were effective against heavy trucks and tanks, or even aeroplanes. And they would be neglecting their duty if they did not concern themselves with means of defence against what is potentially such a valuable weapon. But the results of their potentially vital research have not seen the light of day.

Faults, flaws and flare-ups

Scientists now recognise the fact that certain volcanic upheavals can produce spectacular light displays. An examination of this remarkable phenomena suggests that it could be connected with the origin of UFOs

A CHINESE MOUNTAIN called Wu T'ai Shan may hold a clue to the origin of UFOs. On its southern peak is a tower designed to give a view of a remarkable phenomenon that, in China's Buddhist days, was considered to be a manifestation of the Buddha. Probably the last European to witness it, some time in the 1930s, was John Blofeld. He and his companions were waiting in the tower when a monk entered their room after midnight exclaiming: 'The Bodhisattva has appeared!' Blofeld was led to the tower's window – and gasped with surprise at what he saw. 'There, in the great open space beyond the window,' Blofeld wrote, 'innumerable balls of fire floated majestically past . . . .' These lights evidently appeared with sufficient regularity to have persuaded the monks to build their observation tower; and the monks linked the mountain itself with their occurrence.

It is probable that these 'balls of fire' are in fact related to 'mountain peak discharges' – curious beams of light that are seen from time to time radiating from the tops of high mountains. They have been noticed particularly in the Andes in South America. These luminous effects are sometimes visible over huge distances. In the Chilean Andes mountain peak discharges are usually seen from late spring to early autumn. A constant glow around a mountain can give way to occasional outbursts that look like great

A rare photograph of earthquake lights at Matsushiro, Japan, taken during a local 'swarm' of seismic tremors that took place between 1965 and 1967. There have been frequent and reliable reports of the phenomenon for hundreds of years – but scientists have only recently acknowledged its existence

searchlight beams. Such displays have been reported when the sky is clear and seem particularly closely associated with earthquakes. In August 1906, for example, at the time of a great earthquake in Chile, mountain peak discharges were so brilliant that, as one witness put it, 'the whole sky seemed to be on fire.'

This link with earthquakes is interesting because there are other, though doubtlessly closely related, types of lights that have been noted specifically in relation to seismic activity – the so-called 'earthquake lights'. These odd illuminations take many forms. Just before the strong 1957 earth tremor centred on Charnwood Forest, Leicestershire, England, dozens of people reported 'tadpole-shaped' lights flying through the sky, while in an earthquake that shook Humboldt County in California, USA, in 1932, the lights appeared like 'bolts of lightning travelling from the ground towards the sky'. During another Californian earthquake, near Hollister in 1961, sequential flashes of light were seen being emitted from random places on local hillsides. Later inspection of the locations failed to reveal an obvious explanation for the lights.

Japan is prone to earthquakes, and it is in that country that seismic light phenomena have been most closely studied to date. A researcher named Musya collected no less than 1500 eyewitness reports from a single earthquake that occurred on the Idu Peninsula on 26 November 1930. Various forms of lights were reported – flares like sheet lightning but of longer duration, auroral streamers emanating from a point on the

Left: an illustration from *Earthquakes*, by Arnold Boscowitz, published in 1898: 'The sky streaked with lightning flashes and meteors. The inhabitants regard them with terror, as presages of an earthquake.' Another probable example of what has since become known as 'earthquake lights' occurred at Logelbach in Alsace, in France, in March 1878 (below). The phenomenon finally received the blessing of orthodox science in 1981, when Dr Brian Brady of the US Bureau of Mines at Denver, Colorado, succeeded in reproducing in the laboratory and photographing 'earthquake' lights that appeared as a result of applying huge pressures to a piece of granite (overleaf). Megaliths are huge lumps of stone: could it be that they, too, emit light when subjected to large pressures by natural forces?

horizon, and beams and columns of light at other locations in the vicinity of the quake. Fireballs and straight rows of round masses of light were also observed. The brilliance of some of the lights was such that they cast illumination as strong as moonlight as far as 30 miles (50 kilometres) away. But the most important data on such phenomena have come from another researcher, Yasui, who was able to obtain photographs of atmospheric illuminations associated with the swarm of tremors around Matsushiro between 1965 and 1967.

So it is clear that the geology of our planet can produce extraordinary luminous atmospheric manifestations, even though the mechanisms by which they are created are far from understood by scientists. In their 1977 book *Space-time transients* Michael A. Persinger and Ghislaine F. Lafrenière suggested that UFO events were, in fact, geologically produced lightforms; that in areas subject to low intensity tremors as well as full-blown earthquakes, piezoelectricity – or 'seismoelectricity' – created ionisation effects in the atmosphere close to geological fault lines. Their research in Canada and the United States led them to conclude that 'the data consistently point towards seismic-related sources' for UFOs. The researchers further suggested that the geophysical conditions producing such light phenomena, and possibly surrounding such phenomena themselves, could have a 'scrambling' effect on human brain rhythms, triggering hallucinatory imagery within the consciousness of witnesses.

Years before these suggestions were made, however, certain ufologists had already noticed an apparent correlation between UFO incidence and fault lines. The French researcher F. Lagarde, for instance, made a study of sightings in the 1954 French UFO wave and concluded: 'UFO sightings occur by preference on geological faults.'

Spanish researchers Lopez and Ares similarly noted in their study of the Spanish UFO flap that took place in 1968 and 1969 that a large percentage of UFOs were sighted on or near fault lines. In the late 1960s the Pereiro region of Brazil experienced a plague of UFOs. Tremendous detonations were heard and 'immense' blue-green fiery balls were seen 'flying in all directions overhead'. Conical forms also appeared, and some of the UFOs seemed to direct 'lights like searchlights' onto the ground. Concurrent with these manifestations the region was undergoing almost daily earth tremors. Observers noted that the lights always preceded the tremors by a few hours: 'the balls of light seem to know where and when the 'quakes are coming.'

A history of strangeness

During the period from 1972 to 1976 a wide-ranging study of the central English county of Leicestershire was conducted, in which local researcher Andrew York and the author took part. A thorough archival and field study was made of ancient sites and traditions, seismic and meteorological phenomena as well as alleged UFO events. English counties are particularly suitable for such research, as each has central archives, county research groups, at least one local newspaper and forms a practicable ground area for fieldwork. This particular study located hitherto unknown standing stones and revealed that the county has a rich history of seismic disturbance, with records going back to the 16th century. The study also found accounts stretching back for centuries detailing remarkable atmospheric events in Leicestershire. A typical incident occurred in 1659 in the village of Markfield ('the mark on the field' – named after a standing stone) on Charnwood Forest, a rugged waste of exposed strata of ancient rocks with its own geological fault system, in the north-west

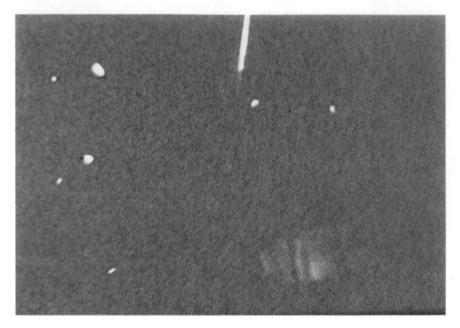

of the county: 'extraordinary flashes of lightning' broke from angry-looking clouds, accompanied by 'terrible' claps of thunder. This went on for some time but no rain fell. At length, hailstones of unusual shapes were precipitated. Then the atmosphere came alive with crackles and bangs 'like muskets', and 'prodigious eruptions of fire' were seen flying close to the ground. Some of these uprooted trees and destroyed houses. Eventually, the strange geophysical display came to an end as mysteriously and suddenly as it had started. Again, in the following century, at the village of Shepshed – also on Charnwood – the local vicar recorded in his diaries that unusual auroras were to be seen in the local skies displaying 'strong vibrations or dartings'. These appeared in all parts of the heavens in every season for nine years, so they were clearly something other than mere 'northern lights'. In more modern times,

exceptional geophysical events have occurred, such as the fall of the largest amount of debris from a single meteorite ever to have been recorded in Britain. This took place on Christmas Eve 1965 at Barwell, about 10 miles (16 kilometres) south of Charnwood. Buildings were damaged by the bombardment from space, and last-minute Christmas shoppers cowered in shop doorways, but no one was injured. Ten years later another extraordinary event afflicted this otherwise normal village: a fireball – presumably ball lightning – bounced down a street in the village. It was described as being about 3 feet (1 metre) in diameter. It eventually came in contact with a house and exploded.

Freak thunderstorms

The Leicestershire study suggested that the parts of the county most likely to experience exceptional seismic and meteorological displays coincide with the main network of the county's faults, in the western half of the shire, particularly on and around Charnwood. This was to be expected with regard to seismic activity, but why should unusual meteorological events also be so associated? Most *normal* thunderstorm activity occurs in the east of the county, so the researchers came to the conclusion that there must be some magnetic or electrical factors in the vicinity of fault regions that in some way cause or enhance exceptional atmospheric phenomena.

Additional support for this hypothesis came when carefully compiled UFO sightings for the county were correlated with the geophysical data. The incidence of reported UFO activity seemed clearly to follow a remarkably similar distribution in the landscape to geological fault lines. It was hard to avoid the conclusion that, whatever the conditions are that produce exceptional meteorological events such as earthquake

Right: two maps of the county of Leicestershire showing the main areas of geological faulting and the peak incidence of UFOs. The result of a research project carried out between 1972 and 1976, the maps show that the patterns of UFO incidence and geological faulting are remarkably similar.
(NB the maps show the county of Leicestershire as it was before the redefinition of English county boundaries in 1974)

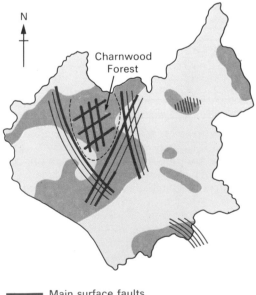

——— Main surface faults
——— Secondary surface faults

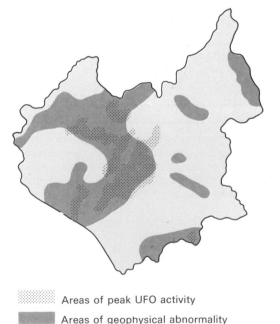

▓ Areas of peak UFO activity

▓ Areas of geophysical abnormality

lights, they also favour the occurrence of UFOs. Are UFOs therefore a special but related type of geophysical phenomenon? Research carried out in the USA, in which the state of Michigan has been subjected to a similar study by the Michigan Anomaly Bureau, has suggested the same interpretation of UFOs.

A British research project has sought to extend the microcosmic study of the type attempted in Leicestershire to a wider context. Over 800 UFO cases were taken from records of 19 separate, randomly selected years from 1904 to 1977. They were plotted as carefully as the available data would allow on a map of England and Wales. This information was then correlated with population information supplied in units of 1 square kilometre (0.4 square miles) by Her Majesty's Stationery Office. The resulting map gives some idea of what a population-corrected picture of UFO incidence in England and Wales would look like. It is important to have such correction in a UFO map because the fact that knowledge of a UFO event relies on witnesses means that population distribution can affect the apparent distribution of UFO incidence. In rural England and Wales there may be fewer than 125 people per square mile (50 people per square kilometre) whereas in a conurbation like Greater London, for example, there can be over 12,500 people per square mile (5000 people per square kilometre). So the chances of a UFO that appears in a rural region being unobserved are many times greater than in an urban region. Moreover, the chances of misperception of ordinary aerial lights are greatly increased in city skies, thus further inflating the likelihood that more UFOs will be reported in city areas.

The resulting map is a symbolical one; it is representative rather than exhaustive, based as it is upon a random sample, but it is the

Above: the Hanging Stone Rocks, Leicestershire, showing the impressive rock strata in this area of Charnwood Forest. In 1957, during an earth tremor centred on Charnwood Forest, many people reported 'tadpole-shaped' lights

Below: a massive rock formation near the village of Shepshed on Charnwood Forest. An 18th-century vicar reported seeing strange lights with 'strong vibrations or dartings'

best available of its kind for England and Wales. It gives an indication of what the actual distribution of UFO activity might be. If this map is compared with one showing the distribution of earth tremor epicentres for England and Wales, a remarkable correlation can be seen. There is more information about epicentres than about UFOs, but the general similarity of distribution cannot be missed.

Miraculous phenomena?

It is interesting to note the positions on the UFO map of the 'window areas' at Barmouth, Dyfed and Warminster. The Barmouth cases occurred during a wave of UFO activity that took place in 1904 and 1905. Many lights in the forms of globes and other strange shapes were reported, witnessed by all sections of the local populace as well as by outsiders in the form of journalists from London. The lights were, at the time, widely believed to be miraculous phenomena produced through the agency of a visionary Methodist preacher, Mrs Mary Jones. Informed analysis of these reports has proved informative because they contain a number of eyewitness accounts that confirm that the lights first appeared close to, or actually emerged from, the ground in a significant number of cases. Three clergymen at Cefn Mawr, inland from the Barmouth-Tywyn area along the valley formed by the great Bala Fault, saw balls of light 'rise from the earth and suddenly burst luridly'. Another witness, at the village of Dyffryn, near Barmouth, saw three columns of light emerge from the ground in January 1905, while in May of the same year a similar manifestation was seen by another man in which the column also produced balls of light. A husband and wife saw balls of deep red light emerging from a field next to a chapel near Harlech on the night of 25 March

account of the 'birth' of a UFO. Another witness saw the same light shortly afterwards, by which time it was flying freely and was intensely brilliant. Could the 'streaks of misty light' be the 'searchlight beams' that are a common feature of UFO reports of more recent times? Could it be that, in these reports, it is only *assumed* that the beams of light come from the UFO? Perhaps they are really some form of discharge streamer emerging from the ground.

Experimental evidence, too, seems to hint that UFOs may be formed in the ground. An experiment carried out in 1981 by Dr Brian Brady of the US Bureau of Mines in Denver, Colorado, has provided laboratory evidence to demonstrate that geology can produce luminous atmospheric effects. By subjecting a piece of granite to immense pressure, he produced and filmed short-lived points of light in the air around the rock sample. They would streak away, hover and sometimes move along fractures – faults – in the piece of granite. This seems to indicate what can occur when rocks affected by seismic action are squeezed and pulled and strange lights are seen in the sky. Enormous forces are involved, even if no actual earthquake results.

Research, testimony and experiment all appear to indicate that UFOs do not come from Venus, alpha Centauri or via holes at the poles – they come from planet Earth, the most mysterious world of them all.

1905. And so on. But a particularly significant sighting took place a little later that year. In July a witness saw 'a ball of misty light in the heavens about 7 or 8 inches [17 or 20 centimetres] in diameter . . . then it got very much brighter, and . . . grew very much larger . . . forming an oval shape . . . it glittered and quivered very much. Then there appeared to be two great long streaks of misty light coming from the ball which almost reached the earth.' This is surely the

Above: artist John Petts's impression of a curious light he saw during a spate of UFO sightings that occurred around St Brides Bay, Dyfed, in 1977

Below: maps of England and Wales comparing selected UFO sightings (blue) to earthquake epicentres

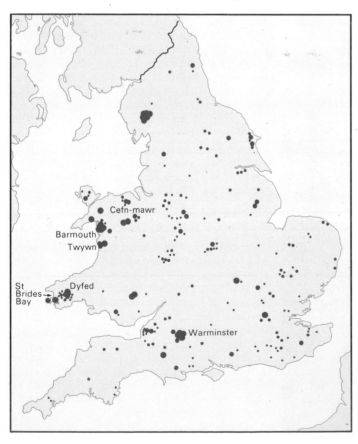

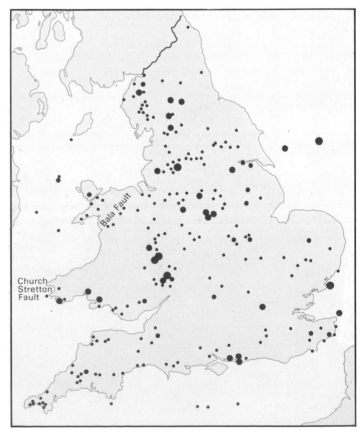

Scientific research suggests that UFOs seen near stone circles may be produced by the energy of the Earth itself. These terrestrial forces may connect sacred sites with seismic activity, electromagnetic fields – and the incidence of UFOs

The fault of the Earth

A BELIEF EXISTS that standing stones mark places of power; evidence to support it comes from folklore, geomancy, dowsing, the response of psychics to such sites and research by electronics experts and other scientists. The British Dragon Project in particular has, since late 1977 been investigating many of these types of evidence at ancient sites. Its findings regarding the geological aspects of the distribution of stone circles are beginning to suggest that there may have been a geophysical dimension to the siting of these ancient holy places and that there may be common factors linking some types of megalithic site with the unusual atmospheric phenomena we call UFOs.

As long ago as 1969 John Michell suggested that stone circles were located in geological fault regions. This, however, was only a 'hunch', and it was not until 1982 that research by geologist Paul McCartney confirmed Michell's suspicion. Britain is an ideal 'laboratory' for such investigation because not only does it have a rich heritage of stone monuments, but it also has an extraordinarily wide range of landscapes of different geological types, all crammed into one small island. The country has undergone a number of mountain-building periods – orogenies – and the landscape has been scarred, fractured, and in some cases overlaid with sedimentary deposits, only to be scarred by subsequent orogenies. The most recent mountain-building episode to leave a really major mark on the British landscape was the Armorican orogeny, which took place about 300 million years ago. It is the pre-Armorican rocks that took the brunt of the disturbances caused by this orogeny, of course, and it is on outcrops of these that we find most of the surface faulting in the British Isles. A glance at a geological map shows that most faults occur in the north and west of Britain.

In the vicinity of faulting there is *mineral enhancement*: the minerals found within rock strata are here compressed into relatively small areas, often with metal ores of different kinds jammed into close proximity to one another. Different metals have different magnetic values, and it is in such places that we tend to find variations in local magnetism.

In the course of these primordial geological upheavals, great *intrusions* of igneous granite have been thrust through the Earth's crust. These have naturally fractured the areas around them and have therefore formed hubs of faulting, folding and general tectonic disturbance, giving the landscape its characteristic appearance.

If certain megalithic sites such as stone circles are, as one theory goes, places of power, it is in geologically disturbed areas, where the energies of the Earth are likely to be at their strongest, that we would expect to find them. And so it proves. If we compare the limits of main stone circle building in England and Wales with the surface-faulted pre-Armorican rock outcrops, we see that the distribution is almost identical. The areas of mineral enhancement also follow a markedly similar distribution.

The correlation between megalithic monuments and fault lines appears to be more than a vague similarity of distribution. The Rollright circle near Oxford, for example, falls outside the main boundaries of stone circle distribution and it is not in an area where surface faulting would be expected. Yet, within about three-quarters of a mile (1.2 kilometres) of the stones, there runs a surface fault – called, appropriately enough, the Rollright Fault. This is a pattern repeated throughout England and Wales, and McCartney's research convinces him that every stone circle in those two countries lies within a mile (1.6 kilometres) of a surface fault or on an associated intrusion.

Research that has been carried out in Scotland indicates that the same principles hold for stone circle distribution there as elsewhere in the British Isles. For instance there is the Great Glen Fault, a huge, extremely ancient fissure that contains Loch Ness. Approximately 50 megalithic sites of various sorts cluster around this feature. Archaeological evidence suggests that the loch itself covers the sites of inundated stone circles. Only the group of circles in Aberdeenshire seem less closely linked to tectonic features. This is particularly interesting because these form a distinct set of sites, archaeologically speaking, characterised by having a recumbent stone in each circle. Some of the recumbent stones are exactly horizontal as measured by a spirit level. It is possible that this peculiarity is in some way related to the fact that the circles lie further from faults than do their counterparts elsewhere in the British Isles.

Places of power

Little research of this kind has been carried out outside the British Isles, but the results of a French research project provide telling confirmation and additional information. Pierre Mereaux has conducted many years' geophysical study of what is probably the world's largest megalithic complex, at Locmariaquer near Carnac in Brittany. Mereaux has pointed out that the thousands of stones comprising the rows of the Carnac region are located on a huge granite platform – an intrusion – that also contains magnetite, or lodestone. (This is also the case with the British circles on the great intrusions of Dartmoor, Bodmin Moor and so on.) Around the edges of this granite upland there is considerable faulting, of course, and it is an important fact that this region of Brittany is the most seismically active in the whole of France. Over the years, Mereaux has been carrying out a unique set of experiments around the Carnac stones – and the results give us a deeper insight into the geophysical reasons why megaliths are where they are. Gravitation is not constant at all places on the Earth's surface, and in specific areas there are anomalous changes in the magnitude of the

Castlerigg stone circle (overleaf above and below) in Cumbria lies in an area of geological disturbance. Most British stone circles lie near fault lines. Maps (below) show similarities in the distribution of highly faulted pre-Armorican rocks (left), stone circles (centre) and areas of mineral enhancement, which tends to create local variations in the magnetic field (right). Can this close resemblance be mere coincidence?

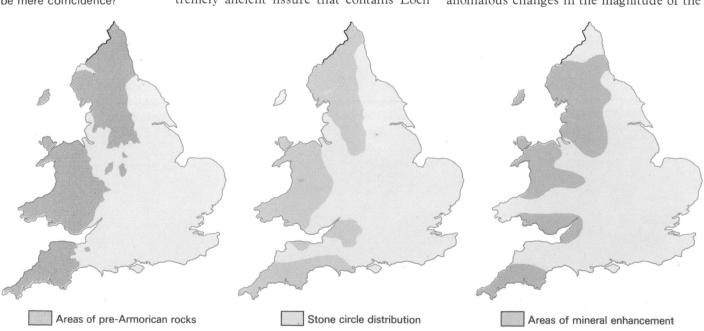

Areas of pre-Armorican rocks   Stone circle distribution   Areas of mineral enhancement

are subjected to surges of seismoelectricity resulting from the piezoelectrical effect – the current that flows when quartz crystals in rock are subjected to physical pressure. As movements in the faults take place, the granite and other rocks within the ground are pressurised, bathing the megaliths in seas of subtle electricity. We do not yet know how this may affect the standing stones in their geometrical layouts, but there is undoubtedly at least one energy input into the megaliths that might, when combined with the presence of underground water, solar radiation, lunar attraction, the presence of human energy fields and any number of other ambient electromagnetic conditions, produce various effects. These might be those enlarged upon in folk tales that tell of healing stones, divination, special meteorological effects and the presence of 'spirits' at such sites.

It is worth noting that when the Sun or Moon cross the horizon there is a 'shear force' (which acts along the ground rather than upwards, as in the tidal pull) exerted on fault lines; thus dawn and sunset are the most likely times for the delicate electromagnetic effects of otherwise quiescent tectonic features to be put into action. Precise knowledge of such geophysical mechanisms could perhaps have been the reason behind the apparent megalithic obsession with solar and lunar astronomy. Another interesting feature is that when faults move, ultrasound can be

force of gravity. Mereaux has measured this force with sensitive instruments across the whole Carnac area and has shown that subtle changes in gravity certainly occur there. He has found that five of the major Carnac row complexes fall along boundaries, or interfaces, between zones of 'positive' and 'negative' gravity anomalies; that is, a coin is lighter in a negative zone on one side of a stone row, and heavier in the positive area on the other side. The difference to our normal senses is minute but, geophysically speaking, the anomalies are there. What is suspected by the French researchers, as by members of the Dragon Project, is that the megalith builders – although not aware of electromagnetism in the way in which we are – could sense changes in the Earth's fields that told them where the places of power were.

Another major finding by Mereaux is that seven of the Carnac row complexes stand precisely on the borders of an area of stable magnetic field, with an eighth row, *Vieux moulin*, placed within it. This calls to mind the magnetic anomalies recorded by Dr Balanovski and Professor John Taylor on and around a twelve foot high Welsh standing stone in the mid 1970s. It would be an unwise sceptic indeed who would attempt to dismiss all this as coincidence.

All megaliths, whether in France, Britain or elsewhere, that are located near fault lines, and particularly those on granite intrusions,

Previous page: the Loanhead
of Daviot near Aberdeen is
one of a number of circles in
the area, each incorporating
a recumbent level stone.
Unusually, the area is not
one of seismic disturbance:
elsewhere, as geologist Paul
McCartney (right) has
established, megalithic sites
are generally associated with
geological faults. Loch Ness
(previous page, below left),
for example, in the Great
Glen Fault, is surrounded by
stone circles

Below right: at the Carnac
complex in Brittany, France,
minerals and faults in the
Earth's surface appear to
cause subtle changes in
gravity

appearing out in the darkness of a prehistoric
night would not have been missed. If such
lights haunted specific areas they would
undoubtedly have been incorporated into the
cosmologies of those ancient societies and it
would be natural to expect that sacred sites
would have been erected within such regions. There is a modern example of this, in
the Lake Manchester area near Brisbane in
Queensland, Australia. This area is said to
have many manifestations of small globes of
light that appear and disappear mysteriously.
Local aborigines, apparently, consider these
lights – which they call '*min min* globes' –
to be spirits of the dead, and they have built a
totem site in the vicinity.

Such reactions to natural phenomena are
not rare among so-called 'primitive' peoples.
It seems likely that the megalith builders
would have reacted in a similar way – and
surely it is not mere speculation to suppose
that they would have taken careful note of
such 'spirits', studied their behaviour and
learned the laws relating to their manifestation. It is difficult to believe that such
phenomena would not have left their mark on
the religious, or shamanistic, practices of the
day. By studying the remnants of the ancient
megalithic societies, the marks they left in
the landscape, it may be possible for us to
learn more about a phenomenon that is as
old as the Earth and yet may be one of
the most remarkable and startling mysteries
still unsolved on the planet.

produced. This may account for the ultra-
sonic measurements recorded by the Dragon
Project.

When rocks are subjected to great pressure
unusual atmospheric lights of some kind may
be produced, as we have seen. Britain's fault
areas tend to attract the highest incidence of
UFO activity, and it has been proposed that
UFOs are, in fact, 'earth lights' produced by
seismic action. The evidence suggests that
these lights, while probably closely related to
phenomena such as earthquake lights and
mountain peak discharges, possess special
characteristics. One of the most important of
these is the ability to *shapeshift*. Some British
researchers believe that it is possible that
these lights, composed of sensitive pockets of
energy, are *consciousness-sensitive*, enabling
their forms to respond to psychokinetic cues
unconsciously generated by the human mind
or brain. This is, at least, a testable theory.

Lights out of darkness
Ley hunters have long speculated that UFOs
are related to leys. There is, in fact, almost no
hard evidence to support this. But the association of particular types of *site* with
geological regions prone to UFO incidence
might be another matter. What we can be
sure about is that if UFOs have appeared in the
skies of our planet for thousands of years,
then the ancient megalith builders would
have been aware of them – mysterious lights

UFOs and the digital computer

Computer processing of photographs of UFOS creates striking and bizarre images, while revealing subtleties that are difficult to discern in the originals. Ground Saucer Watch is the most important UFO group pioneering this new research technique

MOST PHOTOGRAPHS of unidentified flying objects are disappointing. They are blurred, lacking in detail and uninformative at a casual glance. Often they lack the context of landscape or everyday objects that would enable one to judge the size and distance of the UFOs. The few that are sharp and clear usually turn out to be fakes.

It is the task of the UFO photo analyst to sift through this mass of low-grade material, weed out the frauds and the misidentified aircraft, birds and astronomical objects, and call attention to the small residue of photographs that resist all attempts at being explained away.

Traditionally, UFO photo analysts have been limited to a few techniques of study. By measuring shadows they may be able to show that the picture consists of a landscape shot

Top: a swirl of vivid hues is a 'computer eye view' of a glowing disc seen over Colorado, USA (inset). The colours represent different brightness levels in the original image and forcefully portray detailed structure in the UFO and surrounding sky. The lines on the coloured image are 'drawn' by the computer as it makes measurements on the picture

combined with a picture of a model taken under totally different lighting conditions. By studying the focus on the UFO they may be able to show that it is much closer to the camera than the witness claimed, and is therefore much smaller than it appears. By enlarging details they may be able to reveal the presence of a tell-tale 'Frisbee' trade mark. More frequently they can identify the shot as showing some natural object – even that sceptics' favourite, the planet Venus, seen under unusual atmospheric conditions.

But all too often the label 'unidentified' has remained on the photograph because there was apparently too little information to resolve the question 'What is this mysterious object in the sky?' Yet even in the fuzziest photograph there are many subtle clues hidden away. Now a powerful new tool, the computer, promises to disclose them.

One UFO investigation group, Ground Saucer Watch, has applied the computer to the analysis of UFO photographs on a large scale. Ground Saucer Watch was founded in Cleveland, Ohio, USA, in 1957 in order to bring a high level of technical expertise to the study of UFO reports. The group wanted, in the words of a statement made then, to 'see positive scientific action taken to end the elements of foul-up and cover-up in UFO research'. A network of 500 scientific and engineering consultants assists it in this task.

Now the computer is available as an aid. It enabled Ground Saucer Watch, in a study of 1000 photographs that had *prima facie* plausibility, to reject all but 45 as misidentifications or hoaxes. Here are some of the techniques that are used to sift such quantities of material.

The pictures were analysed with a Computer Eye, manufactured by Spatial Data Systems, Inc. It uses a television-type camera that scans a picture and breaks it down into nearly a quarter of a million tiny 'pixels' (picture cells), in an array consisting of 512 columns and 480 rows.

Although the colours of the photographs provide important information, they do not come into our computer analyses. The scanner 'sees' only a black and white picture. The scanner measures the brightness of each pixel and assigns it a rating on a 'grey scale' from 0 (completely dark) to 31 (bright white). So the whole picture is reduced to a quarter of a million numbers, which are stored in the computer's memory. They can be recalled and used to build up a black and white image, a direct copy of the original, on a television screen linked to the computer. But they can also be manipulated in countless different ways to generate new images,

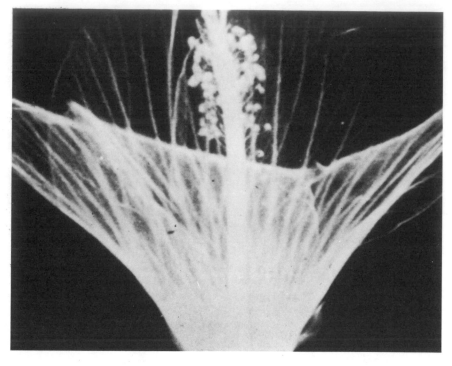

Above: an x-ray photograph of a flower. Lighter areas represent thicker tissues, which absorb x-rays more strongly than the thinner areas. Careful study is needed to see the details

Below: a computer-processed version of the picture above, in which edges separating light and dark areas have been enhanced. Some UFO pictures can be similarly clarified

which reveal unsuspected information in the original picture, or display it in unfamiliar and striking ways.

At the touch of a button the computer operator can do most of the things that the photo technician can do only at the cost of several hours' work in his laboratory.

The computer can instantly enlarge any selected detail of the picture to full-screen size. There are limits to the degree to which this can usefully be done. The picture becomes coarser as the mosaic of pixels becomes more evident. This begins to happen when the picture has been enlarged by about four times, in height and breadth.

The computer can 'stretch' the contrast, brightening the light areas and darkening the shadows, so emphasising the detail in a murky original. (This is what you do to your television picture when you turn up the contrast control.)

Enhancing the image

Measurements of distances and angles on the image become extremely easy. Crossed lines can be superimposed on the picture and moved at will, to identify points of interest. The computer can measure the positions of those points and instantly calculate distances and angles.

All this makes life easier for photo analysts, and enables them to plough through much more material than before. But the computer can also easily accomplish a number of feats that are impracticable, or even impossible, for the photo technician to perform.

For example, the computer can enhance the edges of the features seen in a photo. The effect of edge enhancement is illustrated here with a picture that is a little more conventional than a UFO photo. The x-ray picture of a flower is in black and white. Each shade of grey carries information about the flower – its thickness, and hence ability to absorb x-rays, at that point. In this negative image, the brighter areas correspond to thicker areas of plant tissue. There is a great deal of delicate structure to be seen in the petals and the central pistil.

But the eye's ability to distinguish shades of grey is limited. The result obtained when the edges are enhanced is also shown opposite. Areas of uniform shade in the original are represented as a medium grey in the computer-processed picture. Wherever the original increases in lightness (from left to right) the computer draws a bright line, while where there is a transition from light to dark it draws a dark line. The result is arresting. The flower's structure, which was lost in the subtle, veil-like x-ray image, is now laid bare in a tracery of metallic clarity.

Edge enhancement has little relevance to the indistinct forms visible in many UFO pictures. However, it is revealing when applied to UFO images showing faint detail;

Like an artist with a taste for poster paints, the computer has transformed the x-ray flower picture on the opposite page into a bold pattern of colours. All the detail below is present in the original picture, but is now presented in a form that is more easily 'read' by the human eye and brain

these are generally dark objects seen against the contrast of the daytime sky. But another technique, colour coding, can extract information from the brightness pattern in the original pictures. It exploits the fact that the eye can distinguish colours far more readily than it can distinguish shades of grey.

To colour-code a picture, the computer is linked to a colour television set. Each pixel is assigned a colour according to its brightness. Thus, in the x-ray picture of the flower, the darkest areas are shown as black. The darkest shades of grey (the thinnest parts of the flower) are rendered as shades of violet and red. Increasingly light areas are shown as shades of yellow, green and blue. The lightest areas (the thickest parts of the plant) are rendered as white.

The result is a gaudier flower than nature has ever created, with all the details of structure leaping out at the eye. Radiographers use this type of colour coding on x-ray pictures to improve their view of the interior of the human body.

Astronomers and space engineers apply the same techniques to the photos they take with ground-based telescopes, and to the television images sent back from space satellites and probes. In the original picture, brightness levels may represent the actual brightness of a planet's surface, or the temperature of a gas cloud in space, or the intensity of radio waves from distant galaxies. The patterns in the computer-generated image will represent this information in terms of colour. So, though there is a superficial resemblance in these different types of picture, the information they give is totally different in nature.

An ambiguous message

What does the procedure reveal specifically about UFOs? The brightness pattern of light and dark in the photo image of a UFO is a complex and ambiguous 'message', involving the shape of the object, the amount of light it may be emitting at each point, its intrinsic lightness or darkness if it is being seen by reflected light, the effects of glare and atmospheric haze, and so on. Emphasising the pattern by the colour-coding technique often · reveals the true form of the object immediately. A broken, uneven density may indicate a cloud. A cylindrical shape with protruberances may appear, indicating an aircraft body and wings partly hidden by glare. The contours of a 'daylight disc' (meaning any daytime UFO) are revealed, and often turn out to be suspiciously like those of a camera lens cap, a pie plate, or a hub cap.

Ground Saucer Watch has employed these techniques on thousands of photographs. Take as an example the two famous 'Colorado pictures' overleaf. They show a single UFO sighted and photographed at precisely 6.20 a.m. local time on 28 August 1969 by Mr Norman Vedaa and his passenger while driving north-east on State

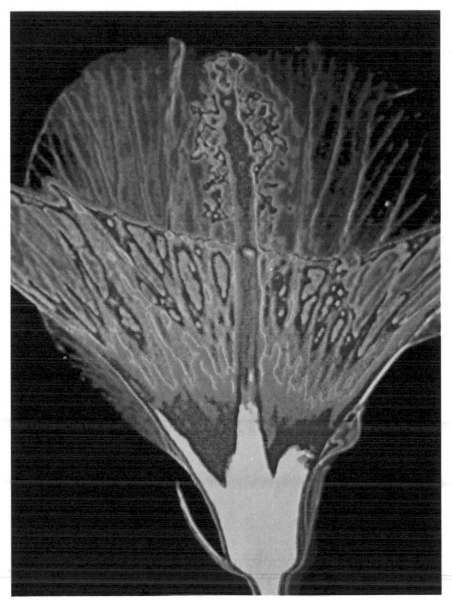

Route 80s, approximately 70 miles (110 kilometres) east of Denver, Colorado. Mr Vedaa described the object as yellow-gold, tremendously brilliant, oval in shape, and soundless. He said: 'The object was bright, hard to look at – and appeared to hover momentarily. The object's glow . . . was producing a reflective light on the clouds below. . . .' Two colour transparencies were taken and do indeed show a bright yellowish glow with well-defined edges, back-lighting the clouds.

The colour-coding technique was used on the Colorado photographs, and the result is reproduced on page 81. Again, lighter parts of the original are represented by white, blue and yellow, while darker parts are represented by red, violet and black.

The light vertical lines in that picture and in the one below are just a different way of showing brightness information. The computer has taken a 'slice' down the picture along the left-hand line. At the right, it has plotted a graph of the brightness of the scene along that line, shown by the fluctuating line. Thus the 'bump' in the wavy line represents the bright centre of the object.

The computer also speeds up the detailed study of light and shadow at any selected region of the picture. Ground Saucer Watch has a 'library' of data on the proportion of light that is reflected by each of a large range of materials. In some photographs of UFOs seen by reflected daylight, everyday objects, such as trees or houses, are visible, with which the UFO image can be compared. This

Top: a tantalising glimpse of a UFO. An American motorist, Norman Vedaa, saw a brilliant disc and stopped his car to photograph it. It is visible near the top centre. The second picture (above) was taken within a few seconds, and was the original of the processed UFO images elsewhere in this article. The disc flew off at high speed

Right: measurements of image brightness made by the computer. The measurements are made along the left-hand line. The fluctuating line at the right shows the brightness: it curves to the right where the photograph is brightest. The curve helped to prove the disc was not a lens flare, weather balloon or aircraft

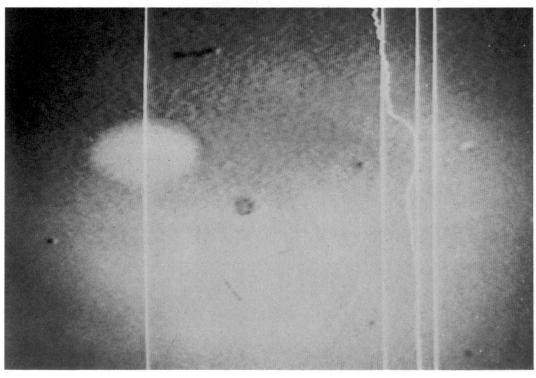

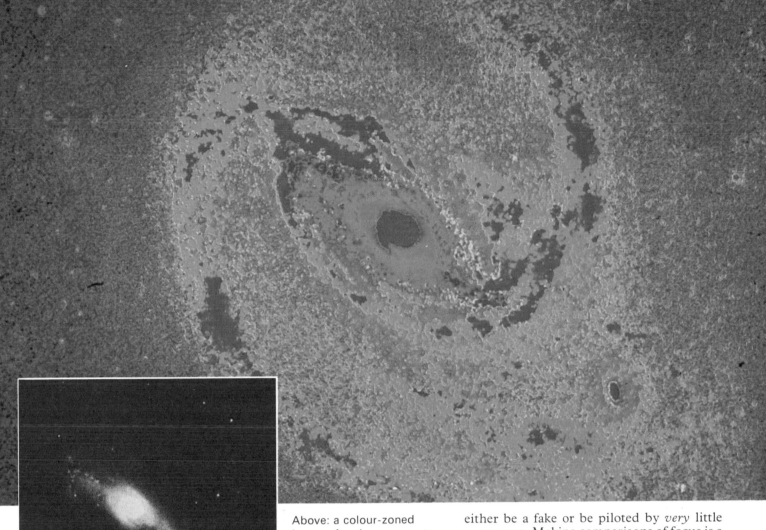

may enable the analyst to make a tentative judgement about the composition of the UFO.

We can compare the contrast in the light and shadowed areas of the UFO image and in landscape features: if there is a serious discrepancy, a composite picture or a model close to the camera is indicated. Essentially the same method can be used to estimate the degree to which atmospheric haze veils the UFO image. The more distant the object is, the lighter and less contrasty it will appear because of light scattered by air molecules, dust and water vapour. This often allows us to make an estimate of the distance of the UFO from the witness.

Careful measurements on the sharpness of various features in the picture are also a valuable indicator of distance. In fact, the annoying fuzziness of most UFO pictures – which are no worse than most holiday snaps in this respect – can be turned to advantage.

Sometimes the image of a UFO in the sky is beautifully sharp, while all ground features more than 50 feet (15 metres) away are slightly out of focus. This shows that the object is close to the camera – and so must

Above: a colour-zoned image of a giant star system reveals the detail latent in a black and white picture (left), itself the computerised average of five photographs. The galaxy, a mass of billions of stars and vast quantities of gas and dust swirling in a spiral, is 40 million light years from us. The coloured image shows its spiral arms extending as far as its companion elliptical galaxy at lower right. Further image processing revealed extraordinary ray-like structures surrounding the spiral galaxy. Astronomers realise the value of the computer in extracting information from their photographs. Scientific UFO study may benefit equally

either be a fake or be piloted by *very* little green men. Making comparisons of focus is a traditional part of UFO photo analysis, now greatly facilitated by the computer.

In its study of the Vedaa pictures, Ground Saucer Watch was able to rule out more and more explanations that seek to reduce the sightings to causes that are well-known and understood. This was no weather balloon, flock of birds or daylight meteor – the brightness distribution was that of a disc. It was not an aircraft hidden in the glare of reflected sunlight – it was too bright for that, and not a trace of tail or wings could be found. Lens flares, reflections from clouds, mirages and other atmospheric effects are all ruled out: the Sun is in the wrong position for them. The object was three-dimensional in form, and it was certainly a long way from the camera.

Objective research will progress with the aid of modern technology, of which the computer is an important component. In the near future photo analysis will be carried out by more sophisticated computer programming, in conjunction with more powerful 'hardware' – faster computers with bigger memory capacity, working with scanners that can break the original image down into yet finer detail. Soon it will become virtually impossible to fake a UFO photograph. Then, perhaps, the UFO mystery will be solved.

Analysing the Trent photos

Computer analysis lends support to two of the best-known UFO photographs. This description of the studies carried out on these classic pictures and the findings of the researchers suggests that the US government has for years sown confusion about UFOS

Above: a huge disc glides silently across the sky over the small Trent farm in Oregon, USA, and is captured in one of the most famous UFO photographs

Above: one of the Trents' pictures of the mysterious object shows its disc-shaped outline. In the Trents' words: 'The object was coming in toward us and seemed to be tipped up a little bit. It was very bright – almost silvery – and there was no noise or smoke'

THE COMPUTER HAS BEEN USED to analyse two of the most impressive UFO photographs to date, taken by an American couple, Mr and Mrs Trent, near McMinnville, Oregon, USA. The computer study has endorsed and extended the findings of the expert appointed by the University of Colorado's Condon Committee – that the pictures show an object that is not explicable as any known phenomenon, natural or artificial.

By the Trents' own account, the object appeared over their small farm in the evening of 11 May 1950 (see page 202). It was seen by Mrs Trent as she fed the farm's rabbits, and she called her husband. The family camera was found, and Mrs Trent took two photographs from positions a few feet apart. There was no sound as the disc glided from the north-eastern part of the sky across to the north-west.

There were a few unused frames left on the roll of film. The Trents attached so little importance to the pictures that they waited a few days, until they had used up the rest of the film, before they had the roll developed. They then ignored the photographs and it was only by chance that the local newspaper heard about them. When they did, however, the pictures caused a sensation, finally being featured in *Life* magazine. They were the only photographs that were not dismissed by the US Air Force's highly sceptical Condon report of 1967, which was scathing about the mass of evidence presented to it. Their investigator, William K. Hartmann, concluded that all the factors he had investigated, both in the photographs and at the scene of the sighting, were consistent with the assertion 'that an extraordinary flying object, silvery, metallic, disc-shaped, tens of metres in diameter, and evidently artificial, flew within sight of two witnesses'. The evidence, he said, did not positively rule out a hoax – which, coming from a member of the Condon team, almost rates as an endorsement of authenticity.

Controversy blew up around these photos, however, as it does around all UFO pictures that stand up to scrutiny (see box). The advent of the computer afforded an opportunity to review the Trent photographs in order to discover more than the human eye can see, even when it is aided by the microscope.

The principles involved in the computer study techniques used to analyse the photographs have already been described (see page 81). A television camera scans the picture, breaking it down into nearly a quarter of a million pixels (picture cells) and recording the lightness or darkness of each pixel as a number stored in its memory. The computer can process these numbers in countless different ways to create new images, which it displays on a television screen. Each such picture has something new to say about the information contained in the original photographic negative.

Colour-contouring the image

The first thing that Ground Saucer Watch, the investigating organisation, did with the Trent photos was to colour-contour the image, converting each shade of grey in the original picture into a different bright colour. The result was to make the distribution of light and shade over the object far easier to 'read'.

The lower surface of the disc shows only a few different shades, confirming an evenly lit, flat lower surface. The second photograph, showing the edge-on disc, disclosed a darker shade in the centre of the object than at the extreme edges, which indicates a circular shape and bevelled disc profile.

The colour-coding technique makes the light-and-shade pattern of the image plainly visible to the eye. Detailed calculations by the computer provide a more sophisticated judgement confirming the detailed shape of the object shown.

Hoax photographs generally show such items as hub caps or dishes, but the obvious

Below: a computerised view of the disc seen in the Trent photographs. Each shade of grey in the original has been turned into a particular colour, making the details in the picture easier to 'read'. The object is seen to have a flat, evenly lit underside

shapes of such objects would be resolved by the colour-contouring technique applied to the magnified image.

The computer technicians measured the lightness of the UFO image and compared it with the shadows that can be seen on the nearby garage. The UFO turned out to be much lighter. The most straightforward explanation of this effect is that the object is at a great distance from the camera. Atmospheric haze over that distance would veil the disc – just as an observer, looking at the distant horizon, finds that it looks paler than nearby foreground objects, even on days when the air is at its clearest. However, other possible factors, including reflected ground light and grease on the camera lens, have been brought into the controversy. But this objection cannot be brought against the estimation of the object's distance by means of the sharpness of the UFO image. The foreground objects, such as the telephone wires and the building, are sharper than the UFO and distant objects on the ground.

The next step in the analysis was to search for wires suspending or supporting the disc, which would imply that the object was a small model, comparatively close to the camera. To

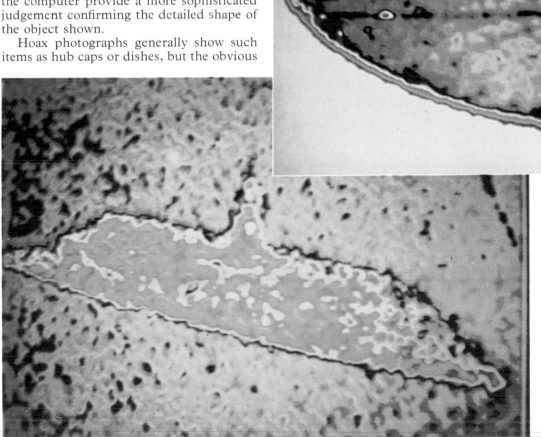

Left: colour-coding emphasises the form shown in the side-on view of the object. This wingless disc, with its curious off-centre tower, is unlike any known man-made aircraft

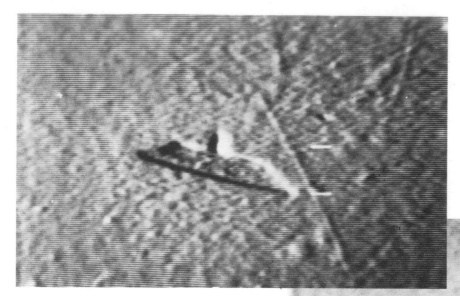

have long asserted that the United States intelligence agencies are aware of the existence and origins of UFOs. For more than 25 years they have maintained that the government knew more than it was telling. On numerous occasions when the government became involved in the investigation of a sighting, evidence would mysteriously disappear or be destroyed. The computer and other modern aids to analysis cannot demonstrate their full potential while vital evidence is withheld.

However, the Freedom of Information Act now gives American citizens powers to do this, the group took advantage of the edge-enhancement facility of the computer.

The resulting pictures have something of the look of a bas-relief carved in rough stone and lit at a low angle. Bright and dark lines now mark the edges of features on the object, and even small flaws in the negatives. The edge-enhancement technique can reveal, under typical conditions, the presence of a wire less than one hundredth of an inch (a quarter of a millimetre) thick, at a distance of 10 feet (3 metres). There is definitely no evidence of such a supporting wire or string in the area around the object.

The edge-enhancement technique not only ruled out the theory of a suspended model: it made it easy for Ground Saucer Watch to make measurements of the size of the image, which, when coupled with the analysts' assessment of the distance of the object, enabled them to draw conclusions about its true size.

Results of the analysis

The accumulated evidence gleaned from the several lines of attack that Ground Saucer Watch followed in its computer study led the organisation to the sober conclusion that the picture shows a flying disc, between 65 and 100 feet (20 and 30 metres) in diameter, and probably made of polished metal (since its light reflection was consistent with laboratory specimens of metal).

The entire UFO phenomenon deserves a properly conducted scientific investigation, undistorted by preconceived opinions. Modern technology has the means to make progress on the subject. However, there is a factor that impedes serious UFO research. Most governments have preferred to conceal the full extent of their own evidence from their citizens. The United States government probably has available to it the largest pool of data that exists anywhere in the world – data that have come from its own employees, military personnel, policemen and ordinary citizens. Civilian UFO researchers

The sceptics put their case

The Trent photographs have been scrutinised intently for three decades. The first scientific analyst, William K. Hartmann, studied the haze, apparently atmospheric, that veils the UFO, and decided the object was about 1400 yards (1.3 kilometres) distant. A sceptical analyst, Robert Sheaffer, claims the haze could be due to grease on the camera

compel their government to disclose the information that its agencies hold on file. The first legal skirmishes have taken place and documents that the CIA would have preferred to keep to itself have been made available to ufologists.

It may prove, as more information is prised from unwilling hands, that the role of the US government has been more active than previously suspected – that the clouding of UFO investigation they have brought about is due to more than the usual torpor, confusion and conservatism of government departments. On the contrary, some small and as yet unidentified group within the government machine may have been manipulating public opinion and the work of ufologists. They could have done this by familiar techniques of 'disinformation' – releasing distorted reports and data, starting rumours, feeding ufologists with 'confidential' but misleading stories – even setting up the occasional spurious sighting. They would have done this to set up a background of widespread UFO belief – at the same time that other government agencies were busily debunking UFOs.

There could be several motives for such a devious strategy. Public attention has occasionally been distracted from other issues by well-timed 'saucer flaps'. For example, a wave of sightings over Texas and New Mexico occurred within hours of the news of the Soviet Union's launching of a second

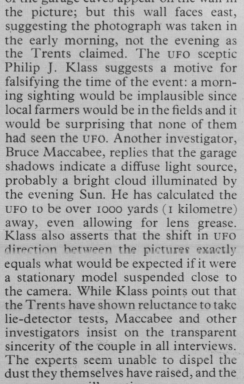

Sputnik in November 1957, at a time when America's Vanguard rockets were failing to get off the launch pad.

The long-running UFO story could also provide vast quantities of data on the psychology of individuals and groups as they found themselves under supposed surveillance by unknown and possibly threatening forces. The official interest in the psychological warfare aspects of UFO scares is documented in secret memoranda only now becoming available.

The plethora of sightings that has grown up during the last 30 years could also serve to bury the occasional sighting of advanced types of aircraft by citizens or unauthorised service personnel.

A UFO tradition

An agency wishing to foment a UFO tradition and the occasional outbreak of UFO hysteria would not need to do a great deal. The enthusiasts and the general public would do it for them, at the stimulus of a few hints, added to the UFO reports made in good faith. Better analysis of UFO data of all kinds, in which computerised image-processing has a large part to play, can improve the situation by countering such a campaign and combatting the extremes of credulity and scepticism. But for this all the evidence hidden in government files is needed.

So, while Ground Saucer Watch adheres firmly to its judgement that remarkable physical phenomena lie behind many of the UFO photographs, it believes that the battle to discover the true nature and origin of those phenomena may be fought out in the courtroom before it can be taken up in the photo analyst's laboratory.

Left: the edges of the features visible in the two Trent photographs are enhanced in these two computer-generated images. Scratches and other blemishes on the ill-treated negatives are clearly brought out – but there is no trace of the wire that would be expected if the object were a model suspended from the telephone wires overhead

Right: colour-coded detail from one of the Trent photographs. The focus of the telephone pole seen here, and of other objects in the pictures, was studied and compared with the focus of the disc images. The comparison indicated that the disc was too far from the camera to be a model

Below left: the puzzling garage shadows, clarified by colour-contouring

Left: during an investigation, William K. Hartmann tries to fake a UFO by a means of a small suspended model

Below: Philip J. Klass, who attacks the authenticity of the Trent photographs

lens, and the object could be close to the camera. He also points out that shadows of the garage eaves appear on the wall in the picture; but this wall faces east, suggesting the photograph was taken in the early morning, not the evening as the Trents claimed. The UFO sceptic Philip J. Klass suggests a motive for falsifying the time of the event: a morning sighting would be implausible since local farmers would be in the fields and it would be surprising that none of them had seen the UFO. Another investigator, Bruce Maccabee, replies that the garage shadows indicate a diffuse light source, probably a bright cloud illuminated by the evening Sun. He has calculated the UFO to be over 1000 yards (1 kilometre) away, even allowing for lens grease. Klass also asserts that the shift in UFO direction between the pictures exactly equals what would be expected if it were a stationary model suspended close to the camera. While Klass points out that the Trents have shown reluctance to take lie-detector tests, Maccabee and other investigators insist on the transparent sincerity of the couple in all interviews. The experts seem unable to dispel the dust they themselves have raised, and the controversy will continue.

UFO photos: facts and frauds

Nine out of ten photographs of alleged UFOs are misinterpreted pictures of everyday events or the work of hoaxers. The range of tests to which such photos are subjected is rapidly increasing as new, sophisticated techniques of analysis become available

WELL-TRIED METHODS of analysing and evaluating UFO photographs will be supplemented, but not superseded, by newer methods of image-processing by computer. In fact the more sophisticated and expensive techniques of analysis are generally reserved for photographs that have survived the more traditional examination. These are a small minority of all claimed UFO pictures. At most, 10 per cent of the photographs that analysts study still seem convincing after they have been exposed to a battery of tests.

A UFO photograph is a report like any other, and requires to be supported in the same way. Many pictures that seem to be authentic cannot be used as evidence for the occurrence of some inexplicable phenomenon simply because of the unsatisfactory circumstances of the sighting. The photographer may have been alone at the time, for example; however strongly a researcher might be convinced of the sincerity of the witness, sceptics can hardly be blamed for insisting on the possibility of a hoax.

Inducements for hoaxers

Financial motives for creating a successful hoax photograph are very strong. One person who took photographs allegedly showing the Loch Ness monster refused to release the negatives for study by experts. Despite this and the fact that there are inconsistencies in his account of the sighting, his photographs were prominently featured in the British press and continue to be used. He has commented that the use of the pictures by the media all over the world would fetch something like £200,000 over the first six months. Income would continue long after that, of course, and there would also be fees for lectures and personal appearances. There are great incentives for providing what the public wants to see.

Among some people, especially bright schoolchildren, it has become a hobby to fake 'flying saucer' photographs. One of the best-known cases is that of Alex Birch, which took place in Britain. In 1962, when Alex was a 14-year-old schoolboy, he produced a photograph of a group of five saucer-like objects. He was interviewed on radio and television and by the Air Ministry. He appeared before the inaugural meeting of the British UFO

Above: UFO hoaxster Alex Birch revealing how he faked a picture of 'flying saucers' that had been accepted as real ever since he took it, 10 years before he made his confession

Above right: the 'daylight discs' that Alex Birch, then 14 years old, claimed to have photographed as they passed over Sheffield, in northern England, in 1962. The shapes were actually painted on the windowpane through which he took the photograph

Right: one of many pictures of flying discs taken in New Mexico by Paul Villa, who claimed to have talked with their crews. Computer studies indicated that the pictures showed small models

Research Association to explain the circumstances of his sighting. It was only 10 years later that his plausible, tenaciously defended and apparently sincere story was admitted to be a hoax.

Hence the vital importance of having independent witnesses to a sighting. The ideal case, from the investigator's viewpoint, is one in which the witnesses are neither friends nor relatives of the photographer, and make full statements of the circumstances of the sighting before the film has been processed. Hoaxers are rarely bold enough to announce their 'sightings' before they have made quite sure that their pictures are sufficiently convincing.

Hard evidence

So the first requirement for a photograph if it is to provide 'hard' scientific evidence is that there should be at least one other witness, who is independent of the photographer. The second requirement is that the original film – whether it is a black and white negative, a colour negative or a colour transparency – be submitted to qualified analysts for examination and evaluation. The whole film roll should be provided, even if only one or two frames show the UFO image. The other pictures may provide valuable evidence about the weather conditions, whether there was grease or dirt on the lens, whether there was stray light in the camera, the characteristics of that particular sample of film, and much else besides.

The third requirement is that there should be reference points in the picture. If it shows an object against a blank sky and nothing more, distance and size cannot be calculated.

The fourth requirement is not obligatory, but it is highly desirable: that there should be a sequence of pictures. A series of still

photographs provides more information than a single one could; and a movie sequence is still more valuable. A movie film is harder to fake than a still photograph, and it provides information about the time elapsed during the sighting. (On some cameras the speed of the film can be varied from the normal 24 frames per second. It is essential that the witness report should specify what speed was used during the filming of the UFO.)

The UFO investigator presented with a photograph will also want to know full details of the camera and film used, the distance, aperture and speed settings, whether there was a filter over the lens and if so, of what type it was, whether the camera was hand-held or tripod-mounted, and any other information that might be relevant.

So a great deal of the investigator's work is done before he or she gets down to a detailed study of the picture. What needs to be done when that analysis at last begins?

The University of Colorado was given a contract in 1966 to study UFOs on behalf of the US Air Force. Many UFO investigators have been sceptical of the value of the report that was finally published under the title *The scientific study of unidentified flying objects*;

Below: a small, near object can produce a photographic image of the same size as a large object farther away. The true size can be calculated if its distance can be determined – for example, by analysis of its sharpness of focus

Bottom: an orbiting 'saucer' photographed from the spacecraft *Aurora 7* in May 1962. This ambiguous image could have fuelled endless speculation about alien observation of human space activity if Scott Carpenter, who took the picture, had not known its true nature: a small clump of ice crystals that had detached themselves when he knocked the side of the craft

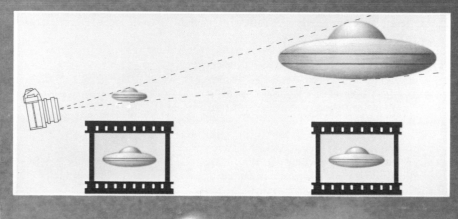

however, the approach that photographic evidence requires was clearly outlined by the Colorado investigators, and can provide a good guide to other analysts. This approach falls into several phases:

Firstly there is a subjective evaluation. Do various photographic factors such as clarity and contrast, combined with the witnesses' testimony, make the picture appear both plausible and informative about a potentially unusual phenomenon?

If a photograph passes this initial qualitative assessment, the second phase of investigation asks whether there is any rational explanation for what is shown in the picture. This question can be tackled only by someone who has wide experience with astronomical, meteorological, optical and photographic effects. Only such a person is equipped to know the surprising forms that can be assumed by aircraft vapour trails, stars and planets seen under unusual atmospheric conditions, lens flares, faulty film processing and countless other straightforward but poorly appreciated effects. Yet such possible causes of a 'UFO' image are so infinitely diverse that even the expert will be fooled on occasion. Nevertheless many photographs will be rejected at this stage of examination as cases of mistaken interpretation.

In the third phase of investigation the possibility of a fake is examined. Even with the best credentials concerning the sincerity of the report, this possibility remains and must be tested by the investigator. Are there any signs of tampering with the original film? Such interference can usually be detected. An elementary question to ask is: do the frames represent a continuous sequence? If the manufacturer's frame numbers reveal that the available pictures are separated by

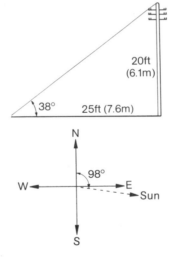

Top: when was the UFO photographed? A hypothetical picture like this has many clues for the analyst. The relation between the height of the telephone poles and the length of their shadows shows that the elevation of the Sun is 38° (centre). An on-the-spot study of the direction of the shadows in relation to landmarks reveals the direction of the Sun (above) as 8° south of east. From this, and the latitude of the site, the date and time at which the picture was taken can be calculated

others, which the witness cannot or will not make available, the suspicion arises that the shots do not belong to a single sighting but were 'set up' on separate occasions – or else that obviously unconvincing shots have been deliberately withheld.

Are the focus, sharpness and contrast in accord with the description by the photographer and others? If the object is alleged to have sped across the sky there should be some corresponding degree of blurring in the UFO image – or, if the photographer panned while taking the shot, there should be some blurring of the landscape.

The focus of the image can provide an accurate estimate of the distance of the object. This is crucial to a judgement of the authenticity of a photograph, since most hoaxes involve small objects positioned close to the camera. Nevertheless, even if the UFO image is judged to be distant from the camera, the possibility remains that the witness knows it to be an everyday object, such as an aeroplane at an unusual angle, but has decided to cash in on the peculiarity of its appearance in the picture.

Clues from lighting conditions

Further tests of consistency between the pictures and the witnesses' testimony can be made. In daytime photographs, angles of sunlight and weather conditions can be checked to see whether they agree with the stated time and date of occurrence of the sighting. If the height of an object appearing in the picture and the length of its shadow can both be measured, the height of the Sun can immediately be calculated, and by the use of an astronomical *ephemeris* or nautical almanac the time of day can be found. The local weather office will have detailed records of the weather on that day. Not only might they confirm or contradict the time of the alleged sighting, but such information as the height of the cloud base can, in some circumstances, give information about the height of the object photographed.

Study of the lighting conditions may also show whether the photographs in a sequence have been taken within a short period of each other. If a sighting is described as having lasted a few seconds, and the Sun is found to have moved through, say, 10 degrees between one shot and another – corresponding to 40 minutes – then the credibility of the witnesses is destroyed.

This investigation may very well be carried on to an examination of the camera itself, if this is available. The true shutter speeds and apertures of most cameras can be substantially different from their nominal values and it can be vital to obtain an accurate value.

It is also highly desirable to visit the scene of the sighting. The purpose of this is generally not to look for physical traces of the UFO – though such evidence, if available, is invaluable – but to make measurements to determine the sizes and directions of objects

candidates – though it seems that controversy concerning such pictures never quite dies down. Some of the most convincing photographs are the stills taken aboard a Brazilian naval ship participating in scientific studies as part of the International Geophysical Year. At 12.15 p.m. on 16 January 1958, while the ship was off Trindade Island in the South Atlantic, large numbers of personnel on the deck of the ship saw a strange object approach the island at high speed, hover over it for a while, disappear behind a peak, reappear and head out to sea. Four photographs taken by Almiro Barauna, a civilian photographer on board at the time, show an object resembling two dishes face-to-face (see pages 200–201).

In many respects this was a near-perfect sighting. There were many witnesses and the negatives were developed immediately, virtually ruling out a fake.

The US Air Force later claimed they had made a detailed investigation and concluded that the affair was a hoax. However, their publicly available file does not contain any evaluation of the case. If they have any

that are visible in the picture.

Of the photographs that run this gauntlet of tests, few survive with their credibility intact. But when they do, the final classification is essentially of a negative kind – the object shown is not a nearby object, not a plane, not a meteor. Unfortunately the ideas often associated with the term 'UFO' – ideas of extra-terrestrial craft – cause misunderstanding between the public and serious-minded researchers. People ask, in all seriousness: 'Do UFOs exist?'. This is tantamount to asking whether anything has ever been seen in the skies that remains unidentified – and this is obviously so. The question that such enquirers really have in mind is: do alien spaceships visit the Earth? And to this we do not have an answer. No firm evidence exists that unambiguously shows the phenomena to be due to this cause.

We might ask, less ambitiously: are there any photographs that have resisted all attempts to discredit them? There are many

information throwing doubt on the pictures, they have kept it to themselves. There is no publicly available evidence against the authenticity of the Trindade Island photographs. The Brazilian investigators decided that the object seen in the pictures was 120 feet (36 metres) across and flying at 560 to 620 miles per hour (900 to 1000 km/h).

Equally remarkable objects are shown in many other photographs such as those described earlier. But whether they are space visitors or something even more exotic, such as thought projections, cannot be discovered by photographic analysis alone.

Many ufologists believe that detecting a UFO on radar is the next best thing to capturing it and taking it into a laboratory. But it becomes increasingly clear that radar evidence, though valuable, is often ambiguous and can raise as many questions as it answers

IN THE SUMMER OF 1952 an air force radar operator on the Isle of Wight, off the coast of southern England, saw a most peculiar trace on his radar screen. Then another one appeared – and then there were nine unidentifiable blips visible, moving across the screen at a rate corresponding to an incredible airspeed. He checked his equipment: there seemed to be no malfunction. Then the targets travelled out of the radar's range at an estimated 7000 miles per hour (11,000 km/h). This was, of course, far in advance of the capabilities of any craft other than experimental rockets at that time.

The operator completed a report on this incident. Shortly afterwards, he says, all the staff were called together and politely but firmly 'advised' that, as far as they were concerned, the incident had never happened. And they were more explicitly reminded of the terms of the Official Secrets Act by which they were all bound, and the consequences of infringing this.

Scanning the skies

The Act is effective only for 30 years in regard to incidents of this kind. So it was in 1982 that the witness, now retired, reported the event to investigators. He also asked whether any visual sighting had been made at the time that would corroborate it. The answer was that nothing is known of such an incident.

There are a number of similar accounts on file with UFO organisations, in Britain and elsewhere. They suggest that the files of the world's armed services are packed with such cases, some possibly strengthened by simultaneous visual sightings. The British Ministry of Defence certainly does not seem in public to attach much importance to such anomalous radar sightings. In fact, in 1982 it stated that it did not retain such reports dating from before 1962. On the face of it such an admission is astonishing. It would mean that the RAF had no record of, say, the highly significant Lakenheath/Bentwaters case of August 1956 (see page 195) – a case that has never been explained, and is widely regarded as one of the best examples in UFO history of a phenomenon of an unknown kind. The alternative – that dozens of intriguing radar cases are lying in a secret file whose very existence is denied – is even more

disturbing, and not only to ufologists.

A radar sighting of an unidentified object is often viewed with great respect by ufologists. It is regarded as virtual confirmation that the object is solid – perhaps even an extra-terrestrial machine with fantastic capabilities. But in fact the question of the interpretation of radar evidence is extremely complex. To understand it the basic principles of radar itself and the way it is used for different purposes must be understood.

The word 'radar' is an acronym for Radio Detection and Ranging. It was first put into use during the Second World War, and its applications, both military and civilian, rapidly expanded during the postwar years. There was much to be learned in those early days about the behaviour of radar waves, and there were teething troubles with new equipment. There seem to be far more instances of radar UFO cases from the 1950s than from either of the following two decades. This inevitably creates the suspicion that many were due to complexities of the behaviour of radar equipment and radar waves that were then not sufficiently understood. However, today's radar systems are far from trouble-free. As one specialist said in 1978, 'The problems and shortcomings of early radar

Radar scanners are instantly recognisable features of every airport. Some are relatively short-range (left); others observe the movements of air traffic over large areas (far left). The parabolically curved dish functions like a lighthouse mirror, reflecting the radar waves forward in a narrow beam that sweeps all points of the compass as the scanner rotates. Between transmitted pulses the scanner 'listens' for radar echoes from objects in the path of the beam. Radar is vital for tracking the movements of aircraft: what can it tell us about UFOs?

Right: the display on an air traffic control radar screen – with 'clutter' (top) and without (bottom). The clutter consists of reflections from stationary objects on the ground: a computer removes these from the display when the operator so wishes. A blip corresponding to a stationary UFO would inevitably be removed at the same time.

Below: 'targets' crowd a radar display of south-eastern England. They are neither aircraft nor UFOs but flocks of migrant birds

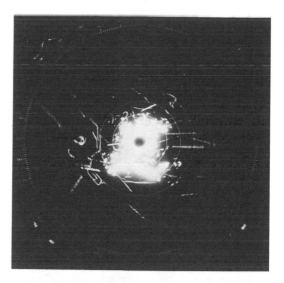

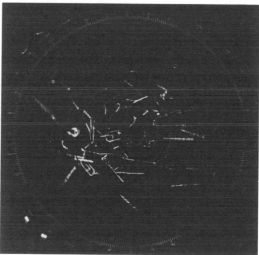

systems are still with us.' Today large radar systems are being increasingly computerised, and such innovations in electronic wizardry might occasionally malfunction.

All radar applications rely upon the same principle. An aerial – usually a rotating one – sends out a narrow beam of radio energy in short pulses. The beam spreads out very slightly, but after it has travelled, say, a few hundred miles it becomes several miles wide. An object in the beam's path will reflect some of the beam's energy in all directions. If the object is sufficiently dense, enough of the radar signal will be reflected to be detectable back at the aerial, which 'listens' for it in the gaps between the emitted pulses. The position of the object can now be worked out precisely. Its direction is, of course, simply the direction in which the aerial is pointing. Its distance can be calculated from the delay between the emission of a pulse and the arrival of the echo at the aerial. The positions of all the objects detected by the beam as it rotates can be displayed on a circular screen, much like a television screen, called a plan position indicator. Primary radar, in which little computer processing is involved, shows blips whose brightness corresponds to the strength of the echo. This is often related to the actual size of the object, but other factors are involved as well – including the shape of the object and the material of which it is made.

In addition, it must be realised that two objects that are relatively close together may not show up as two separate blips on the screen. Suppose that the radar beam spreads at an angle of 3°. At a distance of 25 miles (40 kilometres) from the aerial the beam will be around 1.3 miles (2.1 kilometres) wide. It will also be many miles deep. The beam will not be able to distinguish between objects unless they are widely spaced: they will appear as one blip on the screen.

It should be apparent that the interpretation of images on a radar screen is a skilled job, that requires good eyesight, cool and clear thinking, and considerable experience.

These problems are greatly compounded by the variety of the 'targets' that can appear on a screen. 'Ground clutter' is very common: mountains, oil refineries, tower blocks and so on can reflect the radar beam. Insect swarms and flocks of birds can pro-

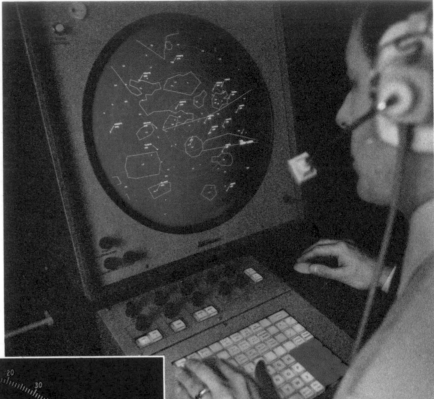

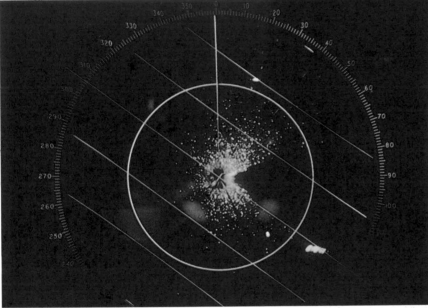

duce blips as well. Even pockets of what is known as 'non-standard air', differing in temperature, pressure or humidity from the surrounding atmosphere, can cause an image to appear on the screen.

Stationary clutter is a problem, since it unnecessarily complicates a display. Consequently, radar systems that handle air traffic often have a special computer 'filtering' system called a moving target indicator, or MTI. When it is switched on it removes stationary blips from the display.

Each of the many different varieties of radar system that may be employed for particular purposes has its own problems. There is an extensive network of weather radar stations throughout the world. However, this operates on short wavelengths, which means it is unsuited to detecting

The radar blips on 'primary' radar (above) are formed by direct reflection of radar waves from objects. In the computer-processed image (top) labels specifying the identity and height of some of the aircraft are shown alongside the corresponding blips. This information is derived by 'secondary' radar: a coded pulse is transmitted by the aircraft's onboard 'transponder', in response to the radar pulses sent from the ground. Outlines of certain important areas are also displayed on the radar screen

aircraft – and perhaps some types of UFO. Generally speaking it is used to track the progress of clouds, rain and snow, and so on. It is particularly liable to spurious echoes from surface features: coastal weather radar is especially prone to clutter, owing to reflections from the surface of the sea.

Squawk, please

Radar systems, both civil and military, vary widely in function but they are all strictly concerned with a localised area, and the task of their operators is to track the aircraft for which they are responsible and guide them safely to their landing or to their next traffic control zone. Nowadays all large aircraft and numerous small ones carry a transponder – a transmitter that can respond automatically to a radar pulse and send back a coded message, carrying information about the aircraft's identity, its altitude and its destination. The radar operator can ask the pilot to 'squawk' by means of the transponder; he will then see the information 'written' on the screen alongside the aircraft's blip. This will pick it out from all the other targets on the screen, which include not only aircraft coming to and going from the airfield that the radar serves but also aircraft in transit, light aircraft flitting about on unscheduled flights, crop-spraying aircraft, and so on. The MTI will cut out anything that is stationary – or even that is moving at speeds that are much slower than an aircraft's. Without using the MTI, the controller would be faced with such a confusing morass of targets he would never

be able to do his job successfully

It is highly unlikely that a UFO would be noticed in these circumstances, let alone investigated. There may be many unidentified, non-transponding targets on the screen, but an operator simply does not have the time to worry about what they *might* be, unless they pose a direct threat to one of his aircraft.

Air traffic moving between airports is controlled by a very similar system. In Britain there are just three main centres: London and Manchester, and Prestwick in Scotland. Life in these radar rooms is even more busy than at an airport control tower. They have to control hundreds of flights every day and must constantly be alert for potential collisions.

Such long-range radar systems do pick up unidentified blips. Some of them might prove, on further investigation, to be extraordinary objects. Unfortunately there are just too many of them. The only occasions on which the operator will take an interest in them is when they threaten to come too close

to one of the aircraft under his supervision. Such a 'conflict alert' opened the film *Close encounters of the third kind* (1977).

Of course, there are other radar systems. A physicist involved in radar study of the upper atmosphere once got into conversation with the author on a train journey. Before disappearing into the crowds, he said: 'We often record unknown objects that appear to be controlled aircraft. We call them UFOs!'

Another type of radar system is the long-distance radar intended to provide early warning of enemy missiles. There are installations in Alaska and at Fylingdales, in northern England. But apart from the fact that, for obvious reasons, they are secret, they are not too valuable to UFO research. They concentrate only on remote objects moving in the highly specific manner of

Below: air traffic controllers at a large international airport. Contrary to what might be thought, they are not in a good position to study UFOs: although unidentified 'targets' may appear on their screens, the operators must confine their attention strictly to the aircraft for whose safety they are responsible

Bottom: huge radomes protect the early warning radar scanners at Fylingdales, on the Yorkshire moors. This station is concerned with detecting missiles launched from the Soviet Union. If anomalous echoes are ever received, the fact is a well-guarded secret

ballistic missiles. An object performing fantastic manoeuvres over a nearby town would elicit no reaction whatsoever from such a radar station.

The American UFO researcher Allan Hendry studied radar establishments in the United States and concluded that radar is much less useful as a tool of UFO detection than might at first be supposed.

But there are occasions when a sighting of a UFO does receive support from radar. In one year at the Center for UFO Studies in Evanston, Illinois, there were five such reports, out of 1300 UFO reports altogether. A typical case occurred at Fairborn, Ohio, where an orange light was seen in the sky. A local radar installation was called, but they had noticed nothing at that spot. However, now alerted, they did pick up one very brief, weak signal. Subsequent investigation showed that the object was a hot air balloon released by a trickster, whom the police apprehended. The radar return had been weak and ephemeral because the balloon was so insubstantial – it would not have appeared on radar at all if it had not happened to have a little metal in its construction. It was a good case of a radar-visual sighting – but it nonetheless ended up in the 'identified' file.

In fact all five of Hendry's radar-visual cases were shown to involve natural objects. Three of them were sightings of balloons, two of stars sparkling and flashing different colours. Yet in these last two cases as well, local radar operators apparently found radar targets in the direction of the 'UFO'. But it is almost impossible for such a radar system to get an echo from a heavenly body. The relationship between what was seen on radar and what was seen by the naked eye proved to be spurious.

Encounters with angels

Ufologists are used to frustration and disappointment in their investigations of mystery objects in the skies – even when they have the benefit of radar evidence. For, as researchers emphasise, what is seen on the radar screen can rarely be interpreted without additional eyewitness evidence

IN THE WINTER of 1979 to 1980 the Manchester UFO Research Association (MUFORA) were faced with a problem. The hilly terrain of the Rossendale Valley, about 20 miles (30 kilometres) north of Manchester, had been providing dozens of UFO observations. Mostly these referred to an orange light in the sky, which became known as the 'Rossendale anomaly'.

The group had excellent relations with local airport authorities – a great advantage in the hunt for a solution to the Rossendale mystery. The chief suspicion was that the 'anomaly' must be an aircraft, as it appeared to a regular time schedule – behaviour most untypical of UFOs. Yet MUFORA investigators had seen the object and remained puzzled as to its nature. What was more, rapid checks after these sightings had brought a response from the airport that no air traffic was on their radar screens in that particular area.

MUFORA considered various possibilities. It could be, for example, that the presence of the hills would act as a filter. If an aircraft were low enough over the hills, its blip could blend into the radar return from them. It could even be expunged from the screen by its proximity to a non-moving target, if the moving target indicator were to be switched on, as we have seen.

Eventually it was decided to attempt an experiment. MUFORA members positioned themselves at two sites in the Rossendale hills and kept alert for the anomaly. They did not see the usual object. But a bright light *was* seen by all the observers. They took it to be an aircraft, despite a curious 'wiggle' in its motion, to which they could attest independently. They had with them a radio tuned to civilian air traffic control frequencies: it suggested that an aircraft might well be in the location in which this light appeared. The time was precisely that at which the anomaly was most active – between 1 and 2 a.m.

Meanwhile Peter Warrington, a member of the group and a UFO radar specialist, was some miles away, at a radar establishment that had extensive facilities with which all air traffic over the Rossendale hills could be seen and logged. Warrington's task was to watch a radar screen for some hours, under skilled

Below: an air traffic controller watches a radar screen. At some airports, when the workload permits, radar operators are willing to search for UFOs in response to telephone calls from witnesses made while the sighting is in progress. One difficulty in trying to find a reported object in this way is that the witness can usually report only its bearing from his position – not its distance

Below: Peter Warrington, an expert on UFO radar anomalies, helped to investigate the mystery light that was seen near Rossendale, Lancashire

supervision, and make a full record of any objects that the teams in the hills might see. But when the data were compared in the cold light of morning it was discovered that nothing had been logged by Warrington that correlated with the phenomenon seen by the observers.

What does this mean? Did the teams observe a UFO that was invisible to radar? This would not be the first time that the Rossendale anomaly had failed to show up on radar, in circumstances in which it seemed unlikely that a radar blip would be masked by the hills' radar trace. The MUFORA observers were convinced that the object they saw was at some distance above and to the side of the hill line – making it unlikely that a radar return from it would be obscured in this way.

However, Peter Warrington points out that the UFO evaluation is a risky one. He argues that the pressure of work in the radar establishment (even at that hour of the night) was such that it was quite possible that an overflying aircraft might have been missed. He could not guarantee that, just because he logged no radar return, there was no relevant blip among the many that were on the screen at any given moment. In their subsequent evaluation of this experiment, MUFORA stated that, primarily because what was seen was consistent with an aircraft (possibly seen under unusual atmospheric conditions), the likeliest conclusion was that it was just that, and its radar return had somehow been missed.

Here there were ideal circumstances for the identification of a UFO: several independent observers seeing an object, with simultaneous radar observation by means of some of the best facilities available, under the auspices of a most experienced ufologist. And yet no conclusive statement could be made. The object seen might or might not have been an aircraft. All the problems of using radar to confirm a visual sighting are thrown into sharp relief by the Rossendale experiment.

The term 'angel' is used by radar operators for a moving radar return that is not readily identified but appears to be caused by a real object – not by some defect in the equipment. The word was chosen because these objects appear to have the ability to fly and to appear, disappear and reappear at will. Some UFO enthusiasts believe that many angels seen on radarscopes are in fact alien spacecraft performing their marvellous feats. The accepted scientific view is that they are the effects of moving pockets of non-standard air or other atmospheric anomalies.

Radar operators at all airports are well aware of the existence of angels. They confront them very often, and inexperienced operators are sometimes fooled by them. Peter Warrington and UFO expert Jenny Randles, while researching such cases, were informed of one occasion where an operator became convinced that an angel was a real object and warned an approaching aircraft. The pilot could see no sign of this 'UFO' – and promptly flew straight through it! Evidently this particular angel was nothing more substantial than non-standard air.

Gordon Thayer, an American scientist, took part in the infamous Colorado University project under the directorship of the renowned physicist Dr Edward U. Condon. This extensive study, with financial support from the United States government, published a 1000-page report in 1969. It looked at over 30 radar-visual cases, Thayer's

special interest, and concluded that over half of them were angels caused by atmospheric effects.

But what of those cases where atmospheric conditions do not seem to indicate anomalous propagation of radar waves? Surely if radar detects an object and an apparent UFO is seen in the same area, then we must have good, hard evidence that the object is of a mysterious kind? Unfortunately not.

On 30 July 1976 a British Airways Trident jet left London Heathrow for Faro, in Portugal. As it neared its destination, with the Sun setting, the crew and some of the passengers observed a very bright light above the horizon in the 3 o'clock position (to the west). Below it a dark rectangular object with a hazy outline appeared. Then, seconds later, a further object appeared by this. The Trident crew's attention had been drawn to the UFO when they overheard a conversation between Lisbon air traffic control and a TriStar airliner, saying a UFO had been reported in that area of the sky. The crew of the TriStar indeed saw the object, as did the crew of a Portuguese airliner.

Two hours later the Trident was on its return flight to England. The crew had noted the position at which they had seen the UFO and, sure enough, their on-board radar detected a very large blip and two smaller blips in that area. They described the largest as several times the size of that given by an

Below: the Rossendale Valley. The light that was regularly seen over this area was investigated by the Manchester UFO Research Association. Observers kept watch from the surrounding hills while Peter Warrington manned a radar screen at a nearby airport. A light was seen, which they thought could be an aircraft – yet no corresponding radar trace was noticed

Right: the Rossendale hills area is at top right in this radar display

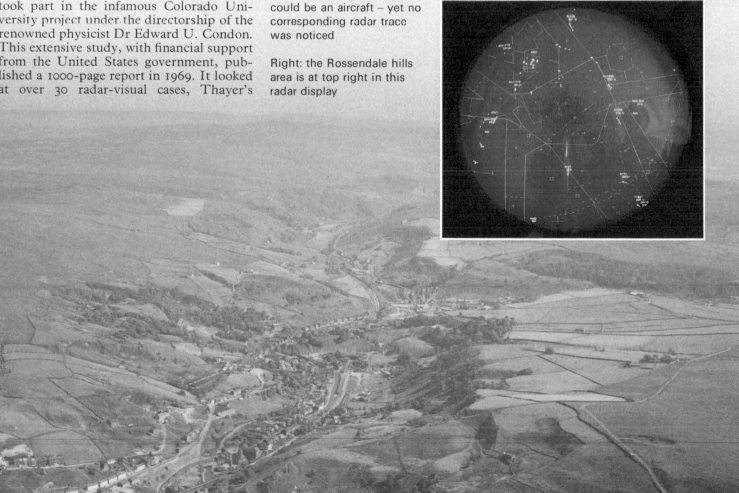

was in fact well over 300 feet [90 metres] in diameter).

But what of the radar blips seen on the return flight? Peter Warrington worked independently on these. While it is possible that they refer to the balloon, this is rather unlikely in the circumstances. The blip sizes implied that the objects creating them were not just big, but impossibly big – miles across, in fact. The radar set's manufacturers were of the opinion that the blips could not have been caused by an aerial target.

It is very feasible that the blips were the product of *ground* returns, probably from the Pyrenees. The mistake was an easy one to make, especially as the crew were expecting to see something. As Peter Warrington points out: 'It is not surprising that they did

ocean-going super-tanker. Peering out into the sky, now quite dark, they failed to see anything corresponding to these returns.

UFO investigators were alerted to this case very quickly, thanks to the aircraft's captain, who contacted Omar Fowler and his Surrey Investigation Group into Aerial Phenomena. They published a report on the story in the British journal *Flying Saucer Review*. Oddly, the media did not pick up the story for many months; then suddenly it was elevated to the status of national news. The affair was hailed as a modern classic radar-visual case. But diligent work by British ufologists began to uncover a conventional explanation.

Philip Taylor, a scientist at the Royal Greenwich Observatory and a co-ordinator for the British UFO Research Association, followed up a lead that looked very promising. It appeared that a high-altitude experimental balloon had been launched over the Mediterranean by a team of researchers on 29 July under the auspices of the British Science Research Council. Dr David Ramsden, a physicist from Southampton University, pointed out that its probable flight path from the launch at Trapani, Sicily, to its intended destination in the United States would take it across Portugal, on or about 30 July.

Taylor obtained data from Italian and Spanish radar: they included two confirmed positions of the balloon on 30 July. From these, and from wind speed and direction, its position at the time of the visual sighting was easy to calculate. The predicted location of the balloon agreed extremely well with the position of the object seen by the aircrews. Taylor reached the very reasonable conclusion that the Trident sighting was explicable in terms of sunlight reflected from this unusually large and high-flying balloon (it

A Trident airliner like this one (top) was involved in a radar-visual UFO incident in July 1976, while *en route* from London to Faro, Portugal. On the outward bound trip the UFO was seen as a bright light with a darker object beneath it. On the return trip the aircraft's forward-scanning onboard radar (above) showed a group of blips in the approximate area of the visible object. Ufologists finally decided that the most likely candidate for the object was a high-altitude research balloon (right), which had been launched from Sicily on a transatlantic flight

not visually confirm the radar reading. Perhaps, had they looked down instead of up, they would have done so.'

This case was a triumph for the hard-working investigators, showing that not all ufologists are set on believing everything they hear – at all costs!

Unfortunately, radar cases have not always been examined in this way. Here is an example that is still widely quoted in UFO books. The case occurred on 30 November 1973, at about 7 p.m. A radar operator at Turin airport in Italy observed a target nearby. He alerted aircraft in the vicinity, and two Alitalia DC-9 jets observed a UFO, in the form of a scintillating light. The pilot of a Piper light aircraft even tried to intercept the object, but it made fantastic 'to and fro' movements and then disappeared into the distance. He had to give up the chase, being quite unable to catch up with the object. On the ground, meanwhile, the radar operator and several other witnesses also saw a light in the right direction.

However, it is easy to become suspicious about this case when a statement of the radar operator is considered: 'Visually it looked to me much like a star.' The colour scintillations are suggestive of this, and none of the other visual descriptions refer to anything that could not be regarded as a star or planet seen under exceptional conditions. Even the 'to and fro' motions would be possible if there were atmospheric turbulence, or perhaps an inversion layer (a layer of warm air lying over cooler air) near the horizon. This would also explain why the light aircraft did not catch up with it!

In fact the planet Venus, being low on the horizon at the time, seems to fit the bill here very neatly. Venus should have been in plain view in addition to the UFO and yet no witness

or investigator refers to it. One is justified in regarding it as a likely candidate. If there were an inversion layer present as well, it could coincidentally have produced a radar angel in the same part of the sky.

It seems probable that this radar-visual sighting was caused by the coincidental occurrence of two different and misinterpreted stimuli. The fact that UFO reports had attracted attention in Italy during the weeks before this suggests a reason why the event was interpreted in the way it was, and why it was then afforded widespread media coverage.

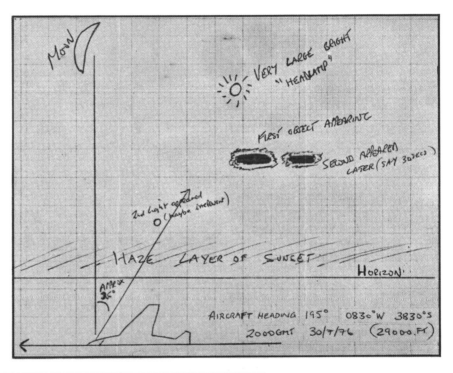

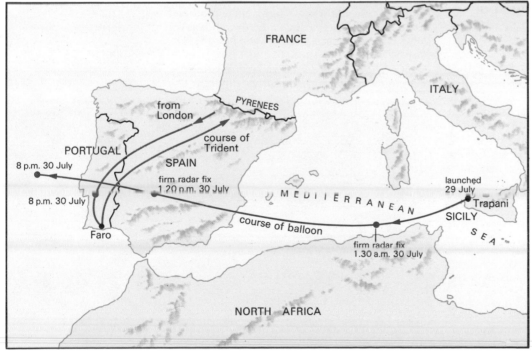

Above: a sketch made by the captain of the Trident airliner. The dark objects could conceivably, he said, have been 'contrails' (condensation trails made by aircraft) but he thought this unlikely since the air was dry and no other trails were being produced by aircraft at the time. He described the light as 'rather like an enormous headlamp in the sky. It was not a star, planet or satellite . . .

Left: the paths of the Trident and of the balloon launched the previous day. All times are GMT. The most probable position of the balloon at the time of the sighting agrees well with the UFO's actual position

Beyond our scope?

Can UFOs become invisible to radar? When they do appear on radar screens, why is it more likely to be at night than during the daytime? Investigators have come to realise that the field of radar and the UFO presents many baffling problems

IF UFOS ARE MATERIAL PHENOMENA, rather than purely psychological ones, then they must be detectable by suitable types of radar on some occasions – *unless* they are some kind of advanced machine capable of becoming invisible to radar. Aircraft that are difficult to detect by radar *are* being developed. One is the US Air Force's B-1 bomber, which is designed to have the smallest possible radar reflective surface. But what if some governmental agency had perfected radar invisibility? Lord Hill-Norton, former Admiral of the Fleet and a member of the House of Lords all-party UFO study group, has suggested that such a development could help to explain the secrecy of governments over the UFO mystery.

This speculation could make sense of a curious aspect of the data on UFO radar cases. The noted UFO researcher Dr J. Allen Hynek has pointed out that nocturnal lights figure

among the cases more frequently than they do among UFO cases in general. Hardly any of them concern daylight sightings of apparently solid or structured objects.

It might be that the only material phenomenon that gives rise to UFO reports occurs in the form of a night-time light, all the other cases being exaggerations, errors, hoaxes, delusions and so on. Or, following Lord Hill-Norton's line of thought, an intelligent agency in possession of radar invisibility techniques may use them during daylight to

Right: a Boeing B-47 jet bomber. One night in 1957 an RB-47 reconnaissance variant of this aircraft repeatedly observed flying mystery lights that seemed to be associated with an object *emitting* radar waves

Left: the UFO interception over Iran in September 1976. One of the two Phantom jets involved closed in on the UFO, which consisted of multicoloured flashing lights. A smaller light suddenly emerged from the UFO and seemed to approach the aircraft. The pilot attempted to fire a missile at the UFO in reply – but lost all power to his communications and weapons control panel

Above: a Phantom jet fighter in the colours of the Imperial Iranian Air Force – the type of aircraft involved in the UFO incident of September 1976

Left: the B-1 supersonic bomber, designed to be difficult to detect by radar. Its body is slender to present as small an area as possible, it is contoured to scatter radar waves rather than reflect them back to the ground radar stations, and radar-absorbing materials are used whenever possible

avoid detection, but not employ them as frequently at night, when there is less chance of being seen.

A number of truly baffling radar-visual cases are on file. One occurred in September 1957 and involved a US Air Force RB-47 bomber flying from a base in Kansas with an experienced crew of six. During one part of their flight they were apparently tailed by an incredibly manoeuvrable UFO. It appeared and disappeared at whim. The pilot, aptly named Chase, did just that, making his aircraft plunge after the object but not being able to match its performance. The story continued as the aircraft flew across the southern states. Ground radar tracked the UFO for an hour or so. The RB-47 was carrying some electronic countermeasures (ECM) gear, highly advanced for the time. Its function in time of war was to detect radar pulses from enemy ground radars. This equipment detected a source of radar-like waves, and tracked its apparent motion. The crew became convinced that the ECM equipment, operated by a crewman deep in the belly of the aircraft, was tracking the same object that the pilot and copilot could see.

Dr James McDonald, a professor of atmospheric science at Arizona State University, concluded that this case was quite inexplicable 'in terms of present-day science and technology'. The University of Colorado study group described the case as 'unusual, intriguing and puzzling'.

But even what seems to be the most rock-solid of UFO cases can be undermined by a determined and sceptical investigator. Philip J. Klass, after lengthy study of the case, claims that the ECM operator was actually detecting a ground radar station, and that the

pilot and copilot successively misinterpreted a meteor, an airliner coming in to land, and bright stars as the visible UFO. The UFO subcommittee of the American Institute of Aeronautics and Astronautics found Klass's explanation of the radar evidence plausible, but his conjectures about the visual sightings hard to accept.

Together with the Lakenheath/Bentwaters case (see page 195), this ranks as a thoroughly investigated, yet baffling, radar-visual case. These two incidents alone might be sufficient to suggest the existence of a strange phenomenon, though nothing beyond the bounds of a peculiar *natural* event is proven. That is why Peter Warrington, the UFO radar specialist, and Jenny Randles have advocated the use of the phrase UAP (unidentified atmospheric phenomenon) for this kind of event, rather than UFO, which for many people has acquired strong connotations of intelligent control.

A UFO interception

Military cases of this type from Britain and the United States have completely dried up – according to official sources. It seems a reasonable suspicion that such cases have not stopped occurring but now simply have a 'higher classification' – that is, are kept more secret.

In other countries with a more open-minded attitude to the UFO question, there have been several striking radar-visual cases. The UFO interception by two Iranian Air Force Phantom jets in September 1976 is one such incident. This object apparently interfered with the electrical systems of the pursuing aircraft (see page 70). A full account of the events of that night merits a place in this discussion of radar-visual cases.

The mystery object had been seen by civilians and military personnel on the ground and both pilots saw a brilliant light in the sky. One got a radar fix on it and began to close in on it. At this point the pilot got his best view of the object, as a sequence of multicoloured and flashing lights. Then it accelerated away with the Phantom struggling to keep pace. Suddenly a small object emerged from the UFO and made straight for the jet. Not surprisingly the Iranian pilot interpreted this as a hostile act and attempted to launch an air-to-air missile. But at that moment he lost the power to his communications and weapons control panel, though not to his other controls.

The ejected object was still heading towards the fighter. Instinctively the pilot turned his aircraft into a steep dive and tried to shake off what looked alarmingly like an enemy missile. This had no effect: the small object changed course to continue its intercept path. But then it changed its course again, circled round the aircraft and travelled back to rejoin the parent UFO. At that moment the pilot regained the failed power supply.

Maintaining admirable composure, the pilot returned to the pursuit. On his radar he watched the object's manoeuvres mirror those that he could see. He had no doubt that the object was very real. Then a second 'missile' was ejected, this time heading straight for the ground. It appeared to land, and poured out a brilliant flood of light, illuminating the ground for a long way around. The UFO meanwhile accelerated to several times the speed of sound, leaving the Phantom behind and giving the pilot no option but to give up and return to his home airfield.

At dawn a helicopter team was sent to the place where the 'missile' had landed. The missile was not there and there was no sign that it ever had been.

A classic saucer

If the pilots' account of this case is accurate, it admits virtually no other explanation but the existence of a fantastic aerial machine. This was clearly no UAP but a classic 'flying saucer'. Certainly the United States government took this story very seriously: the Defense Intelligence Agency, the CIA and the State Department, among others, reported on it. One intelligence officer described it as 'an outstanding report'. It is thanks to the Freedom of Information Act that all this has been revealed. Yet the United States government still tries to convince us that it does not believe UFOs are worthy of investigation.

In Spain the authorities have begun to accord great respect to UFOs. In November 1979, for example, Mirage jets were scrambled to chase a UFO that had been seen and also detected on several radar systems. The object flew so close by a civilian passenger jet

The path of the UFO that was tracked across western England on 1 April 1980. The civilian radar operator at Birmingham Airport claimed that the East Midlands airport first detected it at A and reported it to him. The object flew south-west extremely slowly and was seen by a light aircraft at B. The Birmingham operator tracked it as far as C. Other radar systems detected it, he claims – but none of their staff would admit it. The report of the incident was passed to West Drayton air traffic control centre, where it is now hidden behind official silence

that the pilot became alarmed for the safety of his aircraft and made an emergency landing. The story made headlines around the world. A major government investigation ensued and the Spanish Minister of Transport was quoted as saying 'It is clear that UFOs exist.'

In the light of the Spanish case and many others, this statement seems wholly reasonable. Unfortunately, British authorities have not conceded as much.

On the night of 1 April 1980 a civilian radar operator at Birmingham Airport tracked an object moving across country on a south-westerly course, at a steady speed of a mere 44 miles per hour (71 km/h). (It was *not* following the wind direction.) A light aircraft saw the object and described it as 'like a car headlight shining through mist'. The radar operator says that other radar systems tracked this object, but none admitted it; they referred enquirers to West Drayton, the Civil Aviation Authority centre where all British reports of radar anomalies are sent – and the authorities at West Drayton would say nothing.

The object in this case may have been some unusual military craft. But the highly experienced radar operator said: 'For the first time in 20 years I was stumped for an explanation.' The inconclusive result of the follow-up investigation shows just how difficult the analysis of radar reports can be. Radar evidence is not, unfortunately, a talisman for the ufologist, but as complex and ambiguous in its interpretation as any other kind of report with which the investigator must deal.

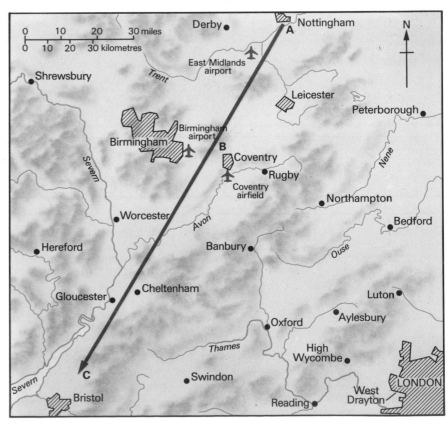

Those mysterious flying machines

conventional aircraft. But when military spokesmen comment, they always exclude the possibility that they might be *accurately* perceived aircraft – aircraft of remarkable capabilities, intended to remain hidden from the eyes of the public.

The UFO sightings of much earlier times might have been natural phenomena of a kind that would have baffled and frightened people less technically developed than ourselves: phenomena such as sun dogs, comets, meteors, noctilucent clouds, ball lightning, mirages, and so forth. But there is considerable evidence to support the suggestion that the modern wave of 'flying saucer' sightings may be based on a new factor: flying machines constructed *here on Earth*.

The first 'modern' UFO sightings were the 'mystery airships' that were seen by thousands of people all over the United States between November 1896 and May 1897. At that time, European inventors were far ahead of their American counterparts in airship experimentation, but neither the French nor the Germans had managed to design an airship that could do much more than hover helplessly. Not until 1904 was the first dirigible – Thomas Baldwin's *California Arrow* – flown, in Oakland, California. Consequently, the mystery airships of 1896 and 1897 were then as inexplicable and frightening as are the UFOs today.

Significantly, the mystery airships were invariably reported as being cylindrical or cigar shaped, and driven by a motor attached

The predecessors of today's unidentified flying objects were mysterious 'airships', sighted in huge numbers in the 1890s. One theory proposes that they – and some later UFOs – are the creations of human engineers, working in secret at the far frontiers of aviation science

THE EXPLANATIONS OFFERED for unidentified flying objects have been numerous and varied. In past ages they have been regarded as supernatural visitants or omens, divine or demonic. In our own technological age, they are surmised to be visitors from distant civilisations in space, time-travellers, or emissaries of dwellers inside the Earth. Those who despair of finding evidence for such conjectures speculate that UFOs might be thought forms created by those who perceive them, or that they are the results of governmental manipulation of mass psychology. Scientific debunkers insist that they are misinterpreted natural phenomena or

Above: a non-rigid airship built by Santos-Dumont of France at the turn of the century. Nothing as advanced as this was publicly known in the USA, where mysterious airships were then being sighted

Right: an aerial object seen over California in 1896, as portrayed in a local newspaper. Witnesses saw a dark body above a brilliant light, apparently descending

to a propeller – in short, they were exactly like the forthcoming airships. They were manned by human beings, not by creatures from another world. In fact, their occupants were often reported to have talked to the witnesses, usually asking them for water for their machine. Perhaps the most intriguing of all such cases were those involving a man who called himself Wilson.

Landing in a pasture

The Houston *Post* of 21 April 1897 carried an account of the first Wilson incident. It had occurred in Beaumont, Texas, two days before, when J. B. Ligon, the local agent for Magnolia Brewery, and his son noticed lights in a neighbour's pasture a few hundred yards away. They went to investigate and came upon four men standing beside a 'large, dark object', which neither of the witnesses could see clearly. One of the men asked Ligon for a bucket of water. Ligon gave it to him and the man gave his name as Mr Wilson. He then told Ligon that he and his friends were travelling in a flying machine, that they had taken a trip 'out of the Gulf' and that they were returning to the 'quiet Iowa town' where the airship and four others like it had been constructed. When asked, Wilson explained that the wings of the airship were powered by electricity. Then he and his friends got back into the passenger car at the bottom of the airship and Ligon and his son watched it ascend and fly away.

The next day, 20 April, Sheriff H. W. Baylor of Uvalde, also in Texas, went to investigate a strange light and voices behind his house. He encountered an airship and three men – and one of the men gave his name as Wilson, from Goshen, New York. Wilson

Top: in 1900 the world's conception of air travel was still dominated by the image of the airship. Here an artist imagines an aerial ironclad of the year 2000, suspended from a somewhat vulnerable gasbag and battling with aeroplanes and ships

Above: one of Samuel Pierpont Langley's designs for a pilotless aeroplane, powered by a light petrol engine. Some of his small aircraft were successful, but in 1903 two of his full-scale planes crashed. The discouraged Langley died a few years later, the butt of the nation's newspapers

then enquired about one C. C. Akers, former Sheriff of Zavalia County, saying that he had met him in Fort Worth in 1877 and now wanted to see him again. Sheriff Baylor, surprised, replied that Akers was now at Eagle Pass and Wilson, apparently disappointed, asked to be remembered to him the next time Sheriff Baylor visited him. The men from the airship asked for water and requested that their visit be kept a secret from the townspeople. Then they climbed into the passenger car of the airship, and 'its great wings and fans were set in motion and it sped away northward in the direction of San Angelo.' The county clerk also claimed to have seen the airship as it left the area.

Two days later, in Josserand, Texas, a 'whirring sound' awakened a farmer, Frank Nichols, who looked out of his window and saw 'brilliant lights streaming from a ponderous vessel of strange proportions' in his cornfield. Nichols went outside to investigate, but before he reached the object two men walked up to him and asked if they could have water from his well. Nichols agreed, and the men then invited him to view the airship. He noticed that there were six to eight crew members. One of these told him that the ship's motive power was 'highly condensed electricity' and that it was one of five that had been constructed 'in a small town in Iowa' with the backing of a large company in New York.

The next day, 23 April, witnesses described by the *Post* as 'two responsible men' reported that an airship had descended where they lived in Kountze, Texas, and that two of the occupants had given their names as Jackson and . . . Wilson.

On 27 April the Galveston *Daily News* printed a letter from C. C. Akers, who claimed that he had indeed known a man in Fort Worth named Wilson, that Wilson was from New York, and that he was 'of a mechanical turn of mind and was then working on aerial navigation and something that would astonish the world.'

Sighting at Deadwood

Subsequently, the Houston *Post* reported that in Deadwood, Texas, a farmer called H. C. Lagrone had heard his horse bucking as if about to run amok. Going outside he saw a bright white light circling around the fields nearby and illuminating the entire area before descending and landing in one of the fields. Walking to the landing spot, Lagrone found a crew of five men, three of whom talked to him while the others collected water in rubber bags. The men informed Lagrone that their airship was one of five that had been flying around the country recently, that theirs was the same vessel that had landed in Beaumont in the first incident, and that all the ships had been constructed in 'an interior town in Illinois' (which borders Iowa). They were reluctant to say anything more because

The German engineer Otto Lilienthal flying one of his biplane gliders. Lilienthal was the first inventor to build and fly successful controllable aircraft. He steered by shifting his dangling body and legs from side to side. He was killed in a flying accident in 1896, soon after this flight. His successes inspired other pioneers, including the Wright brothers

they had not yet taken out any patents on their machine.

By May, the mysterious airship sightings had stopped. What lay behind them? Could such airships have been financed by a powerful company in New York and constructed secretly in the wilds of Iowa or Illinois?

That is certainly a possibility. In the late 1890s numerous inventors in the United States obtained patents for planned airships. But since most of them worried constantly about the possible theft or plagiarism of their designs, they also kept many of their ideas secret. Knowing this, many Americans came to believe that Wilson and his friends had indeed invented successful airships.

Experimentation in aerodynamics was highly advanced by the 1890s, particularly in Massachusetts (an area having numerous

---

Other mystery airships

The American mystery airship wave began in November 1896, when citizens of Sacramento, California, watched a light moving through the night sky. Further sightings came in from all parts of California throughout the month, with a few from farther north, in Washington state and Canada. A dark shape supporting the light could sometimes be glimpsed: it was shaped like a cigar, a barrel or an egg. The airship's motion was invariably slow, and often undulating, suggesting a wind-blown craft. Some newspapers named the inventors who, they speculated, could be responsible. Others floated the idea that the 'airships' were visitors from Mars. Occasionally airships were seen on the ground: in one such case two Methodist ministers saw a 'fiery object' taking off as they approached. Three strange beings, very tall and with bald heads, allegedly attempted to kidnap two men on a country road, and then fled in a cigar-shaped craft.

After a two-month lull the sightings again came thick and fast from all over the United States and Canada. At one point each day saw a score of reports coming in. A citizen of Michigan reported that a voice from above the clouds asked him for four dozen egg sandwiches and a pot of coffee – which were duly hauled up to the unseen craft in a scoop. The main 'flap' was over by mid 1897. But later in the year there were isolated sightings from other parts of the world, including Sweden, Norway and Russia.

mystery airship sightings) and New York, reportedly Wilson's home city. At the Massachusetts Institute of Technology (MIT) there were plenty of informal courses on propulsion and the behaviour of fluids, which is relevant to aerodynamics. By 1896, instructors and students at MIT had built a wind tunnel and were experimenting with it to get practical knowledge of aerodynamics. A man such as Wilson could have attended those courses and then gone on to Cornell University in Ithica, New York, where by the mid 1890s it was possible to obtain a bachelor's degree in aeronautics.

Pioneers in the public eye
Cornell University was noted for its courses in aerodynamics. One of the men who gave a series of lectures at the college in 1897 and 1898 was Octave Chanute, the world-famous engineer. In 1896 he had emulated the successful manned hang glider experiments of the German engineer Otto Lilienthal. The courses included experimental engineering, mechanical and electrical engineering, and machine design and construction. Aeronautical texts would have included the Smithsonian Institute's *Experiments in aerodynamics* (1891), Sir Hiram Maxim's reports on his experiments with engines, propellers and aircraft designs (1893), and the *Aeronautical Annual*, which contained highly innovative contributions from most of the leading aeronautical scientists.

By 1896 the first successful flights of S. P. Langley's flying machines took place in Washington, DC. By the following year numerous patents for other flying machines had been registered.

The scientific advances of the last decade of the 19th century were of staggering magnitude, and laid the ground work for advanced aeronautical experimentation. If a particularly dedicated team of scientists were working on an airship project in secrecy, it

Above: the *Flyer*, built by the Wright brothers, takes off on its first brief journey and inaugurates a new age. Four flights were made on that day, 17 December 1903. They were the first sustained, powered and controlled flights known to history. But could other inventors working in secret have anticipated the Wrights and been responsible for the earlier 'airship' sightings?

Right: Louis Blériot's Number XI flying machine above the cliffs of Dover at the end of the prize-winning cross-Channel flight on 25 July 1909

becomes possible that the sightings all over the country during that period were of man-made flying machines.

No more was heard of the mysterious Mr Wilson. But the following years saw an extraordinarily fast advance in aeronautics. By 1901 Santos-Dumont had flown an airship from St-Cloud to the Eiffel Tower and back in less than 30 minutes; two years later, at Kitty Hawk, North Carolina, the Wright brothers made the first known heavier-than-air manned flight; and by 1906 the American Robert Goddard had begun his experiments in rocketry. On the last day of December 1908, Wilbur Smith flew 77 miles (123 kilometres) in two hours and thirty minutes. Seven months later, the French aviator Louis Blériot flew across the English Channel from Calais to Dover.

Since these were all highly publicised achievements, is it possible that even greater advances were being made away from the public gaze? The numerous UFO sightings of the early 20th century, and the rapid pace of technological development suggest that this may have been so. In 1904, US Navy Lieutenant Frank H. Schofield – later to be Commander in Chief of the US Pacific Fleet – officially reported seeing, from the deck of his ship, three bright lights that were travelling in echelon, remained above the clouds, and *ascended* before disappearing. In 1909 numerous unidentified aircraft were reported over Massachusetts. On 30 August 1919, at about 9 p.m., a long black object flew low over Madison Square, New York City, and was witnessed by hundreds of people. The nature and origin of this object was also never determined.

Scandinavian ghost planes

In 1933 and 1934 what would now be called a UFO 'flap' occurred over Scandinavia. 'Ghost planes' were reported on scores of occasions. They frequently appeared, or were heard, flying overhead in 'impossible' conditions for the aircraft of that time. They were described as monoplanes, usually grey in colour. Sometimes their crews could be glimpsed. Often their engines would cut out, and the aircraft would glide for long periods before their power was turned on again – an unlikely feat for conventional aircraft. Sometimes brilliant searchlights would be directed from them onto the ground below.

In 1934 the Swedish Air Force began a thorough search of the remote areas from which the ghost plane reports were emanating. Twenty-four aircraft took part in the search, and two of them crashed during it. No traces were found of the bases that would be required to support the activities of the intruders. In April 1934 a high-ranking Swedish military officer stated to the press:

Comparison of these reports shows that there can be no doubt about illegal air traffic over our secret military areas.
. . . In every case the same remark has been noted: no insignias or identifying marks were visible on the machine.
. . . It is impossible to explain away the whole thing as imagination. The question is: Who are they? And why have they been invading our air territory?

The same questions were being asked in Norway and Finland, where similar sightings were occurring. But they were never satisfactorily answered.

The 'aeronautical age' outgrew its infancy in a few brief decades. Aeronautics advanced from its first crude experiments with wind tunnels in Massachusetts to the highly complex rocket research at Peenemünde that led to the V-2. On the principle that all scientific research resembles an iceberg – nine-tenths hidden from public view – the possibility arises that secret research in America, Europe, or both, had led to the construction of machines much more powerful and

unorthodox in design than those that were officially put into use. Certainly it is a fact that from the First World War onward, more and more technological research was being financed and controlled by governments interested mainly in the military applications of such research.

Is it possible that citizens of the United States and some European countries had witnessed the clandestine aeronautical experiments of their own leaders?

The pace of aviation development accelerated during the Second World War. Jet aircraft, radar navigation and detection, ballistic missiles and bombers of unprecedented size appeared in response to the desperate necessities of the combatants. And sightings of mysterious 'aircraft' entered a new phase, in the skies over embattled Germany.

Only 40 years after the Wright brothers' first flight, air warfare had advanced to the point where the first rocket propelled, long range ballistic missiles were being readied for use against cities. Here three experimental V-2 rockets stand on their trailers at the Nazis' Peenemünde research centre

The UFO goes to war

Flying discs were built by the Nazis and later by the victorious powers. Despite military denials, there is the suggestion that these unconventional craft are the cause of many UFO reports

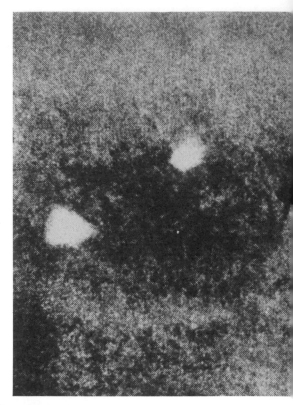

'THE NAZIS HAVE THROWN something new into the night skies over Germany. It is the weird, mysterious "foo fighter" balls which race alongside the wings of Beaufighters flying intruder missions over Germany. Pilots have been encountering this eerie weapon for more than a month in their night flights. No one apparently knows what this sky weapon is. The "balls of fire" appear suddenly and accompany the planes for miles. They seem to be radio-controlled from the ground. . . .' The sightings referred to in this news story showed remarkable

oimilarities. Lieutenant Schlueter of the 415th US Night Fighter Squadron reported being harassed by 'ten small balls of reddish fire' on the night of 23 November 1944 when flying over the Rhine. Pilots Henry Giblin and Walter Cleary reported that on the night of 27 September 1944 they had been harassed in the vicinity of Speyer by 'an enormous burning light' that was flying above their aircraft at about 250 miles per hour (400 km/h). The mass of UFO reports agreed on two major points: the foo fighters invariably appeared to *ascend* towards the aircraft from the ground; and they usually caused the aircraft's ignition systems to malfunction. Other reports, unconfirmed by the Allied forces, suggested that the malfunctioning of the ignition systems had actually caused some aircraft to crash.

At first the Allies thought that the foo fighters were static electricity charges. This theory disproven, they then began to think that they were either German or Japanese secret weapons designed to foul the ignition systems of the bombers. Another theory was that the objects had been designed purely as psychological warfare weapons, sent aloft to confuse and unnerve Allied pilots. Finally,

border. There was much speculation that both the Soviets and the Americans, utilising the men and material captured in the secret research plants of Nazi Germany, were developing advanced disc-shaped aircraft.

Speculation that there might be a connection between Nazi secret weapons and the flying saucers increased when various West German newspapers and magazines began publishing articles during the mid 1950s about one *Flugkapitän* Rudolf Schriever. According to these reports this former Luftwaffe aeronautical engineer had designed, in the spring of 1941, the prototype for a 'flying top', which was test-flown in June 1942. With his colleagues Habermohl, Miethe and Bellonzo, he constructed a larger version of the original 'flying disc' in the summer of 1944. At the BMW Plant near Prague they then redesigned the larger model, replacing its former engines with advanced jets.

A brief description of *Projekt Saucer* and the aborted flying saucer is given in Major Rudolf Lusar's important book *German secret weapons of the Second World War*:

Habermohl and Schriever chose a wide-surface ring which rotated round a fixed, cupola-shaped cockpit. The

Above: a rare photograph of foo fighters in company with Allied planes during the Second World War. Some aircrew described the mysterious spheres as being like silver Christmas tree decorations. The nickname came from the 'Smokey Stover' comic strip, popular at the time, in which the phrase 'where there's foo, there's fire' was often used

Right: the Chance-Vought Flying Flapjack, also known as the Navy Flounder. Although it could take off nearly vertically and fly as slowly as 35 miles per hour (55 km/h), it was reported also to be capable of speeds greater than 400 miles per hour (640 km/h)

Left: the Avro Car, built for the US Air Force and US Army by the Avro-Canada company. It was designed by an English engineer, John Frost. Officially, work on it was dropped in 1960 – despite the early claim that the machine would reach twice the speed of sound

both the RAF and the US Eighth Army, unable to solve the mystery, concluded officially that the foo fighters were the product of 'mass hallucination'. However, the cause was never discovered – officially, at any rate.

The foo fighters disappeared from the skies a few weeks before the end of the war. The next wave of UFO sightings occurred in Western Europe and Scandinavia, where from 1946 to 1948 many people, including airline pilots and radar operatives, reported seeing strange cigar- or disc-shaped objects in the skies. On 21 June 1947 Harold Dahl reported seeing saucer-shaped objects flying towards the Canadian border. Three days later Kenneth Arnold made his more famous sighting of saucer-shaped objects over the Cascades, also flying towards the Canadian

ring consisted of adjustable wing-discs which could be brought into appropriate position for the take-off or horizontal flight, respectively. Miethe developed a discus-shaped plate of a diameter of 42 metres [138 feet], in which adjustable jets were inserted.

Other reports, which sometimes conflict in their details of the overall project, agree on the flying saucer's diameter, and that it had a height from base to canopy of 105 feet (32 metres), reached an altitude of approximately 40,000 feet (12,000 metres) and attained a horizontal flight speed of 1250 miles per hour (2000 km/h).

Rudolf Schriever himself claimed in the late 1950s that he had indeed worked on a wartime research programme called *Projekt*

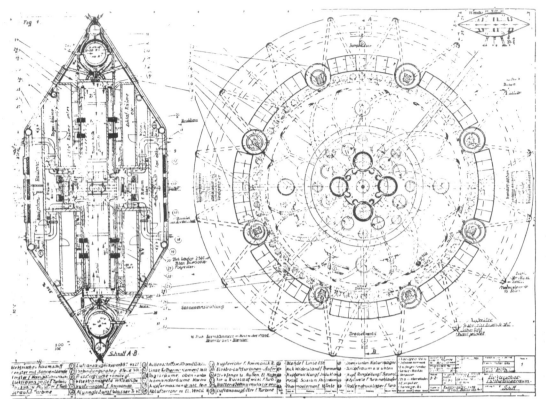

Left: blueprints for a flying saucer. According to the obscure single-issue publication *Brisant*, in which these diagrams appeared in 1978, they are plans for a disc-shaped spaceship, modified by the West German government to make them 'safe' for publication. Although 'electromagnetic turbines', 'laser-radar' and computers are indicated, the design is not a practical one. The diagrams appear in an article on Rudolph Schriever's Second World War designs, and may have been inspired by them

Saucer. His 'flying disc' had been ready for testing in early 1945, but with the advance of the Allies into Germany, the test had been cancelled, the machine destroyed, and his complete papers mislaid or stolen in the chaos of the Nazi retreat.

Schriever died not long after these revelations, convinced to the end that the UFO sightings since the end of the war were proof that his original ideas had been taken further with successful results.

But what were the foo fighters? An identification was proposed by an Italian author, Renato Vesco, in a book first published in 1968. According to him the foo fighter was actually the German *Feuerball* (Fireball), first constructed at an aeronautical establishment at Wiener Neustadt. The craft was a flat, circular flying machine, powered by a turbojet. It was used during the closing stages of the war both as an anti-radar device and as a psychological weapon designed to disturb Allied pilots. Vesco says:

> The fiery halo around its perimeter – caused by a very rich fuel mixture – and the chemical additives that interrupted the flow of electricity by overionising the atmosphere in the vicinity of the plane, generally around the wing tips or tail surfaces, subjected the H_2S radar on the plane to the action of powerful electrostatic fields and electromagnetic impulses.

Vesco also claims that the basic principles of the *Feuerball* were later applied to a much larger 'symmetrical circular aircraft' known as the *Kugelblitz* (Ball Lightning), which could rise vertically by 'jet lift'.

Since neither the British, the Americans nor the Russians are ever likely to reveal what, precisely, was discovered in the secret factories of Nazi Germany, it is worth noting that in 1945 Sir Roy Feddon, leader of a technical mission to Germany for the British Ministry of Aircraft Production, reported:

> I have seen enough of their designs and production plans to realise that if they had managed to prolong the war some months longer, we would have been confronted with a set of entirely new and deadly developments in air warfare.

In 1956, Captain Edward J. Ruppelt, then head of the US Air Force Project Blue Book, was able to state:

> When World War II ended, the Germans had several radical types of aircraft and guided missiles under development. The majority of these were in the most preliminary stages, but they were the only known craft that could even approach the performances of the objects reported by UFO observers.

Post-war saucer projects

The first concrete evidence for post-war flying saucer construction projects came in 1954. The Canadian government announced that the enormous UFO seen over Albuquerque, Texas, in 1951 was similar to one that they had tried to build shortly after the war. Owing to their lack of adequate technology, they had eventually passed the design over to the United States.

Further evidence for United States involvement with saucer-shaped aircraft projects was to be found in the US Navy's Flying

Above: a US soldier guards a V-2 rocket, still lacking its outer skin. This vast underground factory at Nordhausen in Germany was top secret during the war, along with many others whose secrets may still not have been revealed by the Allied governments

Above right: Wernher von Braun, creator of the V-2, with senior military staff at the Peenemünde range

Flapjack. The Flapjack, also known as the Navy Flounder, was a circular aircraft, the design of which was begun during the Second World War. At that time what the Navy desperately needed was an aeroplane that could rise almost vertically so that it could take off from carriers, and could fly at as little as 35 miles per hour (55 km/h).

Little was known about that machine until early 1950, shortly after the US Air Force had ended its UFO investigation programme, Project Grudge (the forerunner to Project Blue Book). As part of an attempt to show that UFOs did not merit further investigation, the Air Force released photographs and vague information about the Flying Flapjack.

Apparently, because the aircraft was wingless, the reduced stability had presented problems. A later model, reportedly designated the XF-5-U-1, solved that problem and was rumoured to be over 100 feet (30 metres) in diameter, and to have jet nozzles – resembling the 'glowing windows' seen on so many UFOs – arranged round its rim. It was built in three layers, the central layer being slightly larger than the other two. Since the saucer's velocity and manoeuvring abilities were controlled by the power and tilt of the separate

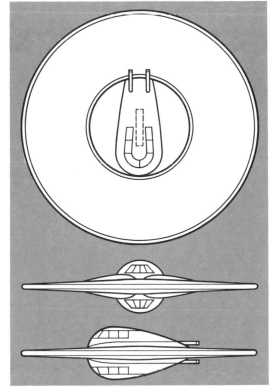

Right: a flying disc designed by Dr Miethe, one of the team of brilliant engineers working on unconventional aircraft designs for the Nazi war effort. This 'saucer' was almost ready for operational use in 1945, when the factories in Prague were overrun by the Allies

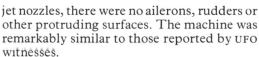

jet nozzles, there were no ailerons, rudders or other protruding surfaces. The machine was remarkably similar to those reported by UFO witnesses.

Research on saucer-shaped aircraft did not stop with the XF-5-U-1. On 11 February 1953 the Toronto *Star* reported that a new flying saucer was being developed at the Avro-Canada plant in Malton, Ontario. On 16 February the Minister for Defence Production informed the Canadian House of Commons that Avro-Canada was working on a 'mock-up model' of a flying saucer, capable of flying at 1500 miles per hour (2400 km/h) and climbing vertically. Then the president

of Avro-Canada wrote in *Avro News* that the prototype being built was so revolutionary that it would make all other forms of supersonic aircraft obsolete. The craft's official name was the Avro Car.

But by 1960 it was being officially claimed that the project had been dropped. The prototype of the Avro flying saucer is now in the US Air Force Museum in Fort Eustis, Virginia. The Canadian and US governments have insisted that they are no longer involved with flying saucer construction projects.

Yet is this necessarily true? The possibility remains that the Canadian, United States or Soviet governments could have continued to work on highly advanced, saucer-shaped, supersonic aircraft. The people directly involved in the projects, understanding the impossibility of testing the machines in complete secrecy, may have opted for creating a smokescreen of confusion, rumour and systematic humiliation of UFO observers, thereby ensuring that they can fly their machines with impunity.

But could man-made machines have such remarkable performance?

We have only to think of the extraordinary innovations of contemporary science and technology – jet aircraft, space rockets, reconnaissance satellites, pulse beam weapons – and then remember that such miracles are merely the tip of the iceberg, and that what goes on behind the guarded fences of our top-secret military and scientific establishments is probably decades ahead of these. Then it becomes easier to answer 'yes'.

Secret weapons and cyborgs

Top secret research aircraft often outrage normal ideas of how an aeroplane should look and perform, and may give rise to UFO reports. Are governments concealing the earthly origins of UFOs for reasons of security?

COULD AN EXTRAORDINARY research project to build flying saucers have been kept wrapped in secrecy since the Second World War? And could our present technology possibly account for the advanced capabilities ascribed to UFOs?

It is entirely possible that the necessary research establishments could have been hidden well away from the gaze of the public or media. The underground research factories of Nazi Germany were gigantic feats of construction, containing wind tunnels, machine shops, assembly plants, rocket launching pads, supply dumps and accommodation for the thousands who worked there; yet very few outsiders knew that they existed. Likewise, the Cheyenne Complex in Colorado Springs, operated by the US Aerospace Defense Command, is virtually an underground city in the heart of a mountain. It rests on giant shock absorbers to counteract the blast of nuclear attack, it is webbed with miles of underground tunnels, it is completely sealed off from the outer world, and invisible from the air – and very few people, other than those who have worked there (all of whom are sworn to secrecy), know what goes on inside the establishment.

Equally large and complex establishments for the construction of highly advanced disc-shaped aircraft could, therefore, exist in other desolate parts of the world, such as the wildernesses of Russia and North America, the Arctic or the Antarctic.

While secrecy might prevail during the construction of the machines, it could not be

Above: this remotely piloted research aircraft (RPRA), designed by NASA, would certainly have confused non-expert witnesses to its flights. Its cigar-shaped wing could be swung to as much as 45° from its normal angle to optimise performance at varying speeds

Right: NASA's 'lifting body' craft lacked wings, since its whole upper surface generated lift. It was launched from a bomber at high altitude

Right: an unmanned probe – not from space but from Westland, a British helicopter manufacturer. This remotely controlled helicopter had rotors 5 feet (1.5 metres) wide, and a body 2 feet (60 centimetres) wide, which could carry a variety of surveillance equipment. The 'feet' could leave marks similar to the circular depressions in the ground often described in cases of UFO landings

reliably maintained once the machines were test-flown or actually used for reconnaissance or other purposes. It is therefore possible that the relevant authorities simply decided to fly them openly while simultaneously creating an international smoke-screen of confusion and incredulity. The systematic harassment and humiliation of UFO observers and the deliberate inefficiency of official UFO investigations could have been their chosen methods of obscuring the issues.

This theory would also go a long way towards explaining such suppressive measures as a US Joint Chiefs of Staff directive of December 1953, which made the unauthorised release of information on UFO sightings a crime under the Espionage Act, punishable by a prison term of 1 to 10 years

Right: first prototype of the British Flying Wing, one of several post-war designs that dispensed with the heavy fuselage of conventional aeroplanes. The resulting crescent shape is reminiscent of many UFO reports, including, interestingly, Kenneth Arnold's sighting of 1947 that began the modern UFO wave

or a fine of $10,000. It might also explain what happened to the only scientifically sound attempts to determine the size and capability of UFOs and whether or not they were intelligently controlled (see box).

Nonetheless, assuming that the saucer-shaped machines are man-made, we are still faced with the second major question: could modern technology achieve the extraordinary capabilities reported by UFO observers and the equally extraordinary physical appearance that some reported UFO crew members display?

In his important book *Ufology*, James M. McCampbell employs his training in engineering and physics to examine in great detail the physical properties that UFOs must possess to be capable of their reported speeds and manoeuvres. According to McCampbell, UFOs probably use some advanced means of propulsion that at present exists only on designers' drawing boards. They might employ ion rockets, in which the exhaust stream consists of ions (electrically

charged particles) accelerated to high speeds by extremely strong electrical fields. Or the thrust might be provided by a nuclear fusion pulse rocket, in which a continuous sequence of H-bomb explosions pushes the craft along. Or it might be that the craft uses anti-gravity shields – perhaps in combination with one of these forms of propulsion.

Ionisation of the air, with accompanying electrical discharges, could account for the glow that so fascinates UFO witnesses. The anti-gravity shield would account for the lack of turbulence and sonic booms associated with the passing of a UFO, and also for the crews' apparent ability to withstand extraordinary changes of speed and direction.

Shielded from gravity

McCampbell claims that the lift-off of a typical UFO would require as much energy as the detonation of an atomic bomb, would cause the body of the machine to heat up to about 155,000°F (85,000°C) and would cause intense radioactivity in the ground and atmosphere – unless an anti-gravity shield is used. In this case a virtually massless body would result and it would require only modest force for the UFO to achieve enormously high accelerations. This would account for the ability of UFOs to disappear in the blinking of an eye, to come to a very abrupt stop, hover in the air and make seemingly impossible right-angle turns.

In this context, it is to be noted that as far back as 1965 at least 46 unclassified projects concerned with gravity were being undertaken in the United States alone – by the Air Force, the Navy, the Army, NASA, the Atomic Energy Commission and the National Science Foundation. Since these were only the *un*classified projects, it is reasonable to assume that even more advanced projects – both in anti-gravity and the forms of propulsion mentioned above – are still being conducted in numerous top-secret establishments.

Another mysterious aspect of the UFO phenomenon is the frequency with which UFOs have materialised on photographs taken

abducted by them, frequently describe how they felt 'drawn towards' the aliens and were 'compelled' to obey them – even when the aliens apparently did not speak. The common factor in such stories is a feeling of remoteness, unreality and divorce from the self. The contactees invariably behave like programmed zombies. Usually, after their initial terror, they are 'pacified' or 'hypnotised' by various means – a beam of light, a metallic object pressed against the neck, the 'laying on' of an alien's hands, a mere wave of an alien's hand, or strange, frequently indescribable sounds. None of this is necessarily extraordinary in the light of present-day knowledge.

Numerous brain wave experiments have

by people who did not see such an object through the viewfinder. This, combined with the fact that the UFOs have never been seen by reconnaissance satellites (at least as far as we know from official sources), has led some scientists to speculate that the UFOs may have the ability to make themselves invisible to human eyes.

Civilian and military establishments may have been experimenting along these lines for years – and it has long been claimed that the famous 'Philadelphia experiment' of 1943 (in which a US Navy ship was said to have dematerialised and then materialised elsewhere) was part of just such a project. However, doubts surround this sensational case and have helped to confuse the issue of government activity in these fields.

So much for the capabilities of UFOs as seen by observers at a distance. What of the evidence provided by witnesses who claim to have had close contact with the craft and their occupants?

A bizarre yet common aspect of contactee stories is the apparent lack of will, or resistance, on the part of the person involved. People claiming to have been in close contact with the occupants of flying saucers, or even

Above left: the Dornier Kiebitz, a tethered experimental helicopter. This robot craft's rotors span 26 feet (8 metres). The craft is designed to relay communications and reconnoitre battlefields. Its airframe is shaped to minimise radar reflections. Invisibility to radar is a prime goal of military research – and an attribute that UFOs often display

Above: the skeleton of another robot Dornier craft, the Aerodyne. The turbine-driven propeller, providing direct lift, is housed in the shroud at the left. Some of the airstream from the propeller is led along the boom to provide guidance. This weirdly shaped assembly was designed to be housed in a wingless robot aircraft

UFOs under wraps

The US Air Force was responsible for the investigation of UFO reports in the United States from 1948 to 1969, during which period the number of cases on file grew to over 12,600. Of these 701, or more than 5 per cent, were classified as unexplained. Critics claimed that Project Blue Book, as the investigation came to be called, lacked staff of the necessary technical and scientific calibre. One of Blue Book's own consultants, Dr Allen Hynek, made vehement accusations of obstruction and incompetence against the Air Force.

One of Blue Book's more vigorous heads, Captain Edward J. Ruppelt, proposed that a number of radar stations be equipped with photographic equipment to make a permanent record of radar screens during the tracking of UFOs. This scheme was aborted by his superiors. Another officer, Major Dewey Fournet, carried out a detailed statistical study of

shown that light and sound can have disturbing mental and physical effects on perfectly normal people. For instance, a light flickering at between 8 and 12 cycles per second, close to the frequency of the brain's alpha waves, can cause extremely violent reactions in the person exposed to it, including jerking of the limbs, faintness, lightness in the head, or unconsciousness. It is therefore possible that the 'beam of light' described by so many contactees flickers on and off at the particular rate that affects the brain's basic rhythmic patterns and encourages hypnosis, hallucination, or both.

It is also a fact that infrasounds, which are just below the frequency limit of human hearing (thus the contactees' confusion as to whether they 'heard' or 'felt' something), can affect human beings in the same way as flickering lights. Indeed, certain low frequency sounds can lead not only to a change in the brain's rhythmic patterns but to actual physical changes, including severe migraine (a common contactee complaint) and temporary paralysis of the limbs.

Deprivation of will

Time and again a contactee reports that the alien pressed the side of his neck with its hand or with a 'metal object' and thereby rendered him unconscious or temporarily without will. This could simply be a standard form of hypnosis known as the 'instantaneous technique', or the 'carotid procedure', in which pressure is applied to a blood vessel near the ear, thus interfering with the circulation of blood to the brain and rendering the subject confused and susceptible to hypnotic suggestion. Hallucination,

Above: a starship driven by the power of the hydrogen bomb. Project Daedalus is a detailed scheme by the British Interplanetary Society for an unmanned interstellar expedition. Fuel pellets from the globular tanks would be 'burned' in a series of H-bomb explosions, driving the ship at an appreciable fraction of the speed of light. This concept exists only on the drawing board – as far as is publicly known

shock, or deliberate confusion through hypnosis are likely causes of such accounts.

It is not stretching credibility too far to suggest that the known advances made in prosthetics, cybernetic anthropomorphous machine systems (CAMS, or humanoid robots) and genetic and cybernetic engineering in general are excelled by an even more frightening secret achievement: highly advanced, disc-shaped machines operated by programmed or remotely controlled 'cyborgs' – half-men, half-machines.

Far-fetched? Not at all. Among projects relating to extended space flight and the exploration of the Moon and Mars, the writer David Rorvik lists a proposed cyborg that would be considerably more agile and certainly far more effective than our present-day astronauts. Since the envisaged cyborg's lungs would be partially collapsed and the blood in them artificially cooled, the cyborg's mouth and nose would be superfluous and hence sealed and totally non-functioning. Chemicals and concentrated foods would be constantly recycled through the cyborg's bloodstream to nourish and protect him, wastes would be recycled to make new foods, and communications would be carried out by radio, the signals originating directly in the cyborg's vocal cords.

If such an experiment has already been completed in any one of our top-secret research establishments, then the frighteningly persuasive close encounters of the third kind could represent contact not with extraterrestrials but with cybernetically modified fellow human beings.

How far this kind of work has progressed we do not know, however, we do know that as long ago as 1967, Professor Robert White of the Cleveland Metropolitan General Hospital was able to state categorically to the eminent journalist Oriana Fallaci: 'We can transfer the head of a man on to the trunk of another man . . . It can be accomplished now with existing techniques.'

the reports to determine the manoeuvring abilities of UFOs. The Air Force was later to deny its very existence.

The celebrated Condon Report of 1966 was the climax of a two-year study carried out by a team from the University of Colorado under contract from the Air Force. In the body of the report at least 20 per cent of the sightings discussed were unexplained. Several individual case discussions virtually conceded the reality of UFOs, or spoke of rare and poorly understood natural phenomena. Yet the conclusions of the study, personally written by Dr Edward U. Condon, the head of the investigation, said: 'Nothing has come from the study of UFOs in the past 21 years that has added to scientific knowledge. . . .' In December 1969 the US Air Force closed down Project Blue Book and officially ended its UFO investigations, yet many of its findings remain secret to this day. In the eyes of ufologists the official US studies of UFOs over the years had been botched – from incompetence or by the design.

UFOs
and the mind

*Can UFO contactee cases be explained
in terms of powerful mind manipulation
by alien powers? Or are flying saucers a
universal symbol, a manifestation of
man's primordial needs buried in the
collective unconscious of our race?*

Saviours from the stars

Will the answers to humanity's problems come from the skies? Thousands of devoted believers in UFOs think they will. There are now a number of 'flying saucer' cults with UFO contactees as their prophets

OPINIONS ON THE true nature of UFOs vary widely, from the theory that they are as yet unexplained natural phenomena to the belief that they are illusions conjured up by demons to seduce mankind away from Christianity. If we bear in mind that such varying conclusions are all said to have been drawn from the same evidence and that such evidence is notoriously unreliable, then it appears that evidence and reason play a less important role in UFO belief than faith.

When faced with the unknown, the frightening, or the inexplicable, mankind tends to try to make it into a part of his religion: worships it, or damns it. UFO experience is no exception. Erich von Däniken believes that our religious history is actually one of UFO visitation and its misinterpretation. Arthur Shuttlewood, the chronicler of the mysterious events around Warminster, Wiltshire,

Members of the Aetherius Society charge a 'prayer battery' with spiritual energy on Wimbledon Common in London. They believe that the energy, when released under the direction of the Interplanetary Parliament, can assist troubled parts of the globe to struggle against spiritual danger

in southern England, believes that some UFOs are 'the giants of past ages in modern guise, ever reminding us that mankind faces many challenges before he completes his final life-cycle at the very hub of our wonder-filled universe'. Lord Clancarty, who writes under the name of Brinsley le Poer Trench, believes in the 'Sky People', who left Earth after the sinking of Atlantis, and who are occupied now in helping us raise ourselves to a better state of life in the next millennium. There may well be a common source and stimulus for reported UFO, spiritist, ghostly and religious events, and this source is likely to be identified one day, with a resulting dramatic effect upon the world's beliefs and religious philosophies. But one can no more prove that one is right in these suspicions than can von Däniken, Shuttlewood or Trench. It is all assumption, guesswork, and a certain amount of faith or wishful thinking.

This type of belief about UFOs, while not capable of proof, seems justifiable and necessary; without it there would be little experimentation, few advances in understanding. So long as the believers remain

flexible and open-minded, there is no harm to come of it. But there is another form of UFO belief for which there is much less to be said, where reason seems to be wholly suspended, and where detailed and inflexible beliefs about UFOs – their origin, nature, occupants, and purpose – become an overwhelming form of religious faith or personal philosophy and outlook. The belief itself becomes a preoccupation, and a justification for all sorts of actions.

Such beliefs take a variety of forms. Some groups see ufonauts as seeking to co-operate with certain chosen individuals on the Earth, for the improvement or continuation of the quality of our life here. According to the teachings of such groups, the UFO people do not wish or promise to take their followers away. Two American 'contactee cults' are quite typical of many others.

The One World Family, founded by Allen-Michael Noonan, is a California-based cult that has attracted some following. Many of its features recur in numerous other groups. In Noonan's case, it is said that he was working on a billboard when he was suddenly transported to another planet. He found himself surrounded by angelic creatures, seated around a fluorescent throne. A voice boomed: 'Will you agree to be the Saviour of the world?' Noonan agreed. He has since remained in contact with an extra-terrestrial known as Ashtar, has made trips to an inhabited Venus, and regards himself as the Messiah. He is writing a massive reinterpretation of the Bible, the 'Everlasting Gospel', which his followers help him produce. He believes that he is the only mouthpiece for communications from Ashtar. Hallucinogenic drugs and the exercise of psychic abilities feature in the cult.

A new Messiah

Noonan also claims that, with the practical help of the aliens, the One World Family will eventually take over the government of the USA and the running of the United Nations; but only after all professing Christians have been, as they ambiguously phrase it, 'eliminated'. Allen-Michael Noonan is one of the least wholesome characters to have founded a UFO cult and it is impossible to tell whether or not he believes his own claims. But there is no doubt that his followers believe in both the claims and the individual, and try to act accordingly.

A less sinister, but none the less remarkable, cult group was the Institute for Cosmic Research, founded in Michigan, USA, in 1967 by a young man known as 'Gordon'. This group was developed around the supposed construction of a flying saucer that would actually fly – the *Bluebird* – and the group lasted as long as its members had faith in the unique achievement that would climax its slow and painstaking creation. Gordon claimed that his birth was supernatural: he arrived in his mother's arms, clad

Above: this flying disc was filmed by Daniel W. Fry (right) in Oregon, USA, in 1954. As a result of his many alleged contacts with space people, Fry works to enlighten mankind through an organisation called Understanding, Inc.

Above right: one of the earliest contactees, George Adamski, met a Venusian in 1952 and was subsequently instructed in the Cosmic Philosophy

in white muslin, while a UFO hovered over the house. He was, he said, one of the seven Great White Brothers (a common type of claim in pseudo-Eastern movements). He also affirmed that he, and he alone, was in contact with extra-terrestrial entities from Io, one of the moons of Jupiter. There, he said, he had represented Earth at meetings of the 'Intergalactic Council'.

He told his followers that the Space Brothers had warned him that 'Earth's vortex is about to break because of an excess amount of hatred on this planet.' However, the Space Brothers had a plan: in order to change the ways of mankind they had chosen 'to provide Gordon with the technology to build a small flying saucer.' Potential members of the institute were told that only highly developed souls could be involved in work on it. They were to build the saucer and fly it into the skies. They would be joined by saucers from other planets and together would circle Earth for three days, darkening the sky. People would look up and wonder

why – and then would fall on their knees and start practising 'universal law'.

In Gordon's cosmology, the Sun was cold, and the stars, all of them, were inhabited planets. Despite all this, which surely must have been hard to believe, it is clear that Gordon had considerable charisma. The group lasted seven years before the basic untruth of the claims dawned on his adherents. Even then, many of the group members were unwilling to accept the fact. It is desperately hard to admit that you have been *so* wrong, for *so* long. The group had expended time, money, energy and faith: in some ways it was easier to go on believing than to have to cope with reality.

The great majority of UFO contactee cults come from the USA and British ufology is largely free of such extreme beliefs. But the most famous and long-lived contactee cult of all was started in Britain in about 1955. The Aetherius Society, which now has its headquarters in the London suburb of Fulham, has established itself in several of the world's major cities and has members in over 40 countries. Hundreds of devoted members attend the society's activities in Britain and the USA.

The story of the Aetherius Society and its development is very much that of its founder, George King. He built the society from nothing and now is held in the highest esteem by its members. It is worth considering, in a field where cults and belief groups are mostly transient and ephemeral, why the Aetherius Society has achieved a relatively wide appeal and has lasted so long. The key elements of the society's doctrine are very similar to those of the One World Family and the Institute for Cosmic Research. It offered its adherents a cosmology that was then beyond scientific disproof. (It asserted that most of the solar system was inhabited.) It provided an explanation for a mystery that held a widespread fascination: the flying saucers being seen all over the world. Many of them, it was said, represented a benign and concerned force – the Interplanetary Parliament. The doctrine imposed a task on the society's members: to store up, in conjunction with the extra-terrestrial entities, 'spiritual energy' in 'spiritual batteries'

Above left: Allen Noonan, founder of the One World Family, based in California. He receives communications from an extra-terrestrial called Ashtar and regards himself as the Messiah

Left: Frank E. Stranges, president of International Evangelism Crusades, Inc., received guidance from a Venusian called Val Thor, who had come to 'help mankind return to the Lord'

Far left: a well-known New York broadcaster, Long John Nebel (holding photographs), with George W. van Tassel, who founded the Ministry of Universal Wisdom to pass on teachings gleaned from regular UFO contacts

metaphysical studies, even though we believed that we were on the verge of discovering a new method of cancer treatment which could cure certain forms of this malignant scourge. Nevertheless, this command came out of the blue in such a way that no receiver could do anything else but listen and obey .... Quite soon after the deliverance of the Command, I was able to tune in and receive, telepathically, information which was relayed over millions of miles of etheric space. A message from Venus was recorded on our tape recorder. . . .

To be a little sceptical, it might have been better for the world if George King had persisted with his work on cancer, for much of the information he said he had received and the experiences he claimed to have had, implausible enough at the time, have since been rendered utterly absurd by the discoveries of space exploration. King wrote of his travels to Venus and Mars, and stated that Mercury was the only uninhabited planet. He detailed a battle he fought on a massive flying saucer of an interplanetary space fleet, 40 million miles (64 million kilometres) from Earth. In public meetings he gave trance messages from entities such as Mars Sector 6, the Master Aetherius and even the Master Jesus, who was apparently living on or near Venus. Without this last claim, the society might have been taken a little more seriously.

However, in spite of the utter lack of verifiable evidence for any of King's claims,

located in high places all over the world. This energy could then be discharged to prevent hardship, disease and disaster around the world. Lastly, the society possessed a priest: a go-between or communicator who alone had the ear of the Interplanetary Parliament, who would pass on the messages of the extra-terrestrials, and in turn would represent his followers to the mightier powers beyond. That communicator was, of course, George King.

The roots of the Aetherius Society lie in King's fascination, prior to 1954, with yoga and Eastern philosophy and metaphysics. His early life is not well-known, but he was born in Shropshire in 1919 and at various times worked as a fire service employee and a hire-car driver, and ran a healing sanctuary.

The publicity material has it that one day in May 1954, when King was alone in his flat in west London, he heard a voice say: 'Prepare yourself! You are to become the voice of Interplanetary Parliament.' Eight days later 'an Indian Swami of world renown [who] had obviously walked straight through' the locked door gave him information and instruction that dramatically changed his life and led to the founding of the society. In *You are responsible* King, not known for his humility, explains that he had to forsake his

Above: Jupiter's innermost moon, Io. According to one 'Gordon', who founded the Institute for Cosmic Research in 1967, this world, slightly larger than our Moon, was the meeting place of the Intergalactic Council. If so, they chose a singularly inhospitable place. Space probes have discovered a world in violent turmoil, coloured reddish by sulphur spewed out by volcanoes larger than any on Earth

Right: publicity material of an Italian UFO contactee group, with a photograph allegedly showing their extra-terrestrial master. In 1976 this group wrote to US President Jimmy Carter, whose UFO sighting of a few years earlier had been widely reported. They told him that the authority he enjoyed had been 'granted from above'

The Venusian Candidate

Study Center of Cosmic Fraternity
DELEGATION OF THE U.S.A.
P. O. BOX 5 - 95028 VALVERDE (CT) ITALY

REAL PHOTOGRAPH OF
ADONIESIS
FROM THE HEAVENS TO EARTH

I am not of this world: Listen to me!
Non sono di questo mondo: Ascoltatemi!
Je ne suis pas de ce monde: Ecoutez-moi!
No soy de este mundo: Escuchadme!
Ich bin nicht von dieser Welt: Hoeret auf mich!

his meetings grew larger. A regular journal, the *Cosmic Voice*, was launched soon after the society's inception. The messages relayed by King in an apparent trance state were taken seriously and acted upon though, like this example from Mars Sector 6, they were not always very clear: 'Take those m-ions inside of yourself, then your brain cells will release an opposite female magnetic energy. This will counteract the hurricane-force.'

That the society still thrives may seem surprising, but members, who seem often to be selfless and determined, concentrate much of their efforts on the 'task' previously mentioned. They have made pilgrimages, often in difficult and dangerous conditions,

picked up by Adepts 002 and 003 [extra-terrestrials] in position in their (invisible) Space Craft above the central base of operations in Los Angeles.' George King reported during the operation that 'the Great White Brotherhood Retreat in Kilimanjaro, East Africa, had now joined in the release pattern.' At the end of the operation, Mars Sector 6 informed King that 'there was a heavy resonance of Spiritual Energies over the whole of Poland.' Perhaps the society is mistaken in trying to explain the mechanics of how prayer works. Older, possibly wiser, faiths keep the whole matter as vague and obscure as they can.

Though good will and a sense of common purpose hold the Aetherius Society together, one feature seems sure to limit severely the number of those who take it seriously. From being plain George King in 1954, the leader of the Aetherius Society had by the end of 1981 become the holder of such titles as Knight Commander, Doctor of Philosophy, Doctor of Divinity, Doctor of Sacred Humanities, Metropolitan Archbishop of the Aetherius Churches and Count de Florina. Some of these titles are conferred by the Aetherius Society, others are awarded by what are said to be ancient chivalric orders. Similarly, the society is deep in Knights, Ladies, Reverends and Doctors. Even this, the most respectable of the UFO cults, seems unable to understand what impression such excesses make on outsiders.

to a number of the world's mountains to fulfil the aims of plans bearing such names as Operation Sunbeam, Operation Bluewater and Operation Starlight. They have charged the spiritual energy batteries in such places as Ben Macdhui in Scotland, Mount Kilimanjaro in Tanzania and the Madrigerfluh in Switzerland. On the night of 27 June 1981, for instance, batteries E-1 and E-3 were charged at Holdstone Down, in south-west England. The 160 members of the society who were present stored a total of 219 hours and 28 minutes of prayer energy in battery E-1. Meanwhile, the extra-terrestrials put 1100 hours into battery E-3. On the same weekend, as part of Operation Sunbeam, 6000 prayer hours of energy were sent from Jupiter to the Psychic Centre in Scotland.

It is easy to make fun of such behaviour. But if there is any element of truth in what the society believes, then its members deserve credit for their selfless efforts. In a recent *Cosmic Voice* it was reported that a discharge under Operation Prayer Power was sent to Poland on 23 April 1981. It was intended to help prevent a Russian invasion.

The mechanics of the discharge were complex. The Los Angeles battery had to be substituted for the inadequate Detroit one because: 'the Prayer Energies were not being

Apocalypse now?

Messianic UFO contactees often give detailed warnings of impending disasters. But the cults invariably insist that only their own chosen few will be saved – a promise that attracts hopeful devotees

MOST UFO CULTS have appeared in the United States, long the home of countless eccentric religious and near-religious groups. The story of one of these cults is told in full by a trio of sociologists, Leon Festinger, Henry Riecken and Stanley Schachter. They 'planted' observers in a developing group centred on a UFO 'communicator' in 'Lake City', Utah. (The authors used fictitious names throughout, in order to protect their subjects.) The communicator was 'Marian Keech', who believed she had received the initial message from her late father. She sat quietly and regularly thereafter, waiting to produce automatic writing. She was soon contacted by 'higher forces': first by 'the Elder Brother', and then by entities from the planets Clarion and Cerus (neither of which is known to conventional astronomy). She received communications especially from one Sananda of Clarion, who claimed to have been Jesus in an earlier time.

Mrs Keech did not publicise her messages enthusiastically, but others from existing UFO groups and mystical or occult groups soon showed an interest, and in August 1954 a press release was issued. This summarised

not only the more philosophical part of the communications, in which the media took little interest, but also predictions regarding a coming physical disaster of vast proportions. The nature of the event, as reported by Mrs Keech, varied at times, but as interest in the group grew its details became more firmly fixed. At the end of September the *Lake City Herald* published this typical report:

Lake City will be destroyed by a flood from Great Lake just before dawn, December 21st, according to a suburban housewife. Mrs Marian Keech of 847 West School Street says the prophecy is not her own. It is the purport of many messages she has received by automatic writing, she says . . . . The messages, according to Mrs Keech, are sent to her by superior beings from a planet called 'Clarion'. These beings have been visiting the Earth, she says, in what we call 'Flying Saucers'. During their visits, she says, they have observed fault lines in the Earth's crust that foretoken the deluge. Mrs Keech reports she was told the flood will spread to form an inland sea stretching from the Arctic Circle to the Gulf of Mexico.

By now Marian Keech was referring to a group of communicators whom she called the 'Guardians', though Sananda remained the most important. Once the media had

Left: in a television science fiction play a throng of young people, controlled by armed police, gather at an ancient stone circle in the expectation that UFOs are about to take them to a new existence beyond the Earth. Invocations of 'space people' have taken place at pop festivals and UFO enthusiasts' gatherings – where badges such as these (inset) find a ready market. Many older and rather more staid people, however, have also expected to be contacted by UFOs and delivered from imminent cataclysm

started to publicise the group, Mrs Keech and her associates began to be afflicted by the problems that always beset UFO contactees. Increasing numbers of visitors called at her house, often when group members were present. She had explained to the group that if they did the right thing and were gathered together, ready, at the appointed time, they would not be drowned in the forthcoming flood but would be carried away in one or more flying saucers. The extra-terrestrials could come to make contact at any time and in any way: so Mrs Keech and her group had to decide whether or not visitors were extra-terrestrials and also whether they were good or evil extra-terrestrials.

The last days

The cult had now fallen into the classical pattern: it had a communicator, an explanation for the UFO mystery, a message of great importance, and a 'task' for its members – not so much to publicise the disaster as to prepare themselves to survive it. As the chosen date approached, the visitors became more frequent and more outlandish. Members of the group gave up jobs, possessions and relationships, and some took up unusual diets. All who could came together to await the fulfilment of their expectations. One condition of escape required by the Guardians was that all metal should be removed from the participants' persons. This led to some interesting arrangements for trousers and brassières, and a lively discussion about dental fillings.

The last few days before 21 December were traumatic for the group members, as their hopes were first raised and then dashed by increasingly strange messages and predictions, all proving to be inaccurate. The

Above: salvation from ageing and death was promised by George van Tassel, the 'Sage of Giant Rock'. On instructions from extra-terrestrials he built this structure, the 'Integratron', at Giant Rock Airport in California, USA. It was intended for research into 'the unseen truths of life', and to develop techniques of preventing and even reversing the processes of ageing in the human body. The structure, four storeys high, was made mostly of timber, and contained no metal

greatest shock came on the day itself, when no flood arrived, nor any spacecraft to save them from it. The group fell prey to disillusion and in due course dispersed.

Another group that purveyed warnings of catastrophe transmitted from space beings called itself the 'Light Affiliates'. They were active in the late 1960s in Burnaby, British Columbia. Their launching statement read:

We wish to notify all those interested that a phenomenon has occurred here in Vancouver. A young girl, age 22, suddenly began channeling on 23.10.69. Her source is a being identifying himself as Ox-Ho, who is relaying transmissions from a galaxy close to our own . . . . Her material is phenomenal in that she has been informed of the coming disasters, when to expect them, and what to do pertaining to the necessary evacuation of the danger areas and food supplies, etc, that will be needed.

The real name of the 'channel' was Robin McPherson, but she was renamed 'Estelle' by the 'being'. Her mother Aileen became 'Magdalene', her friend Sally became 'Celeste'. A young man involved in the early communications was given the evocative name 'Truman Merit'.

Ox-Ho explained that 'the day of judgement would begin during 22 November 1969. In these final hours Man would be 'given a last opportunity to repair his decadent house before the terminal series of disasters'. If mankind did not take the opportunity to change, 'the Space Brothers would remove the Chosen and return them to Earth after the planet had once again "crystallised", and been spiritually, as well as physically, restructured.' The 'restructuring' would involve the tilting of the Earth on its

during the 1970s was called HIM – Human Individual Metamorphosis. This group appeared in California in 1975 and appealed to some of those who had dabbled in the drug culture, personal spiritual development and 'New Age' mysticism. The movement was run by a middle-aged man and woman. They adopted names that were modest enough: Bo and Peep. Their teaching offered the advantages of life after death without the inconvenience of dying. Instead the adherents were to ascend physically. One of the cult's publicity posters read:

> UFOs – why they are here. Who they have come for. When they will land. Two individuals say they were sent from the level above human and will return to that level in a spaceship (UFO) within the next three months. This man and woman will discuss how the transition from the human level to the next level is accomplished, and when this may be done . . . . If you have ever entertained the idea that there might be a real PHYSICAL level in space beyond the Earth's confines, you will want to attend this meeting.

axis and the disappearance beneath the sea of large land areas. The members of the Light Affiliates were exhorted to evangelise wherever possible.

Nothing seems to have happened on the predicted date to fulfil the expectations of the Light Affiliates. Robin McPherson ceased to communicate, but her mother continued the task. In an interview with the writer Brad Steiger in the mid 1970s, she explained where the predictions had gone wrong:

> We misinterpreted them, Brad, because it all happened so suddenly. The first visions I was given of destruction were very upsetting. I can see things now in a much broader perspective . . . . The thing is that it is the first ascension, and it is a *mental* ascension. The Brothers are trying to get as many people as possible into the Kingdom . . . . You know, I've been told by the Brotherhood that Earth is like an encounter therapy centre for the psychotics of the Universe . . . . I have been shown that the Earth is also wobbling very drastically on its axis.

It is sometimes less painful to find ways of showing that your beliefs are fundamentally correct by means of some elaborate re-interpretation than to concede that they are simply mistaken.

Claims that intelligent beings can visit us from the planets of the solar system have been made implausible by space exploration. Alien entities must come from distant star systems, even from other galaxies, of which science presently knows little. Some UFO cults – though by no means all – have adapted to the growth of knowledge by placing the source of their communications in suitably remote places.

The group that made the greatest impact

Above: Joan Culpepper tells reporters about her life with Human Individual Metamorphosis (HIM), the UFO cult run by the Two (below right). HIM offered its followers the prospect of being transported physically to a realm beyond the Earth's atmosphere. Joan Culpepper left the cult and set up a 'half-way house' to assist other disillusioned former adherents. Her two companions in this picture – still believing members of the cult – had taken the names 'Levi' and 'Moriah'. The Two called themselves Bo and Peep – but at the time the photograph was taken they bore their original names: Marshall Huff Applewhite and Bonnie Lu Trusdale Nettles. At the time they were under arrest by Texas police on charges of car theft and credit card fraud

More than human

Bo and Peep – formerly known as M.H. Applewhite and Bonnie Nettles – had convinced themselves that they were more than human, and had the strength of will and personality to maintain that impression; converts were clearly quite overwhelmed by them. At first they claimed that they would

one day be assassinated and then would be resurrected – after three days. Later these claims were set aside. As in other such groups, members were expected to make sacrifices: to give up their names and possessions, abandon the use of drugs, alcohol, radio and television, and not to indulge in sex – or even read books. The members generally lived in semi-permanent camps. The words of Bo and Peep in an interview recounted by Brad Steiger make their attitude to the family and other personal relationships clear:

Husband and wife can take the trip at the same time – but not together. It would be impossible to become an individual if you went together on the trip . . . . In order to leave this Earth's atmosphere, you must go alone and overcome whatever needs you have for any other individual or thing of this Earth. Anything for which you depend on another human being or any thing on this Earth must be overcome.

Being a member of HIM was more like being a Moonie than participating in a traditional religion or even a traditional UFO cult. But the structure of the group was like that of other groups already described: there was a communicator, a message, a task.

No one has yet ascended to another physical realm above the atmosphere. Not many people seem to have got their money back, either. It turned out that Bo and Peep had met each other in a psychiatric hospital, where she was a nurse and he was a patient. Yet plenty of people remained willing to

believe them and to accept their discipline. Like so many fringe religions, it seems to have met spiritual needs shared by many people at the present time.

Let us look, finally, at one further vision of salvation by UFOs – one that has been experienced in dreams by Sue and John Day, an English couple. They claim to have been taken on board an alien spacecraft near the village of Aveley, Essex in October 1974. In their dreams they saw a deep red Sun and a dark sphere hanging in a blood-coloured sky. Columns of weary men, women and children made their way through a devastated landscape towards the summit of a high hill.

There they waited for perhaps days, until their eyes caught the first glinting reflections from a formation of shining UFO-like craft appearing over the murky horizon, heading slowly in their direction. As they drew nearer a number of these craft broke away and descended over the hilltop, then began to lower ramps. The people seemed to know that at last 'they' had come. Come at last to take them away, away from the devastated planet Earth.

The Days identified the area in the dream as Dragon Hill, near Uffington. It seemed to them to be a presentiment of a possible, but avoidable, future – a future holding disaster, but also salvation for a fortunate few through the intervention of UFOs.

Dragon Hill, near Uffington in Oxfordshire, is one of England's most mysterious ancient sites. It was recognised by two contactees, John and Sue Day, as the scene of dreams they had that seemed to foreshadow some future disaster for the world. UFOs figured in the dreams as saving a disease-ravaged remnant of the human race

Reaching for the sky

Flying saucer cults may be no more than a haven for cranks – but is their interpretation of UFOs much odder than those of certain experts? The ideas entertained by some ufologists can stretch credibility to its limits

CULTS BASED ON UFO CONTACTEES have much in common – in their activities, in the way their leaders receive communications, and in the general tenor of those communications. But the specific claims made in the messages from 'space people' differ wildly from each other. The extra-terrestrials who guide them rarely even come from the same planet. However well-intentioned or warm-hearted the members of the groups may be, the divergences in their claims must lead the outsider to conclude that there is little reason to take them seriously. Whether or not the religious impulse that inspires them is authentic, the scientific trappings that they often don are distortions of valid science.

Yet the claims made by the cults are, if anything, less fantastic and disturbing than some of the theories that have been put forward by respected ufologists who have *not* surrounded themselves with followers and made claims to infallibility.

For example, although some of Brad Steiger's books should not be regarded as expressing his own opinions, the material in which his own attitude *can* be discerned seems to indicate a strong belief in the idea of

Above: UFOs descended on a French village in 1974 – but left no clue to their origin

Below: popular science writer Brad Steiger, who seems to believe that many historical figures were in touch with space beings

'Space Brothers' or 'Star People'. In one of his books the final chapter is contributed by his wife and is entitled 'How to contact multidimensional beings'. It states that 'Socrates, Napoleon, George Washington, Joan of Arc and Bernadette of Lourdes had contact with these beings.' Steiger himself has said:

> I am . . . convinced that there is a subtle kind of symbiotic relationship which exists between mankind and the UFO intelligences. I think that in some way, which we have yet to determine, they need us as much as we need them.

This begins to hint that mankind does not have control over its own destiny, but Steiger nevertheless believes that the higher beings with whom we are in contact are benevolent. Other writers have more frightening ideas. They believe that alien powers can control the experiences we have and the way we respond to them. Hypotheses of this kind are known as the 'control system theory', which is generally associated with Jacques Vallée:

> UFOs are the means through which man's concepts are being arranged. All we can do is to trace their effects on humans. . . . I suggest that it is human belief that is being controlled.

That is what Vallée wrote in *The invisible college*. He went further in *Messengers of deception*:

> I believe there is a machinery of mass

Above: D. Scott Rogo, whose account of UFOs includes the notion that the intelligence behind the phenomenon knows what humanity is thinking, and that contactees are 'the tools of a global plan'

manipulation behind the UFO phenomenon . . . UFO contactees are the tools of a global plan. These silent agents are walking among us unseen, placing social time bombs at strategic spiritual locations. Some fine morning we may wake up from our 'scientific' complacency to find strangers walking through the ruins of our Establishments.

Jerry Clark and D. Scott Rogo are a little plainer in their account:

Let's begin by supposing that somewhere in the universe there is an intelligence or force – we'll call it the Phenomenon for want of a better word – that's beaming projections of various kinds into our world. . . . Whatever its nature, it has some deep sense of what human beings are thinking, and it provides us with visions that reflect the concerns of the human mind.

Writing on his own account, Rogo has stated: UFO abductions are physically real events. But they are dramas materialised into three-dimensional space for us by the Phenomenon. They are dreams that the Phenomenon made come to life in very frightening vividness. . . . Once someone has entered into psychic contact with the Phenomenon the link may become permanent, and reactivate periodically.

This is heady stuff, coming from figures of

such stature and influence in the UFO field. But even Dr J. Allen Hynek, who has done so much to help make ufology respectable and acceptable on both sides of the Atlantic, has commented:

There are people who've had UFO experiences who've claimed to have developed psychic ability. There have been reported cases of healings in close encounters, and there have been reported cases of precognition, where people had foreknowledge or forewarning that they were going to see something. There has been a change of outlook, a change of philosophy in persons' lives. Now, you see, these are rather tricky things to talk about, but it's there.

Many people, like Jacques Vallée and I, to some extent, feel that it might be a conditioning process.

No hiding place

The control system theorists are not writing about occasional isolated incidents but about the worldwide evidence of a system to which mankind is bound and from which it cannot escape – a system that, they claim, existed before humanity appeared and will in turn outlive it.

John Keel's theories are perhaps the most terrifying of all. For him the control system, which he calls the Eighth Tower, is no longer running the show intelligently, but instead

CLAUDE VORILHON 'RAEL'

SPACE ALIENS
TOOK ME TO
THEIR PLANET

TRUE STORY

the most important revelation in the history of mankind
THE BOOK WHICH TELLS THE TRUTH

The last days of the world

In *Messengers of deception* Jacques Vallée suggests that the UFO contactee cults are part of a sinister plan to undermine the power of rational thought for political

ends. While the desire to change the world is plain enough in the 'teachings' of contactees like Claude Vorilhon (left and, below, his book), will many people act on them?

Vorilhon claims to have been chosen by extra-terrestrials because he is French, from 'the country where democracy was born', but in order to survive the 'last days' of the present age we must 'eliminate elections and votes' and disband the military everywhere. The 'Elohim' – a Hebrew word meaning 'the gods' – will then return and give us the benefit of their wisdom.

The space people also gave him a new name and his peculiar insignia – a swastika set within the star of David. As if this were not enough, Vorilhon (now 'Rael') naïvely recounts other benefits of his position such as his romp in a bathtub with no less than five singularly lovely extra-terrestrial female robots! All this is told in the course of appealing for funds to build a mansion to house the Elohim when they return.

Do Vorilhon's simplistic and contradictory notions hold any political dangers? Probably not – but this century *has* seen far more irrational ideas turn into hideous reality.

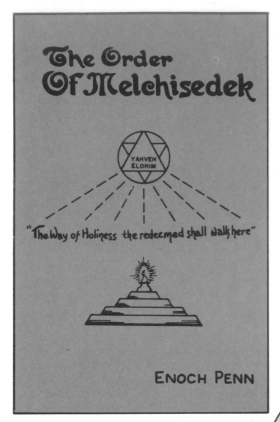

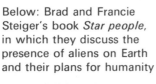

Left: the cover of a book by Ernest Penn, a member of the now-defunct American religious sect, the Order of Melchisedek. From its writings it is clear that the group expected to gain earthly power, though the means to gain that power (among other things members were enjoined to refrain from orgasm, for example) were not calculated to gain it much popularity. Some of the ideas as well as the name of the sect have been taken over by contactee cults in the USA and elsewhere. The pentacle (below) was given to author Jacques Vallée by the French Melchisedek group

Below: Brad and Francie Steiger's book *Star people*, in which they discuss the presence of aliens on Earth and their plans for humanity

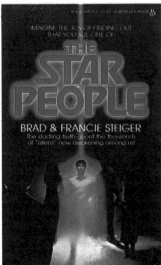

has gone out of control and is blindly following some preordained plan:

> The human race has always been aware that it was serving as a pawn in some cosmic game. . . . We have been programmed well, but the Eighth Tower is dying of old age. The manifestations around us are not the work of the gods, but of a senile machine playing out the end game.

This implies that humanity has only the illusion of free will in the conduct of its affairs – a view more pessimistic than all but some extremely Calvinistic forms of traditional religion.

Certain Christian groups, particularly among the evangelical movements, have viewed the UFOs as sinister, though not as controlling human activity. The respected *Journal* of the Spiritual Counterfeits Project devoted an issue to UFOs and concluded thus:

Current UFO phenomena, insofar as they complete the patterns of fallen human speculation discussed earlier, while playing to that ignorant dynamism which drives us to the stars (to the neglect of our souls) cannot but be suspected of having their origin with Satan and his companions in spoilage and deceit. Add to this both the theological and statistical improbability that an extra-terrestrial race ever would (or could) visit Earth, and the odds lean greatly in favour of the possibility that UFOs *do* represent a visitation, but of extra*dimensionals* – demonic spirits which have gained the power to actually perform materialisations in the physical realm.

Setting Satan's stage

John Weldon and Zola Levitt, authors of a number of books on the paranormal written from a Christian viewpoint, have said:

> Quite simply we think the demons are preparing the coming of the Antichrist. . . . To properly set the stage for the Antichrist, who really is a supernatural personality, the world has to be made ready to think in terms of the new and the strange. . . .

Meanwhile, an English clergyman, the Reverend Eric Inglesby, comments:

> As psychic phenomena (which many UFOs are) the subject is interesting and potentially dangerous; in their spiritual aspect, involving the destiny of immortal souls, whether by false belief, or by spirit possession, or even by abduction, UFOs are not just dangerous – they are deadly. In some respects they are visible manifestations, to those who actually see them, of those principalities and powers which St Paul clearly identified as evil, not good.

Are UFOs as damaging as this mass of diverse opinion suggests? There is no convincing evidence to support the contention that they are physically or psychologically dangerous in a *direct* way: they cannot control our minds. But we can *make* UFOs dangerous to ourselves by bringing our own desires and fears to bear on the mass of recorded UFO data. Any of us can find material in that enormous accumulation to support our own personal opinions. The people who have created UFO contactee cults have built their own elaborate superstructures of belief.

We must regard the over-speculative interpretation of UFO data as a kind of temptation from which even the most intelligent, experienced and knowledgeable of commentators are not immune. The information we possess about UFOs makes a whole that is self-contradictory, confusing, outlandish and, often, incredible. We need to keep that simple fact in mind before building up our speculations on some selected part of the evidence.

Symbols in the sky

Many believe passionately that UFOs originate beyond the Earth. The psychologist C.G. Jung, however, proposed the theory that their true significance lies in the depths of human subconscious

UNIDENTIFIED FLYING OBJECTS fascinated Carl Gustav Jung, the wayward genius of psychology who developed the idea of the 'collective unconscious'. Since they seemed to him to be perfect examples of his main psychological doctrines, it was natural that in 1959 he should devote a short book, *Flying saucers*, to them.

Jung was a pioneering psychologist who based much of his work on the concept of *archetypes* – vastly significant symbols, motifs or figures that seem to carry much the same meaning for everyone. These symbols are liable to rise spontaneously from the depths of the unconscious, manifesting themselves in any human creation and evoking powerful emotional and imaginative responses. To understand their nature and implications, Jung marshalled an astonishing array of parallels from the areas of human activity where the 'non-rational' holds sway – religion and mythology, ancient and primitive ritual, occult systems like alchemy and astrology, and much more. At the same time, to prove that such archetypes were alive and well in the psyche of modern Man, he showed how they emerged again and again in the dreams of his patients and in the art, folklore

Above: the characteristic 'flying saucer' form is evident in this American photograph of a UFO. This sighting was clearly not a delusion, though the possibility of a fake remains. Carl Jung (inset) believed that, whatever their true nature, the power of the 'saucers' over the modern mind stems from the symbolic meaning of the disc

and popular myth of the 20th century.

The eight-year-old daughter of a psychiatrist friend, for example, had a series of dreams with striking imagery of, Jung believed, great antiquity. In one of them a horned, snakelike monster appeared, which Jung identified with a horned serpent referred to in 16th-century alchemical literature. Then, in the same dream, God 'came from the four corners' – presumably of the world, though the young girl did not make this clear. Jung relates this to ideas of a fourfold divinity antedating the concept of the Trinity, but almost forgotten since the 17th century. The little girl was drawing, as he saw it, on 'libraries' of symbolism – the archetypes – available to all mankind throughout history in the collective unconscious.

Jung believed that one of these archetypal images was the disc, of which the UFO was a modern variant. At first he put to one side the problematic question of whether what is seen in the sky is actually there. Certainly people believe that they see UFOs, just as they have believed in other 'non-pathological' visions, like the angels of Mons. Many soldiers reported having seen these apparitions during the fierce fighting accompanying the British retreat from Mons in 1914. It is an instructive parallel, for, if they were imaginary, the angelic warriors were given reality in the minds of soldiers because of the unusually powerful emotional state induced in them by the horrors of the war. People in the

Left: British soldiers in retreat from Mons in 1914 believed that angelic figures had defended them. Although this painting shows the angels as shoulder-to-shoulder with the Tommies, they were actually seen in the sky over the German forces, apparently restraining them from attacking. Soldiers on the opposing side, however, reported interventions by pro-German angels. Jung suggested that UFOs may similarly express the desires, conscious or not, of those who see them

search, with all its accompanying tensions, terrors and despairs, leads frequently to collective projections – resulting in visions, rumours, mass panics, outlandish beliefs. In them Jung delightedly discerns the visible process of the formation of a myth. (The subtitle of *Flying saucers* is *A modern myth of things seen in the sky*. A myth may be defined as 'a story of gods or heroes, especially one offering an explanation of some fact or phenomenon'; or, equally tellingly, as 'a story with a veiled meaning'.) At the heart of the new myths, as of the old, lies one or more of the archetypes, providing the motive power and essential form.

Projections and portents

So Jung is suggesting that UFOs are such myth-projections. Indeed, they may well be another herald of some current and far-reaching upheaval within the collective psyche of mankind. Some see such an upheaval foreshadowed in the current Western passion for the occult; others see it in the worldwide spread of communism; or it may be something as yet unimagined. Such transformations, throughout history, have always been accompanied by major upsurges, in religion, art and literature, of the most dominant and potent archetypes.

The flying discs or saucers, in Jung's view, are modern versions of perhaps the mightiest archetype of all, named by Jung the 'mandala'.

The word is Sanskrit, and the art and religion of the Hindus are filled with these symbols. But mandalas occur literally everywhere – from modern children's art to ancient circles of standing stones, from the ring featuring in the solemn marriage ritual of the Christian Church to the circles of Dante's inferno and the marginal scrawls and

grip of such emotion, says Jung, will tend to see collective visions. And such visions will be *projections* – a key word – taking the form of some answer to their emotional needs.

In a nutshell, and to oversimplify, modern Man is 'in search of a soul' – as stated in the title of one of Jung's most effective analyses of the world's present malaise. And that

Left: a mandala forming the centrepiece of a 19th-century Buddhist painting from Nepal. It symbolises the perfection that has been attained by the eight-armed figure at its centre: a bodhisattva, which has completed its ages-long series of incarnations, but delays its entry into the bliss of Nirvana in order to aid the creatures who still suffer. A mandala also appears in the 14th-century German altarpiece (right), where it frames another being of perfect wholeness: Christ in majesty, surrounded by the Beasts of the Apocalypse and an assembly of the blessed

doodles of busy office workers. The mandala is basically a simple circle, though the variations are legion, and can include important additions like a central nucleus, or a quartering, or further concentric circles. And it carries the meaning – again to oversimplify – of a sought-after completion, totality, and *wholeness*.

That brings us abruptly back to poor suffering modern Man. We live in a 'dissociated' world – split like the mind of a schizophrenic, with little or no true communication between the parts. It is split outwardly into two monstrously threatening international blocs. The advanced technology that sustains our lives simultaneously threatens them with imminent holocaust. The darker, irrational impulses of human nature, disowned by reason and believed in the 18th and 19th centuries to have been finally vanquished by the progress of civilisation, have returned and repeatedly triumphed in the 20th.

Inwardly, too, we are split, to our grave cost. Our science and materialist values have given us our high standards of living – yet within that civilisation they have devalued all

the areas of the non-rational: the emotions, the instincts, the imagination, the religious impulses and so on. The nominally Christian world can no longer draw strength from its religious tradition; in Jung's words: 'Our myth has become mute, and gives no answers.'

We need not dwell on the description of our chronic dissociation, for Jung does not pretend that his view of a sick world is anything but obvious. It is the *effect* that matters – because dissociation causes tension, illness, monstrous deformation of the non-rational areas that have been split off and downgraded. So the dissociated mind cries out to be healed – cries out for a reunion

Above: a UFO sighting of the 16th century. In the broadsheet from which this woodcut comes, an eyewitness reports that on 7 August 1566, in Basle, 'many large black globes were seen in the air, moving before the sun with great speed, and turning against each other as if fighting. Some of them became red and fiery and afterwards faded and went out'

of its parts, for a re-creation of healthy and harmonious equilibrium between them . . . that is, for wholeness. And out of that unconscious yearning, wretched, soul-starved modern Man projects mandalas everywhere, even into the sky.

It is a fascinating analysis, with some rewarding sidelights. Naturally, Jung is at pains to seek the mandala motif in places other than the 'symbolic rumours' of recorded UFO sightings, in order to prove its universality and validity. He finds it, inevitably, in dreams and modern art, and explicates these at length.

Nor does he overlook possible alternative explanations. Some of the UFO sightings or mandala dreams, he says, may carry with them elements of sexual symbolism. But he is, as always, drily dismissive of the Freudian tendency to go very little further in search of understanding, having once discerned the symbolic shape of sex organs in the spacecraft of our dreams.

Far more important, for Jung, are the unique elements of the UFO-mandala, which he finds to be a variant of the archetype that is highly suitable for our time. What more likely image of a healing wholeness, for this technological age, than a mysterious machine, a piece of heavenly hardware?

Saviours from space

Furthermore, the 'heavenly' part of the UFO projection is just as central to Jung's analysis. He was especially struck by the 'unnatural' behaviour and flight patterns of UFOs in all the reports of sightings that he studied. He had no doubt about the significance of the implication that these space-travelling mandalas are not of human origin, for those who have professed to see them. And while sometimes the observer (or dreamer) may have felt threatened, more often the UFO visitation is taken to display the existence of advanced extra-terrestrials, superpowerful and *friendly* beings from the sky, who are watching and worrying over Man's self-destructive twitchings down on planet Earth.

Jung also notes some of those occasions when people have claimed to have had closer encounters, even to have been picked up and carried briefly off by the kindly and godlike beings. He does not give much credence to these tales, but instead concludes that here the yearning for wholeness has taken on the more precise and personalised form of a longing for and dreaming of a *saviour* – some being who is more than human, who will descend to help us find the respite and healing that we cannot find for ourselves.

In this part of his analysis, Jung makes the illuminating point that 'things seen in the sky' existed throughout history, long before they took on the 20th-century guise of mysterious spacecraft out of pulp science fiction. Unnaturally mobile flying spheres, globes and discs occur prominently in annals of strange visions and inexplicable phenomena seen during troubled times of the past.

Again and again Jung makes the point that it matters not at all whether there actually *was* anything there, in the sky, or whether there is today. If UFOs did not and do not exist in objective reality, then they can be defined as projections of all the complex and powerful emotions described above. And if they *do* exist, they can *still* be seen as projections – just as we unconsciously project a huge burden of symbolism, with all the potency of the archetypes, onto many real items or individuals around us (like jewellery or weaponry, film stars or political leaders).

In the last analysis Jung does *not* wholly discount the possibility that there may be some objective, physical basis for the 'symbolic rumour' of the UFO. We might forgivably dismiss as dream or hallucination some of the more far-fetched tales of trips into space with tall robed beings who promise to save the world. But radar screens and cameras do not dream or hallucinate – and Jung was well-aware of the solidly authenticated instances when recorded blips and photographs have seemed to confirm the existence of UFOs. As he puts it: 'Either

Right: the qualities seen in sex symbols, as in other symbols, are largely 'projected' onto them by those who hold them in awe. Moviegoers saw Marilyn Monroe as warm, soft and yielding, and Jane Russell as 'mean, moody and magnificent'. The real personalities of these screen goddesses were irrelevant to the millions whose hopes and desires they symbolically fulfilled

Below: a universally recognised symbol of power and prosperity. To millions who will never ride in one and know nothing of its qualities, the Rolls-Royce is the supreme expression of status and success

psychic projections throw back a radar echo, or else the appearance of real objects affords an opportunity for mythological projection.'

He is of course being ironic: he does not believe that psychic projections can affect radar screens. But the point has to be laboured because of the relentless urge, among the media and other defenders of the rationalist *status quo*, to take every opportunity of decrying Jung as some wild-eyed, credulous crank, hip-deep in what Freud scornfully called the 'black mud of occultism'. His detractors have consistently misunderstood and misrepresented Jung's investigations of alchemy, astrology and the 'irrational' in all its forms. Inevitably they

have also had a field day with their own inadequate comprehension of what he had to say about flying saucers.

Jung, conversely, always persisted in keeping his mind open to an enormous range of material that might in some way contribute to furthering his understanding of the human unconscious. He perceived and analysed, towards this end, the symbolic relevance of the UFO.

But he also perceived that, in all the continually amassing reports on and studies of UFOs, there remained a core of 'hard' data that could only make sense if there were real objects up there, even if they were misinterpreted by those who saw them.

In the years after the publication of his book on flying saucers, Jung was often in touch with one of his nieces in Switzerland, who is something of an expert in her own right on UFO sightings. And according to Gordon Creighton of *Flying Saucer Review*, Jung came to move even more firmly beyond the position that UFOs might be 'merely' symbolic projections of a powerful archetype. Whatever our unconscious wishes might make of them, whatever effects they might have upon the depths of our psyches, Jung apparently grew more and more firmly convinced that there was something very real behind the phenomena.

Jung did not see himself as a prophet, in any sense, but as a psychologist, a scientific observer. Yet history is full of instances where a scientist, from objective study and observation, has 'prophetically' perceived a truth at which his blinkered contemporaries, without examining the data, continue to scoff. Will Jung's view of the UFO one day prove to be another example?

When dreams come true

Tales of close encounters often seem to describe some kind of psychic, rather than 'nuts and bolts', experience. In cases where the paranormal and ufology appear to overlap are there any common features?

MANY REPORTS of encounters with UFOs and ghosts contain curiously similar or even identical elements, which suggest to the objective researcher that both kinds of experience may be psychic phenomena that originate in the mind. All such experiences are strongly subjective and often defy scientific explanation. Frequently entities of one kind or another appear to a single person, while others also present notice nothing. Physical effects are noticed by witnesses: tingling sensations and humming noises are linked with UFO sightings, while a marked drop in temperature is often said to accompany the appearance of ghosts. And the vast majority of such encounters occur at night, often when the witness is alone or in some way 'vulnerable'. The two types of experience may be very different but, as the following examples show, the similarities give cause for reflection.

In 1960 a well-to-do businessman of Manchester, England, was spending the night with a girlfriend when he felt the bedroom invaded by a curious tingling sensation. The air was full of an electromagnetic humming. Worried, he glanced around the room; he noted the time, just after 3 a.m. Then a figure appeared, standing by the bedside and blocking out the light that

Below: Pendle Hill, traditional meeting place for witches, near Nelson in Lancashire. On 9 March 1977 Brian Grimshawe and a friend saw a dark, cigar-shaped UFO with flashing lights appear over the hill. It approached them, then drifted away

Overleaf: a 'doughnut-shaped' UFO pursued 15-year-old Frank Earp and two friends at Wollaton, near Nottingham in 1966. Then a huge, furry creature with 'legs that faded away into nothingness' appeared – but only two of the boys saw it

Overleaf below: Cairo Mill, Oldham, where John Byrne worked as a security guard. One night in 1972 he distinctly saw a huge humming UFO hovering above him – but his colleague, who was nearby, saw nothing

filtered through the window. It was a woman, only inches away from him and as plain and solid as the mattress on which he lay. His mind absorbed her features and her dress. Then he cried out. Quickly, the image melted into the blackness of night and he sheepishly awoke his sleeping companion to tell her of the ordeal. She knew what he had seen, for it was not the first time such a phantasm had appeared. The description perfectly matched the girl's dead mother.

It was not long after 3 a.m. on 9 March 1977. Brian Grimshawe and a fellow night shift factory worker were driving to the factory through the almost deserted streets of Nelson in Lancashire, England. Suddenly, a light appeared over Pendle Hill, famous for its long association with witchcraft. A dark cigar shape, flashing different colours, floated through the sky towards them. As it approached, both the engine and lights of the car cut out. The men became frightened. They felt a strange tingling sensation, and an electromagnetic hum filled their ears. They tried desperately to escape the hovering UFO, but the car was dead. Then, just as suddenly as it had come, the UFO drifted away southwards. The car's lights and engine jerked back to life and the oppressive sensations disappeared. The two men sped back to the factory and soon developed pounding headaches as a result of their terrifying experience.

The materialisation of a ghost and the sighting of a UFO . . . is that what these two events were? Perhaps, but the similarities between them are most intriguing and they are duplicated time and again in other strange encounters.

Witness Frank Earp gives a graphic account of his own encounter in 1966 at Wollaton, near Nottingham, England, in the February 1981 issue of *Northern Earth Mysteries*. He was 15 at the time and playing with two friends beside a disused canal. He admits that they were looking for UFOs. As darkness came, a mist began to rise from the watercourse. This was not unusual. But then a cloud, the size of a fairground dodgem car, detached itself in the shape of a doughnut (without a central hole). It drifted towards them. Becoming disturbed they set off for home, quickly breaking into a trot as the apparently intelligent 'cloud' pursued them. They could all see it, glowing inside with a strange luminescence.

Friend, foe – or fiend?

As they approached the edge of the village they decided to stop. Frank was delegated to confront the intruder for they were now close enough to home and could escape, should anything go wrong. Frank turned, to find the cloud just 20 feet (6 metres) away. He tried to ask if it was friend or foe, but his words were cut short by one of his friends, clearly terrified, tapping his shoulder and urging, 'When I say run – *run*!' He looked ahead into

the gloom and understood the reason for this fear. For there stood a 6-foot (1.8-metre) furry figure, silhouetted in front of the glowing object. In claw-like hands it gripped two red 'pencils', and its legs faded into nothingness. The third boy stood only inches from the creature. As the other two fled he called after them, bemused. It later transpired that although he was almost touching the figure he had not seen it. But he had seen the cloud.

These experiences pose a difficult question. Just where is the dividing line between different types of paranormal event? Does a dividing line even exist? Was the strange humanoid figure met by Ken Edwards of Risley a UFO entity or a ghost? Did the boys at Wollaton chance upon a boggart (a furry figure), a ghost or a 'sasquatch'? There are no easy answers. For once again there are features that are common to them all.

At Cairo Mill, Oldham, England, on 8 October 1972, John Byrne, a security guard

at the Ferranti engineering works, saw a massive UFO hovering above him. It emitted a strange blue light and a high-pitched humming whine, but his fellow guard, just yards away, saw and heard absolutely nothing – just as Frank Earp's friend did not see the furry creature.

At Machynlleth, Wales, in July 1975 a terrified teenager saw a landed disc and undulating jelly-like entities. The experience so shocked him he suffered from persistent hysterical blindness for a long time afterwards. The disc became transparent in parts and blended into the surroundings before vanishing entirely – just like the Wollaton boggart or the traditional ghost, which it is claimed one can see through.

Ordeal for animals

Another common factor in stories about ghosts is the manner with which animals allegedly react, even before the presence is confirmed by a human observer. A family in Gorton, Greater Manchester, were plagued by a poltergeist in June 1981. The invisible force upturned settees, threw planks of wood around the living room and scrawled messages in toothpaste on household mirrors. Before these outbursts, the family's Alsatian dog had become disturbed, running about, barking madly, and leaping into the air as if to attack an unseen adversary.

A dog plays a part in the following case, but this time there was no apparent ghost or poltergeist. Instead there was a very peculiar figure, wearing a spacesuit.

The witness was an Army NCO, stationed at Dakelia barracks, Cyprus, in September 1968. At 3 a.m. his dog, a fierce Turkish wolfhound, suddenly sat up and began growling, its fur standing on end. Fearing a possible terrorist attack the soldier went to the door, then a high pitched humming

At Dakelia barracks, Cyprus (above), an NCO and his dog – a fierce Irish wolfhound – were reduced to nervous wrecks by the sudden appearance of a ghostly creature that floated up the stairs after them (below). Yet this 'ghost' seemed to be wearing a spacesuit

filled his skull. The dog was by now under the bed, whimpering and cowering. Out on the landing the soldier saw to his horror the head and shoulders of a creature floating up the wooden stairs. It was humanoid and clad in a light blue suit. It had an eerie face that glowed orange, huge round eyes and a tousled shock of red hair. It could swivel its head 180°.

The soldier rushed back to the sanctuary of his room. He sat on the edge of his bed, shaking uncontrollably, as the whining outside rose to a crescendo. Now he could hear a sliding sound as if the creature were approaching the door. He snatched up his underwater speargun, loaded it and aimed it at the door; the sliding noise faded away. An hour or so later, the soldier was found, still sitting on his bed and trembling with fear. And overnight the dog turned into a quivering wreck.

A woman called Mary was driving her car near Norwalk, Connecticut, USA, in the summer of 1973 when the radio was suddenly filled with strange static interference. She heard a man's voice inside her head and found herself within a huge 'spacecraft'. How she got there she has no idea. Standing before her was a tall entity with fair hair and dressed in a silver one-piece suit. It conversed with her by telepathy, or directly from mind to mind. She was greeted with the strange words, 'Welcome my friend, Mary Angel.' During the time the witness spent on board this 'craft', before being returned

mysteriously to her car, the 'alien' gave her a tour of his UFO. It was supposedly peopled by no fewer than 200 crew, who came from what they called 'the galaxy of Guentatori-Elfi'. The aliens prophesied specific floods that would occur in the USA. In due course the prediction came true.

But the aliens do not always display such insight. A woman in Belfast, Northern Ireland, was taken on board a UFO in 1976. She was told that Princess Anne would have twins and that Canada was about to join the European Common Market. Needless to say, five years later these extremely unlikely events had still not come to pass.

Yet, perhaps it is a relief that these aliens can be remarkably human in their fallibility, for some of their prophecies are not so amusing.

Two men in their late twenties were returning from a night at a friend's house in Palos Verdes, southern California, during a summer in the early 1970s. As they were about to drive off, their headlights illuminated two weird shapes on the road. They were the size of basketballs and looked not unlike giant human brains. After observing them for a few seconds they manoeuvred the car around them and hurried on their way. After taking his friend home (a five-minute journey) the driver continued on to his destination (another five minutes), only to

One night in the early 1970s two young men saw 'giant human brains' on a Californian road (above). Later, under hypnotic regression, one witness recalled humanoids with 'webbed features' (below)

discover that two and a half hours had gone by instead of the expected 10 minutes.

The man, whom investigator Ann Druffel calls John Hodges, was put under regressive hypnosis in 1976 to try to restore his detailed memory of the event. He was anxious to find out what had happened to him. In this condition he described how, when alone in his car, he was taken into a room and conversed telepathically with one of the brains. 'The voice comes within me . . . but it sounds like you are talking to me,' Hodges said. Some grey-skinned humanoid creatures with 'webbed' features were also present, apparently acting as crewmen. The giant brain showed Hodges 'advanced three-dimensional holograms' depicting nuclear explosions, and explained that atomic power was being misused on Earth. Hodges later 'remembered' that the humanoids were in fact the real controllers and the brains simply acted as translation devices (alive, and yet not quite alive). A miniaturised 'translator cell' was implanted in Hodges's brain on the night of the contact, which would allow information to flow freely in the future. Eventually he was returned to his car, but his memory was blocked and he felt a curious 'buzzing and tingling' all over his body.

A third world war

Since 1976 John Hodges has received numerous messages via his 'translator'. These include detailed information about a world war that will erupt in the Middle East and then spread to Europe between 1982 and 1984. Nuclear weapons will be used. After the war ends and a world government is created, the aliens will land in 1987 and trigger the thousands of people who, like Hodges, have been implanted with 'translators' without their conscious knowledge.

Such a story sounds utter nonsense, yet so do most of the other alien contact incidents that are reported. At the very least, however, they demand a reasonable hearing.

There is a considerable problem in trying to trace a common source of these incredible events for they are presented in many different contexts. They involve ghost-like beings, weird monsters, spirit entities, and a veritable menagerie of aliens from all over the Universe. Yet all of them share an underlying theme and many consistent internal characteristics. Are intelligent extra-terrestrial beings contacting us and behaving like skilled impressionists? Or could these experiences stem from a source that is somewhat closer to home – namely ourselves?

Consider this statement by John Hodges. 'The words . . . actually come from within the mind . . . loud, clear, crisp. The voice sounded male, but it's odd. It sounded as if it was the same voice I have to myself, when I *think*.'

Variations on a theme

A woman described being abducted by a UFO as it was happening – but no one else saw it. How many other close encounters take place in the mind, 'real' only in a subjective sense?

CAROL AND STEVE W. are a young married couple from Gateshead in north-east England. In August 1979 they had cause to become very worried when their home was suddenly invaded. This was no ordinary plague of mice or rats disturbing the normality of their lives; instead it involved tiny UFOs and strange alien beings.

It began on 17 August. Carol was alone in the house with her three-year-old daughter as her husband was working on the night shift. She was unable to sleep because of a searing toothache; the time was about 2 a.m. She went downstairs, made a cup of tea and sipped it while sitting on her bed. A red light shone in through the curtains. Puzzled, she got up and drew them apart – and was amazed to see a cymbal-shaped object above the rooftops opposite. The UFO hovered for a while, displaying multicoloured lights, and then spiralled upwards into the sky.

Back in bed, Carol became distressed when a low rumble announced the return of what looked to be the same object – this time in miniature – appearing *on* the curtains and flying *into* the room. In its wake was a trail of glittering specks. She felt a tingle on her body and heard a buzzing as the swarm of

lights fell towards her. The specks then returned to the 18-inch (45-centimetre) disc and left the room through the open door.

The mini-UFO reappeared to Carol 13 nights later when she went into her daughter's bedroom to settle her back to sleep. The tingling returned and she screamed to her husband. He arrived just in time to see a flash of light outside the window. The disc had flown out through the window, although it was shut and remained undamaged.

Four nights later Carol decided that her husband's next night shift could not be tolerated alone so she went to stay with her mother, who lived nearby. At 4 a.m. she was again paralysed by the buzzing and tingling as the mini-UFO entered the room. This time it was accompanied by 12 weird human-like creatures, 2 feet 6 inches (76 centimetres) tall. They wore white suits and had pale, feminine features. Their hair looked unreal and reminded Carol of an Action Man doll. Some of the beings approached the bed, showed interest in her eyes, and conversed in clicking sounds.

The invasion continued for over two months. Carol's family felt the tingle and paralysis at least once, and the dog was sent into a frenzy whenever the buzzing noises enveloped the house. Then, just as suddenly as they had begun, the experiences mysteriously stopped.

This is an amazing story, which one must

Previous page: at 2 a.m. on 17 August 1979 Carol W. from Gateshead, was drinking a cup of tea to help her sleep when she became aware of a mysterious red light shining through her bedroom curtains. Drawing them back to investigate, she was startled to see a cymbal-shaped UFO hovering over the rooftops (top). It flashed many-coloured lights before spiralling upwards and disappearing from sight. Back in bed, the witness was alarmed to see what appeared to be the same UFO *but in miniature* coming into her room through the curtains, trailing brilliant 'specks' behind it (bottom). She tingled all over her body and heard a buzzing sound as the tiny lights turned towards her. The specks then retreated into the disc, which left through the closed window. Four nights later, although Carol was in a different house, the UFO visited her again – and this time brought along its crew as well

either accept or reject. There is no reason why the family should have willingly placed themselves under so much strain, and they continually asked for no publicity. But the events pose many questions. Just how could a UFO appear inside a bedroom? How could a dozen figures 2 foot 6 inches (76 centimetres) tall come from a disc only 18 inches (45 centimetres) in diameter? How could it fly through a closed window? The most obvious solution is that no object was ever physically present. What Carol observed was perhaps a projection, akin to a moving hologram or three-dimensional image, shone into the room from some unknown projector.

All too often in UFO encounters the un-bending physical laws of nature are shattered beyond recognition. Solids cannot pass through solids without trace. Objects do not travel faster than sound without creating sonic booms. Yet these things, and many more, are described in UFO reports with a regularity that is remarkable. But if the UFO or entity were in fact just a film show, projected into our natural environment, then most of these 'problems' would not arise. Think of the movie we all star in at night, with its screen inside our heads. Dreams

Above: on 5 July 1972 a huge blue UFO hovered over Mrs Maureen Puddy's car near Frankston in Victoria, Australia. Twenty days later it returned as she was driving past almost the same spot; this time it stopped the car. She heard a voice in her head that urged her to make her story public and assured her that 'we mean no harm'. Six months passed, then Mrs Puddy heard the voice again; it told her to visit the scene of the sighting once more. Two investigators, Judith Magee and Paul Norman, accompanied her there, where she described a UFO, its crew – and an attempted abduction. Yet the others saw nothing, and Maureen Puddy remained in the car all the time. Was something or someone projecting images into her mind, trying to control it?

have no need to follow the laws of physics. Anything is possible provided our subconscious is capable of imagining it.

On 5 July 1972, 27-year-old Maureen Puddy saw a UFO on the Mooraduc Road near Frankston, in Victoria, Australia. The object was a huge blue disc, which hovered above her car as she returned from visiting her son in hospital. Twenty days later, at almost the same spot, it returned. This time it seemed to drain power from the car, causing it to stop; indeed, the car appeared to steer itself to the roadside. A voice in her head told her, 'All your tests will be negative.' It then said: 'Tell media, do not panic. We mean no harm.'

Judith Magee, a respected researcher, investigated the case and about six months later received a telephone call from Mrs Puddy asking for an urgent meeting. She said that a voice had called her name and told her to return to Mooraduc Road. Judith Magee went with fellow investigator Paul Norman to meet Mrs Puddy at the scene of the sighting. Mrs Puddy said that on her way to meet the ufologists a figure in a golden suit had materialised in the car beside her.

As the investigators sat talking to the woman at the site, she claimed that the entity had returned and was standing in front of the car headlights. Neither researcher could see anything. Mrs Puddy began to describe the scene inside a UFO that she claimed was nearby. Over the next few minutes she kept alternating between being 'here' (in the car) and 'there' (inside the UFO), although all the time she was physically present with the investigators. Maureen Puddy claimed the being wanted her to go with it, which she violently opposed. The researchers sensed the battle going on within her and saw her tears as the situation got too much. Yet, if the testimony of the investigators is anything to go by, although Mrs Puddy felt she was 'inside' a UFO and 'observing an entity', this experience had no reality outside her mind.

Just how many other UFO abductions occur at this same subjective level?

The story of the Sunderland family from Oakenholt, North Wales, is a complex and incredible one. It provides a neat encapsulation of the many difficulties in trying to suggest how such experiences occur.

Every member of the family (both parents and all five children) has claimed involvement in at least one paranormal event, during

Below: the Sunderland family of Oakenholt, North Wales. Every member claims to have had some psychic experience between 1976 and 1981 and three of the children, especially Gaynor (standing at the back), say they have met 'aliens' and have been taken by them to visit other realms of being. Author and UFO investigator Jenny Randles (centre left) believes that people with a psychic background are likely to see UFOs and report close encounters

Bottom: an alleged alien footprint, photographed in Florida, USA, by Ron Whritenour in 1966. If the print is authentic then some extra-terrestrial beings are real enough to leave physical traces and, therefore, cannot be 'all in the mind'

What is particularly interesting is that Gaynor says she has always been 'psychic'. Since a baby she has seen what might be called UFOs or ghosts. She claims to see the aura round the human body. At first she assumed all these things were normal; she had no cause to suspect she was different. Gaynor has been observed in the middle of one of her 'trips' to an alien world. Her mother saw her at the time and says she was in bed in a strange, trance-like sleep.

It does seem that the alien contacts experienced by the Sunderlands have a direct relation with the other paranormal events. It is reinforced by the fact that in an amazingly high percentage of UFO contacts the central percipient has a history of claimed psychic experience, which continues after the events that they initially report.

A form of expression

There seem to be two broad possibilities: either something external is trying to get in (perhaps aliens, who find psychic people the easiest channel of communication), or something internal is trying to get out.

John Hodges in California (see page 135) would have us believe the first answer is correct. So would most of those who say they have seen aliens, for that is what the aliens tell them. George Adamski claimed to have been advised in the 1950s that they come from Venus', and in 1964 a Bolton woman met 'aliens from Pluto'. But now science has ruled out these planets as abodes of advanced forms of life and modern contactees have reported different origins for their aliens. All this sounds very suspicious. If there is no reason to trust the aliens when they tell us where they come from, what reason is there to trust them when they tell us they are aliens? Since all belief in ufonauts as interstellar voyagers stems from this one source, there is little justification for accepting such an explanation.

An internal origin for these contacts, however, would explain the puzzling relationship between paranormal phenomena. All of them would be essentially a similar

the period 1976 to 1981. On occasions more than one person witnessed the same event but most often it was a solitary experience. These events took many forms, most importantly UFO sightings but also mild poltergeist outbreaks and a vast assortment of associated anomalies. Three of the children claim to have had independent contact with different alien races, including ground landings, communication and even actual trips to other realms of being.

The principal focus has been the eldest girl, Gaynor, who has experienced direct contact, has visited an alien zoo, been taken for a ride on board a disc-like UFO, taken a guided tour of an alien city, suffered time dislocations and even produced apparently paranormal effects on photographic film.

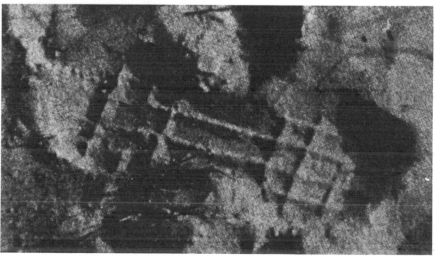

UFOs and the mind

Right: diagram explaining the theory of subconscious projection. This relies on the idea that everyone possesses a store of subconscious archetypes that change only in context. For example, in the past these probably included angels and demons, whereas today they are replaced by benign or malevolent humanoids. According to this theory, something triggers off a projection of a paranormal encounter, peopled by archetypes and experienced as objective reality by the subject. This fits in well with the ideas of author and researcher Hilary Evans who believes that paranormal experiences can be located on a continuous spectrum with dreams at one end and solid, everyday reality at the other

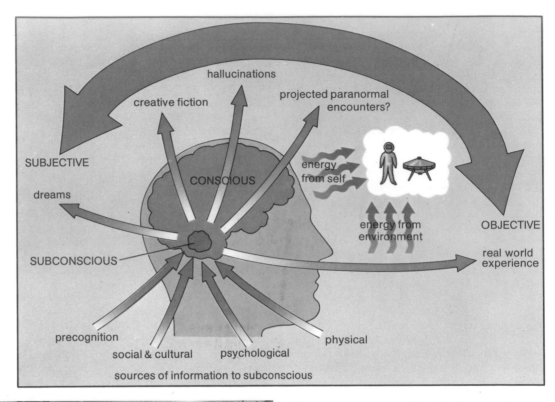

Above: George King and his wife in London in October 1957. King, who founded the Aetherius Society in 1956, claimed to have been called 'to become the voice of the Interplanetary Parliament'. The voice he heard was not psychic, he stressed, but was 'completely physical'. It told him that spiritually advanced 'masters' live on other planets and are concerned about the welfare of mankind. King is seen here with the tape recorder he used to record the messages from the 'masters'

process, clothed in terms to suit the personal beliefs and imagination of the witness. If he wants aliens from zeta Reticuli, then he gets them. If he is more inclined to believe in ghosts, then he gets them instead (or nowadays perhaps both things together). Such a concept would explain why these contacts vary so widely from case to case, and yet remain within a basic pattern. It would give us a means to understand how a ghost can be created by rumour, and endowed with substance by the gullible people who perceive it, as in the case of the invented vicar of Ratcliffe Wharf. It would also provide a reason for the obvious subjectivity of most of the contacts (real to Maureen Puddy, but not to those with her).

There are many comparisons between

alien contacts, out-of-the-body experiences (ESP projection), and the deep hallucinations known to occur on the threshold of sleep and wakefulness. For example, time lapses, jumps from scene to scene, and certain internal features are found in all of these. And there is also the peaking of experiences at 2 or 3 a.m., when the mind is most relaxed and brainwave patterns most receptive, a time when normally we dream our deepest dreams.

For this possibility to be accepted two strong objections need to be overcome. What about the occasional physical evidence of UFOs, such as the stopping of car engines or marks on the ground? If we are willing to accept psychokinesis (the moving of objects without visible or known force) and we believe that Chicago bell-hop Ted Serios and others can mentally impress images on to photographic film, then it is possible that the effects found in some UFO contact cases could be caused in a similar way, perhaps by psychic people when their brainwaves are most receptive. The source of these productions could be deep and uncontrollable.

Dreams emerge from the depths of our subconscious, translated into images that have symbolic meaning to us personally. There seems justification for a belief that UFO contacts may work in a similar manner, and that dreams, hallucinations, and possibly something just a little beyond that are all portions of a continual spectrum emerging from ourselves and our internal or collective needs. It may be that UFOs are images in our minds, not travellers from space. In some cases these images may become so powerful that they are projected by the mind and seen as semi-material entities.

The UFO casebook

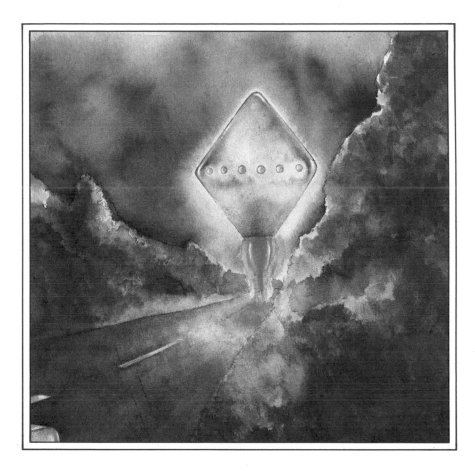

The most significant and best-documented case histories of UFO sightings are established by collecting and examining, with great care and scrupulous objectivity, the mass of detail in each separate account of the experience.

Three young Frenchmen hit the news headlines in early December 1979 with a tale about a UFO abduction at Cergy-Pontoise. But was their amazing story a fabrication? Is it possible to sort out the facts from the fiction?

'FRENCHMAN BACK TO EARTH with a bump' was the headline in the London *Times* – and across the world the media reported the news with the same uncertainty whether to take it seriously or not. But this much was certain: Franck Fontaine, who had allegedly been kidnapped by a UFO a week before, had been restored to friends, family, and a wondering world in the early hours of Monday, 3 December 1979.

Where had he spent those seven days? The world, hoping for a story that would make the Moon landing seem tame, was disappointed. Fontaine's recollections were few and confused. It seemed to him he had simply dropped off to sleep for half an hour: he was astonished and dismayed to find he had been away for a week. He attributed the strange images in his mind to dreams: he was bewildered to learn that he might have been abducted by extra-terrestrial aliens and carried to their distant world.

Police search a field in Cergy-Pontoise, France, for clues to the disappearance of Franck Fontaine, reported as having been abducted by a UFO. Fontaine's two friends, Jean-Pierre Prévost and Salomon N'Diaye, said they had witnessed the kidnapping early one morning in late November 1979. In the background is the block of flats in which Prévost and N'Diaye lived and near which the event occurred

Fontaine was no less dismayed to find himself the focus of the world's attention. During his seven-day absence, it had been his friends Salomon N'Diaye and Jean-Pierre Prévost, witnesses of his abduction, who had been the objects of attention. Ever since their first startling telephone call to the police – 'A friend of mine's just been carried off by a UFO!' – they had been subjected to interrogation by the police, by the press, and by UFO investigative groups ranging from the scientific to the bizarre. If Fontaine's return brought renewed publicity and fresh problems, at least it cleared them of the suspicion that they were responsible for their friend's disappearance – perhaps even his death.

The life-style of the three young men was not of a sort to dispel suspicion. All three – Prévost, aged 26, N'Diaye, 25, Fontaine, 18 – scraped an uncertain living by selling jeans in street markets. They drove an old car that was unlicensed and uninsured, none of them having a driving licence. Prévost was a self-declared anarchist. He and N'Diaye lived next door to each other in a modern block at Cergy-Pontoise on the outskirts of Paris. Fontaine lived 2 miles (3 kilometres) away.

According to their account, Fontaine had

Mystery of the lost weekend

spent Sunday evening in Prévost's flat because they wanted to be up by 3.30 a.m. to travel the 35 miles (60 kilometres) to the street market at Gisors. The market didn't start until 8 a.m. but they wanted a good place. Besides, their Taunus estate car had been acting up lately, so they thought it prudent to allow extra time. At 3.30, after only about four hours' sleep, they were up and ready to load the car with clothes.

First, though, they gave the car a push-start to make sure the engine would function. Having got it going, they decided that Fontaine should stay in the car to make sure it didn't stop again while the other two got on with the loading. Fontaine had leisure to look about him, and so it was that he noticed a brilliant light in the sky some distance away. When his companions arrived with their next

enveloped in a sharply defined sphere of glowing mist, near which a number of smaller balls of light were moving about. While they stood watching, they saw the larger globe absorb all but one of the smaller ones. Then a beam of light emerged, which grew in size until it was like the cylindrical shape they had seen earlier. The large sphere seemed to enter this cylinder, which shot up into the sky and disappeared from sight.

The two hurried to the car, but found no sign of Fontaine. He was not in the car, in the road, or in the cabbage field beside the road. Prévost insisted on calling the police immediately and N'Diaye went off to do so. Prévost, remaining near the car, was the only witness to the last phase of the incident: a ball of light, like those previously moving about

load, he pointed the object out. It was cylindrical in shape, but otherwise unidentifiable. When it moved behind the block of flats, N'Diaye rushed upstairs to fetch a camera, thinking he might take a photograph of the object to sell to the newspapers. Prévost went in to get another load of clothing while Fontaine, hoping for another view of the mysterious object, drove up onto the main road that ran close by the flats.

Hearing the sound of the moving vehicle, his companions looked out of the windows of their respective flats. Both saw that Fontaine had stopped the car on the main road and noted that the engine was no longer running. Prévost, angry because they would probably have to push-start the car a second time, rushed downstairs again. He called to N'Diaye to forget about his camera because the UFO had vanished. N'Diaye came after him saying that in any case he had no film in his camera, and adding that from his window it had looked as though the car was surrounded by a great ball of light.

Outdoors again, the two young men stopped in amazement: the rear of their car was

Top: Franck Fontaine leaving the police station after being questioned upon his safe return. He said that his 'missing week' was a blank in his mind

Salomon N'Diaye (above) and Jean-Pierre Prévost (right) reported the UFO incident to the police at once – a fact that convinced many they were telling the truth

the car, seemed to push the car door shut. Then it too vanished.

Such was the account that the two young men gave to the police on their arrival a few minutes later. Because UFO sightings are a military matter in France, the police instructed Prévost and N'Diaye to inform the gendarmerie, which comes under the Ministry of National Defence. The two spent most of the day with the gendarmes, telling and retelling the story. The interrogators stopped for lunch, during which time the witnesses telephoned the press with their story. Later, Commandant Courcoux of the Cergy gendarmerie told the press that there were no grounds for disbelieving the young men's story, that he had no doubt 'something' had occurred, and that he could give no indication of what that 'something' might be. In a later interview he admitted, 'We are swimming in fantasy.'

For a week, that was all the world knew. During that week, the young men were questioned over and over again. Some people accepted the UFO story as it stood. Others suspected it to be a smokescreen, perhaps a cunning plan to help Fontaine avoid doing his military service, perhaps something more sinister. But one fact stood out clearly: Prévost and N'Diaye had informed the police promptly and voluntarily. Given their backgrounds, wasn't this convincing proof of their sincerity?

When Fontaine gave his version of the story, there seemed no reason to question his sincerity either. He told how he had woken to find himself lying in the cabbage field. Getting to his feet, he realised he was just across the main road from the flats, close to where he had stopped the car to watch the UFO. But the car was no longer there. His first thought,

Jimmy Guieu, well-known science fiction writer and founder of a UFO group. The trio put themselves into his hands exclusively; other UFO investigators found them to be very unco-operative

as he hurried towards the still-darkened building, was that somebody had stolen their car and its valuable load of clothing. Neither Prévost nor N'Diaye was to be seen, so he rushed upstairs and rang the bell of Prévost's flat. When there was no reply, he went to N'Diaye's. A sleepy N'Diaye appeared, gawped at him in amazement, then flung his arms round him in delighted welcome. Fontaine, already surprised to find his friend in his night clothes, was even more amazed to learn that an entire week had gone by since the morning of the Gisors market.

He had little to tell the press or the police. The world's media reported his return but reserved judgement till they heard what the authorities had to say. But the police declared it was no longer their business: no crime had been committed. Apart from the inherent improbability of Fontaine's story, they had no reason to doubt his word or that of his friends.

Besieged by ufologists

So now it was up to the UFO organisations to see what further light could be thrown on the case. From the start, the witnesses had been besieged by the various French groups; there are dozens of these, most of them fiercely independent and reluctant to co-operate with the others. One of the most reputable of all is Control, to whom we owe most of what we now know of the inside story of the Cergy-Pontoise case.

But another group declared its interest before Control, while Fontaine was still missing: the *Institut Mondial des Sciences Avancés* (World Institute of Advanced Sciences). Its co-founder and spokesman was the well-known science fiction writer and author of two books about UFOs, Jimmy

Right: the cylinder-shaped UFO seen by the three friends appeared to have a diameter larger than that of the full Moon that night. It had a rounded front end and a tail that trailed off into a hazy cloud. It was when Fontaine went closer to the UFO – alone – that he disappeared

hypnotised, but the young man obstinately refused to submit to hypnosis. Then Prévost suggested that he should be hypnotised instead. What resulted was truly amazing. It now emerged that Prévost, not Fontaine, had been the true object of alien interest. Now, speaking through him, the aliens explained all. Fontaine had simply been the means to establish communication: Prévost was the channel through whom they could communicate to help save Earth from impending disaster. The aliens identified themselves as 'the intelligences from beyond' but gave no clearer clue to the whereabouts of 'beyond' than that it is 'a planet not like yours'. Their spokesman was Haurrio, a friendly if somewhat garrulous character.

In Guieu's book, Prévost becomes the hero of the story and the only evidence we have for the events is his word. His two companions seem to have become irrelevant.

Guieu. Before he had carried out an investigation, Guieu affirmed his belief in the story: 'No question of it, Franck Fontaine has been abducted on board a UFO,' he stated in an interview. 'Admittedly I haven't questioned the young man's two companions, but I hold their account to be true a priori.'

Delighted to have their story accepted without reservation by so eminent an authority, Fontaine's two friends agreed to co-operate with Guieu. When Fontaine returned, he too was taken under IMSA's wing. Guieu offered them a secret refuge in the south of France where they could work on a book together, Guieu writing it and all sharing the proceeds.

Guieu's book, *Cergy-Pontoise UFO contacts*, was rushed into print with astonishing speed, appearing a bare four months after Fontaine's return. Thanks to the combination of Guieu's name and the intense interest in the case, it was an instant best seller. But readers hoping for a conclusive verdict were disappointed. The book was padded out by Guieu's journalistic style and digressive accounts of other cases, and there was an almost total absence of first-hand testimony from the principal witness – the abducted Fontaine – whose story the world wanted to hear. Such revelations as the book contained were of quite another nature.

Guieu had hoped that Fontaine would be able to recall more of his adventure if he were

Jimmy Guieu's book *Cergy-Pontoise UFO contacts* (top) and Jean-Pierre Prévost's book *The truth about the Cergy-Pontoise affair* (above). Both were published speedily after the alleged kidnapping of Franck Fontaine. Both were long on fantasy and short on facts, disappointing all who hoped for some clarification of what had really happened

This book having raised more questions than it answered, much was hoped for when Prévost announced that he was writing his own account of the event. But *The truth about the Cergy-Pontoise affair*, published later that same year, was even less satisfactory. It was a rambling, incoherent farrago in which great doses of alien 'philosophy' – transmitted by Prévost – show that pious platitudes about the need for more love and less science are not confined to planet Earth.

There is virtually no mention of Franck Fontaine's abduction: indeed, he and Salomon N'Diaye are scarcely referred to. But Prévost's visit to a secret alien base is described in some detail, and this gives us a good yardstick for evaluating the rest of the material. It seems that one morning soon

Above: a group of people anticipate a close encounter with aliens at Cergy-Pontoise on 15 August 1980. They gathered there when Fontaine revealed that he had made an arrangement to meet on that day with his abductors of the previous December

Left: a being named Haurrio allegedly contacted Prévost on behalf of the 'intelligences from beyond'. On one occasion Haurrio was dressed in a one-piece silver garment, looking decidedly 'like an alien'. On another he had long blond hair and looked like a masculine woman in a suit. He was said to be friendly and very talkative

there. So Prévost, though surprised at the stranger's offer, cheerfully accepted it. The salesman dropped him off at the village and he set off up the hill towards a particular site that had always fascinated him – a railway tunnel containing an abandoned train carriage from the Second World War.

Arriving at the tunnel in late evening, Prévost found that other people were there before him: a group of young men gathered round a fire in the open. One of them called out his name; he was from the Sahara and had recently written to Prévost. It turned out that he and the others had come there from many parts of the world, thanks to the 'intelligences from beyond'. Each spoke his own language – but was understood by the rest.

When Haurrio, the alien representative, arrived, he informed them that they had been chosen to spread the philosophy of the 'intelligences' on Earth. A beautiful female alien then took them on a tour of the tunnel, now being used as a UFO base. They saw several spacecraft, similar to ones that Prévost had seen as a child. After their tour, the young men returned to their camp fire and went to sleep on the ground – which, on a December night in the mountains, must have been less than comfortable. Next morning Prévost found his friendly salesman waiting to chauffeur him back to Cergy.

Whether Jimmy Guieu and Jean-Pierre Prévost seriously expected their accounts to be believed, we may never know. But the more they provided in the way of checkable statements, the harder it became to accept the original account of the alleged abduction. Doubts grew even more when an investigative team from Control persisted in taking up the case without the co-operation of the witnesses – checking all the conflicting statements and fragmented testimony as best they could.

after Fontaine's return, there was a ring at Prévost's door. The caller was a travelling salesman, a total stranger who said he had to make a trip to Bourg-de-Sirod and invited Prévost to come along. Now, Bourg-de-Sirod is a small village near the Swiss border some 225 miles (360 kilometres) from Cergy. On the face of it, there is no conceivable reason why a salesman should go there, nor why he should think that Prévost might wish to go there given that they were strangers in the first place.

However, there was a reason for interest by Prévost. Bourg-de-Sirod was a specially significant place for him because as a child he had gone to a summer camp nearby and had later worked there. More recently still, he and Fontaine had spent a camping holiday

Long after the much-publicised disappearance of Franck Fontaine from Cergy-Pontoise, confusion still reigns over whether he was abducted by a UFO. Was it all a put-up job by him and his two friends? Or did it really happen? The truth may never be known

THE ABDUCTION OF Franck Fontaine by a UFO, though unsubstantiated by scientific evidence, seemed a plausible story on first hearing. Had he and his friends Jean-Pierre Prévost and Salomon N'Diaye been content to tell that story and nothing else, they might have convinced an interested world of its truth. But the two books on the case – one by the well-known science fiction writer Jimmy Guieu and one by Prévost himself – raised questions that cast suspicion on the entire affair. Moreover, there were many interviews and conferences in which widely divergent material was put forward. And Prévost, who had pre-empted Fontaine as the hero of the Cergy-Pontoise UFO affair, even published a short-lived journal in which he kept the public informed of his continuing dialogue with the 'intelligences from beyond' who he claimed had contacted him.

All this increased the doubts of the sceptics. Michel Piccin and his colleagues of the Control organisation had detected inconsistencies and contradictions in the witnesses' statements from the start. And the more they probed, the more discrepancies they found.

It began with trivial, marginal matters, like Prévost's insistence that before the encounter he had no interest in or knowledge of UFOs. The Control investigators found that his brother was a French representative of the American UFO organisation APRO. Even if Prévost did not share his brother's interest in UFOs, he could hardly have been unaware of them. Besides, in his own book, Prévost had said that he saw several spacecraft similar to ones he had 'seen as a child' when the 'intelligences' took him to their UFO base. He also denied seeing a magazine in which a UFO abduction story, very like Fontaine's, was being serialised. Yet Control established that this very magazine was in Prévost's flat at the time of the Cergy-Pontoise abduction.

The events of the night before the abduction became more confused the more they were investigated. Control discovered that there were five people – not three – in

Below: the cabbage field in which Fontaine awoke on his return to Cergy-Pontoise

Fact, fraud or fantasy?

Above: Franck Fontaine, whose disappearance for a week – allegedly as an abductee of aliens – stirred worldwide interest. He was never very forthcoming about what had happened to him

Prévost's flat that night. Why had the published accounts almost completely failed to mention the presence of Corinne, Prévost's girlfriend, and Fabrice Joly? One reason suggested itself: knowledge of the presence of the fourth young man, Joly, might throw doubt on one of the facts most favourable to Prévost and N'Diaye. They had claimed that they had gone straight to the police when Fontaine vanished from their car, even though they knew they might get into trouble because they were driving without a licence. But Joly was there because he had a valid licence and had agreed to drive the three friends to the market at Gisors.

Discrepancies abound

Why were Corinne and Joly never questioned about what happened? Did they see and hear nothing? They could certainly have straightened out some of the contradictions, for Fontaine, Prévost and N'Diaye could not even agree on who had been at the flat on the night before the abduction – surely one of the most memorable of their lives. First the three had said they spent the night together. Then Prévost recollected that he had watched a television film with friends elsewhere.

Other discrepancies force us to ask how far we can trust their account. They said that they were dubious about their car's ability to start and pushed it to get the motor running, then left Fontaine in the car to make sure it didn't stop. Why didn't Joly, the only licensed driver, do this so that Fontaine could lend a hand with loading the jeans for the market? Did they really sit outside the block of flats at 4 a.m. with the motor running without any complaint from the neighbours? None of the other residents seem even to have heard the sound. What about N'Diaye's completely opposing statement that they

loaded the car first and only then started the motor? Whom should we believe?

The account of the one neighbour who did witness anything only makes matters more confused. Returning home at the time the young men were supposedly loading the car, he said he saw two people get into the Taunus estate car and drive away. Yet the three involved said that Fontaine was alone when he drove up onto the road to get a better view of the UFO they had spotted.

Even though UFOs are notoriously difficult to describe, the three accounts of the one at Cergy-Pontoise are particularly far apart. One saw 'a huge beam', another 'a ball', the third 'a flash'. One said it was moving fairly slowly, taking two minutes to cross the sky; the others said it was moving fast, gone in a matter of seconds. There was further disagreement about the direction in which it was moving.

The circumstances of Fontaine's return a week after his supposed abduction are no less confused as several stories emerged. One of the journalists covering the case was Iris Billon-Duplan, who worked for a local newspaper and lived close by. Apart from the special interest of a case that had occurred almost on her doorstep, the fact that she lived nearby meant she could follow it personally. As a result, she became closely involved with the witnesses. Indeed, she spent the night before Fontaine's return with Prévost, preparing a definitive account of the case.

According to the journalist's published account, N'Diaye went off to bed shortly after midnight, leaving her with Prévost. He told her that he had no food or money because his involvement in the UFO affair was keeping him from working. So she suggested that they go to her flat where she could give him a meal while they continued to work on

---

Space briefing

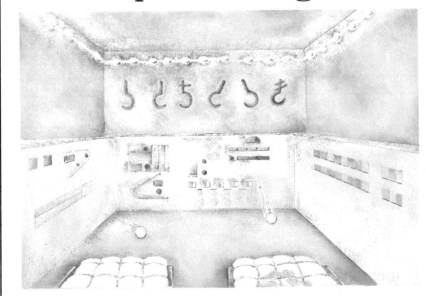

Franck Fontaine remembered things that had happened to him during his week 'out of this world' only slowly and bit by bit, but refused to undergo hypnosis to speed the process. However, strange – and sometimes very disturbing – dreams helped him to recall his experiences, he said.

In one instance that he recalled, he was in a large white room with machines that went all round the walls. They were all the same height and had opaque white glass fronts that lit up and went out almost simultaneously. He was lying on a sort of couch and two small luminous spheres – the extra-terrestrials – were talking to him about problems on Earth and how to solve them.

His abductors, who were always kind, told him that he would be the sole judge of what to reveal of his adventure. He seems to have decided to say as little as possible.

Top: Jean-Pierre Prévost with Patrick Pottier of the Control group. Control carried out as thorough an investigation as they could without the active co-operation of Prévost and the other two involved

Above: Salomon N'Diaye in front of the Taunus estate car which, he said, he and Prévost saw enveloped by a UFO just before their friend Fontaine disappeared

the article. This explains why Fontaine did not find Prévost in when he returned and went to Prévost's flat. We know that Fontaine then went to N'Diaye's flat and succeeded in rousing him. But according to the journalist's account, N'Diaye then left Fontaine and hurried round to her flat to tell her and Prévost the news.

Should we believe Iris Billon-Duplan or Salomon N'Diaye? For his statement, made to the police, flatly contradicts hers.

His story was that he happened to wake up at about 4.30 a.m., looked out of his window and saw a ball of light on the main road. When he saw a silhouetted figure emerge from it, he recognised his friend Franck Fontaine. He then hurried to a telephone to report the return to Radio Luxembourg, believing he would get a reward for information about Fontaine's whereabouts. (In this he was mistaken; it was Europe Numéro 1 that had offered a reward.)

Radio Luxembourg later confirmed that such a call had been made, but not at 4.30 a.m. because there was nobody on duty at that hour. The implication is that N'Diaye telephoned later than 4.30 a.m. and that he waited to inform the police until he had attempted to claim the reward money – not saying much for his concern about his friend. In the event, it was Radio Luxembourg staff who told the police that Franck Fontaine had returned. According to them, they had received an *anonymous* call from a man who, just as he was going to work, saw Fontaine coming back. Surely N'Diaye would not have made an anonymous call if he wanted to collect the reward.

These contradictions are just a sample from Control's 50-page report. There is confusion, if not outright deception, at every stage of the affair. Some of the discrepancies can be attributed to faulty memory, but such an explanation can hardly be stretched to account for Prévost's extraordinary visit to the tunnel. As a case history, Cergy-Pontoise is so ambiguous that few will be ready to give it serious credence. Yet it caused such a sensation that it is still worth asking what really happened. If the abduction was not genuine, was it a put-up job from the outset? Or did the witnesses gradually distort what was fundamentally a true UFO experience? If so, at what point did deceit and contrivance begin? There are several ways to answer these questions.

An elaborate tale

We may believe that Franck Fontaine was abducted as claimed, that all the witnesses were doing their best to tell the truth and that contradictions crept in because of defective memory. However, the extent of the discrepancies makes it easier to believe that the trio elaborated the story for their own purposes, adding sensational details that they may or may not have believed actually happened.

Alternatively, we may surmise that Franck Fontaine was not in fact abducted, but that he sincerely believed he was. He may have been in, or put into, some altered state of consciousness in which he experienced the illusion of the abduction. That this can happen is an established psychological phenomenon, so we cannot rule it out altogether. But it does raise questions about Fontaine's two friends. If he was deluded, where do they stand? Were they also in an altered state of consciousness, experiencing or being made to believe in the same illusion? And does this explain the contradictions? If so, who fed them the illusion and made them believe in its reality?

While neither of these explanations can be ruled out entirely, we may consider it most plausible that the whole affair was a fabrication from the start – that there never was any abduction and that the three young men put the story together for fun, for gain or for some undiscovered ideological motive. We know that the trio immediately co-operated with Jimmy Guieu in a commercial enterprise. We learn from Control that Prévost, clearly the dominant one of the three, was noted for practical joking at school. Indeed he told the Control investigators, 'You bet I'm a clown!'

More questions than answers

The reports are consistent with the hypothesis that Prévost persuaded his two companions to stage a hoax, but that Corinne and Fabrice Joly refused to go along. Perhaps none of them expected their story to attract so much attention and they were forced to improvise beyond their prepared narrative. This could explain such muddles as the contradictory accounts of Fontaine's return.

Another question then arises: was Guieu a party to the deception? Did he suspect the story from the start but, as a professional writer, recognise its money-making potential? Did he start by believing them, as he claimed to do, then discover the hoax but decide to go along with it – perhaps because he was already committed? Or did he believe that the affair was genuine? The last supposition seems unlikely in the light of Guieu's long involvement with ufology, unless he was unusually gullible. On the

other hand, it is hard to believe that he would risk his reputation by endorsing a case that he knew to be a fake. We are probably left with the surmise that he discovered a hoax but decided not to reveal it for reasons of his own.

If the Cergy-Pontoise contact was indeed all a hoax, it would explain why the trio committed themselves to the uncritical Guieu and his *Institut Mondial des Sciences Avancés* (World Institute of Advanced Sciences). IMSA has little following or reputation, but Guieu offered the backing of a big name, sympathetic support and the chance to make a substantial profit from a book bearing his name. And other UFO organisations might have uncovered the deceit in a short time, if deceit it was.

In the absence of any definite proof, all this is merely speculative. Will the truth ever be established? There are hopes that it may be. During their researches, Control came across a tantalising clue that they were unable to follow up. It seems that during Fontaine's disappearance, a school in Cergy-Pontoise was working on a project about it with the local newspaper – the one that was later to carry Iris Billon-Duplan's version of Fontaine's return. Some of the children learned that one of the school workers was an aunt of Fontaine and interviewed her as part of their project in the presence of one of the teachers and one of Iris Billon-Duplan's colleagues from the paper. During the interview, Fontaine's aunt said angrily that she knew perfectly well where her nephew was. He was, she said, staying with a friend.

Was she stating a fact or simply saying what she thought to be true? Who was the friend and where did he or she live? The answers to these questions could settle the Cergy-Pontoise mystery. But until we learn if someone knew where Fontaine was all the time, the case must remain open.

Right: a UFO base in a disused railway tunnel, as described by Jean-Pierre Prévost in his book on the Cergy-Pontoise affair. The tunnel also contained an abandoned Nazi train carriage left over from the Second World War. Prévost, always the dominant member of the trio of witnesses, quickly became the 'star of the show' and the other two receded into the background – for, said Prévost, the aliens had simply used Fontaine to establish contact with himself

A terrifying encounter with a flame-belching UFO on a lonely road near Huffman, Texas, resulted in appalling injuries for the three innocent victims. This bizarre case has been the source of much speculation

LATE ONE CHILLY EVENING at the end of December 1980 two middle-aged women and a young boy were driving along a lonely road in the Huffman area of east Texas, USA. It was the Christmas season and they were in a festive mood. Suddenly a bright light appeared in the sky a little way ahead. A few minutes later the light had turned into a huge diamond-shaped object, shooting out from its underside intermittent bursts of fire. This alarming apparition seemed to be trying to land on the road ahead, making it impossible for the three people in the car to continue on their way.

For the occupants of the car it was to be a terrifying encounter. The intense heat from the UFO burned their skin and the bright light injured their eyes. When the object eventually left the area, a large number of helicopters filled the sky in close pursuit, making a deafening noise that hurt the witnesses' ears.

'A diamond of fire' was how one of the witnesses described the huge glowing object that hovered over the road, blocking their way. Ringed with lights at the centreline, it emitted bursts of fire from its underside that threatened to set light to the surrounding forest

For the three spectators it was like being caught in the middle of some strange battle for the skies.

Earlier that evening, Betty Cash, Vickie Landrum and Colby Landrum had visited several small towns in the Piney Woods area of east Texas in search of a bingo game; but to their disappointment they had discovered that all bingo games had been cancelled while the clubs prepared for the New Year's Eve celebration. Instead the three of them had settled for an evening meal at a roadside restaurant in New Caney. It was soon after this that the terrifying events of the evening began.

Betty Cash, who was driving her new Oldsmobile Cutlass when the trio encountered the UFO, was then a 51-year-old business woman who ran a restaurant and a grocery store. She was planning to open a new restaurant the very next week. A year or so earlier she had undergone a heart bypass operation, and had made a complete recovery. Within the next hour she was to sustain physical injuries more debilitating than any caused by the cardiac surgery.

Vickie Landrum, then 57, is a pleasant,

Blind terror in Texas

It was about 30 minutes later when the three noticed the bright UFO above the treetops some distance away. Colby, an alert youngster, was the first to see it. He pointed it out excitedly to Betty and Vickie as it glowed brightly above the trees about 3 miles (5 kilometres) ahead. As they approached, it appeared to get larger and larger, rather than diminishing as an aeroplane would appear to do as it flew further away. As they realised the object was approaching the road only a short distance ahead their apprehension increased. Nevertheless they hoped to get by in time and leave it behind. But before they could do so, the object had straddled the road, blocking their way.

Vickie screamed, 'Stop the car or we shall be burned alive.' Her warning was probably correct. The object, many times larger than their car, remained hovering at treetop level and sending down an occasional large cone of fire like a rocket blast. In between these blasts it would settle downwards some 25 feet (7.5 metres) or so, only to rise again on the next cone of fire like some huge science-fiction spaceship in trouble. Vickie's vivid description of it was that it was 'like a diamond of fire'.

When Betty eventually brought the car to a standstill the object was less than 65 yards (60 metres) away. It looked as if it were made of dull aluminium, and it glowed so brightly that it lit up the surrounding forest like daylight. The four points of the diamond were blunted rather than sharp, and blue spots or lights ringed its centreline. Had the UFO not come to rest over the road, the cone of fire that periodically emanated from its lowest point would have set the forest on fire. In addition to the blast of the fire, the UFO emitted an intermittent beeping sound.

hard-working woman who worked for Betty in the restaurant and also occasionally as a school meals assistant. She is a committed Christian, and does not believe in UFOs or extra-terrestrial life. When the bright object appeared in the sky, she thought it was the coming of the end of the world. Because she expected to see her Saviour come out of the bright cloud, she gazed intently at the UFO. Her reward was not to meet her Saviour, but to sustain severe eye damage.

Colby Landrum, Vickie's grandson, was being brought up by her. He was a healthy and active lad, and at seven years old he had already earned several trophies for baseball, bowling and other sports. The encounter left him with severe physical and emotional scars. It is difficult to tell whether he was more frightened by the UFO or by the overpowering noise of the helicopters thundering overhead.

The day of 29 December 1980 had been cold, damp and overcast in Texas. In the Huffman area there had been periods of light rain during the day, but by night-time the rain had stopped and the sky had partially cleared. Light from the third-quarter Moon, supplemented by an airglow from lights in the surrounding area, made the sky bright and the visibility good. Because the temperature was only 40°F (4.5°C) the victims were wearing coats and the car's heater was keeping the winter chill at bay.

After leaving the restaurant some time between 8.20 and 8.30 p.m., the three drove along Highway FM1485, a road normally used only by people who live in the area because it is so isolated. Although only about 30 miles (50 kilometres) from the metropolis of Houston, the area is sparsely populated and is covered by oak and pine trees, and dotted with swamps and lakes.

Above: the lonely tree-lined road where Betty Cash and Vickie and Colby Landrum saw the UFO

Below: a map of the region north-east of Houston showing the Huffman area where the incident occurred. The three victims had dined in New Caney about half an hour earlier and were driving home to Dayton when the UFO appeared on the road ahead

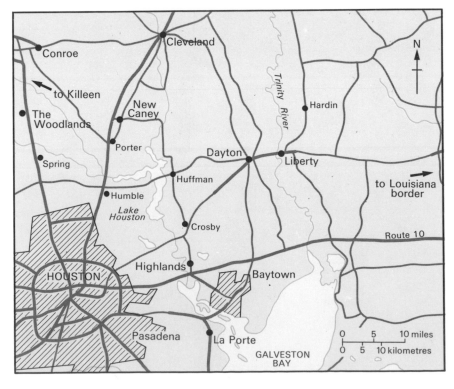

It is not clear whether Betty turned the car engine off, or whether it just died. Whichever it was, the three of them got out of the car to take a closer look at the thing that was blocking their way. Vickie stood by the open door on the right-hand side of the car, with her left hand resting on the car roof. She stared intently at the UFO.

Colby plucked at his grandmother's clothing and begged her to get back inside the car and hold him. Two or three minutes later, in response to his pleading, she did so; but she told him not to be afraid, for 'when that big man comes out of the burning cloud, it will be Jesus' and Jesus would not harm them.

As Vickie held Colby to comfort him she screamed to Betty to get back into the car with them. But Betty was so fascinated by the UFO that she walked round to the front of the car and stood there gazing intently at the bright object. She seemed to be mesmerised by it. Bathed in the bright light, she remained standing there even though the heat was burning her skin. Even the skin on the finger beneath her ring was burned. Eventually, as the object began to move up and away, she responded to Vickie's calls and walked back to the door. When she touched the door it was so painfully hot that she had to use her leather jacket to protect her hand while she got in the car.

As the three of them watched the departing UFO, a large number of helicopters appeared overhead. As Betty said, 'They seemed to rush in from all directions . . . it seemed like they were trying to encircle the thing.' Within a few seconds the UFO had disappeared behind the trees lining the highway. It was then that the victims became aware of how hot the interior of the car had

A number of small, single rotor helicopters of the Bell Huey variety, similar to the one shown above on a military exercise, were seen with the Huffman UFO

surrounding area and illuminating the helicopters.

By this time the helicopters were spread out over a 5-mile (8-kilometre) area. One main group was still near to the UFO, but moving in an erratic flight path. The others were clearly visible in a steady trail formation. At one point one of the large 'choppers' flew directly over the car engulfing it in the roar of its engine and flap of its rotor

become. Instead of the heater, they now switched on the air conditioner to make the environment more comfortable.

When the effects of the bright light had worn off, Betty started the engine and they sped off down the darkened highway. After a mile or so of twisting road they joined a larger highway and were able to turn in the direction of the departing UFO. This was about 5 miles (8 kilometres) and five minutes later. The object was clearly visible some distance ahead, and looked like a bright oblong cylinder of light. It was still lighting up the

Heavy, double rotor helicopters like the CH-47 shown above were identified by several witnesses as being present in large numbers at Huffman

blades. As they watched from this new vantage point the victims counted 23 helicopters. Many of the helicopters were the large double rotor type, with four wheels, and a large housing to the rear (these were later identified as CH-47 Chinooks, manufactured by the Vertol division of the Boeing company). Others were smaller, very fast, single rotor helicopters. These were never clearly identified, but they appeared to be of the Bell Huey variety. There was also a suggestion that there may have been a single even larger helicopter in the middle of the group. Whatever the exact number of helicopters, a lot of aircrew members must have seen the UFO that night.

As soon as the UFO and the helicopters were a safe distance ahead, Betty drove on cautiously. When she reached an intersection, she turned away from the flight path of the UFO and drove towards Dayton, where the three of them lived. By this time they had been involved with the UFO and the helicopters for at least 20 minutes, perhaps longer.

Betty dropped Vickie and Colby at their home at 9.50 p.m. and went home herself. A friend and her children were waiting there for Betty to return, but by then Betty was feeling too ill to tell them about the incident. Over the next few hours Betty's skin turned red as if it were badly sunburned. Her neck swelled, and blisters erupted and broke on her face, scalp and eyelids. She started to vomit and continued to do so periodically throughout the night. By morning she was almost in a coma.

Some time between midnight and 2 a.m. Vickie and Colby began to experience similar symptoms, although less severe. At first they suffered the sunburn-like condition, then diarrhoea and vomiting. It was a miserable night for all three victims.

Colby tells all

The following morning Betty was moved to Vickie's home, and all three were cared for there. Betty's condition continued to deteriorate, and three days later she was taken to a hospital casualty department. The casualty staff assumed that Betty was a classic burn victim, and treated her accordingly. They were not told about the UFO until several days later when Colby blurted out to a doctor that he knew what had burned them.

The burns and swelling altered Betty's appearance so radically that friends and relatives who came to visit her in hospital did not recognise her. Her hair started to fall out and she was eventually to lose more than half the hair on her head. When her appearance was compared with the photograph of her taken just before Christmas, it was impossible to believe that it was the same woman. Treatment was further complicated by the fact that Betty and the others had intense headaches and painfully swollen eyes; in fact Betty's eyes were so swollen that she was unable to see for nearly a week.

The appearance of helicopters at UFO sightings is becoming a common event, as are also strange animal mutilations at such scenes (see page 42). The large number of helicopters at the Huffman incident is just another link in the chain. One thing is certain – it is virtually impossible to be mistaken about the presence of CH-47 helicopters when you are directly beneath these large noisy craft.

The evidence of all the witnesses to the Huffman event was consistent. All were interrogated separately, not only about the UFO but also about the helicopters. They

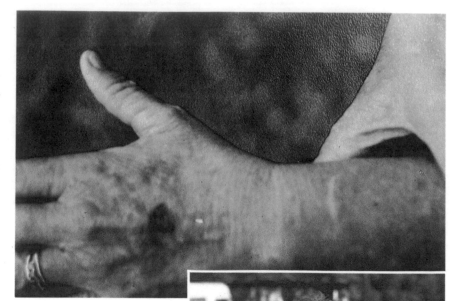

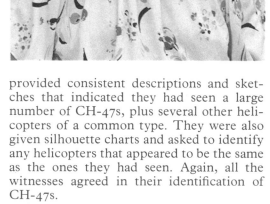

Months after seeing the UFO the victims were still suffering the results of their encounter. Above: the burn on the back of Vickie's hand. Right: a year and a half after the event, Vickie's face showed lasting damage, particularly around the eyes

provided consistent descriptions and sketches that indicated they had seen a large number of CH-47s, plus several other helicopters of a common type. They were also given silhouette charts and asked to identify any helicopters that appeared to be the same as the ones they had seen. Again, all the witnesses agreed in their identification of CH-47s.

Locating the source of the helicopters proved to be a much more difficult task. According to an official of the Houston Intercontinental Airport Federation Aviation Administration, about 350 to 400 helicopters operate commercially in the Houston area. All of these are single rotor type units; there are no CH-47s. The official also said that because helicopters fly on Visual Flight Rules (VFR), they do not need to contact the airport control tower. Other information provided by Houston was that outside a 15-mile (24-kilometre) radius from the airport, helicopters must stay below an altitude of

1800 feet (550 metres), and that due to technical limitations the Houston control radar is restricted to a minimum altitude of 2000 feet (600 metres) around Lake Houston (the Huffman area).

At the US Army's Fort Hood near Killeen, Texas, press officer Major Tony Geishauser told the *Corpus Christi Caller* that no Fort Hood aircraft were in the Houston area on 29 December 1980. 'I don't know any other place around here that would have that number of helicopters,' he said. 'I don't know what it could be . . . unless there's a super-secret thing going on and I wouldn't necessarily know about it.'

At the Robert Gray Field near Fort Hood a spokesman said they might have 100 helicopters from the field home in at one time 'for effect', but he claimed they avoided the Houston area. And all other bases in Texas and Louisiana denied they were responsible

for the helicopters seen at the Huffman UFO incident.

Is it possible that the witnesses were all mistaken about seeing and hearing the helicopters? The descriptions and sketches provided by Betty, Vickie and Colby indicate that they all clearly saw helicopters of a particular configuration, which is common only to CH-47s. As far as the noise is concerned, witnesses had been accused of wrongly identifying helicopters at an earlier UFO incident on 22 March 1978, which was reported in the St Paul, Minnesota, *Dispatch*. That newspaper quoted Dan Meyers, supervisor of the Army Reserve Aviation Support Facility at Holman Field, as saying 'Just one of those helicopters at 1500 feet [450 metres] would sound like a humming chain-saw from the ground. With five helicopters up there, you would have tremendous amplification.'

In another (possibly related) incident the day before the Huffman event, helicopter activity had also been noted when UFOs were

Eighteen months after the Huffman sighting Betty Cash (top) and Colby Landrum (above) were still suffering from facial burns and other injuries

being observed. Dozens of residents of Ohio county, Kentucky, had seen strange moving lights. But when a helicopter arrived in the area, the UFOs left. Again, all military installations denied having any helicopters airborne that night.

Betty, Vickie and Colby were not the only witnesses to the strange happenings at Huffman. An off-duty Dayton policeman and his wife were driving home from Cleveland through the Huffman area the same night and also observed a large number of CH-47 helicopters. A man living in Crosby, directly under the flight path, also reported seeing a number of heavy helicopters flying overhead.

Oilfield labourer Jerry McDonald was in his back garden in Dayton when he saw a huge UFO flying directly overhead. At first he thought it was the Goodyear airship, but he quickly realised it was some unidentified object. 'It was kind of diamond-shaped and had two twin torches that were shooting brilliant blue flames out the back,' he said. As it passed about 150 feet (45 metres) above him, he saw that it had two bright lights on it and a red light in the centre.

The same evening bakery clerk Belle Magee was in her home in Eastgate, about 8 miles (13 kilometres) west of Dayton, when she saw a bright light in the sky heading in the direction of New Caney.

Certainly Dr J. Allen Hynek, founder of the Center for UFO Studies in Evanston, Illinois, was convinced the witnesses were not mistaken. 'We are dealing with a real event,' he said, 'but we're not sure if it's a government exercise or a UFO sighting. There is a lot of top secret stuff going on that most people don't know about.' He added, 'Something sure as hell happened. Those women didn't pull out their hair and blind themselves. The connection with the event is clear-cut.'

Anguish of the UFO victims

In one of a flurry of UFO sightings at the end of 1980, three people in Texas received injuries that resembled severe radiation poisoning. Do the events at Huffman indicate that contact with aliens can be dangerous?

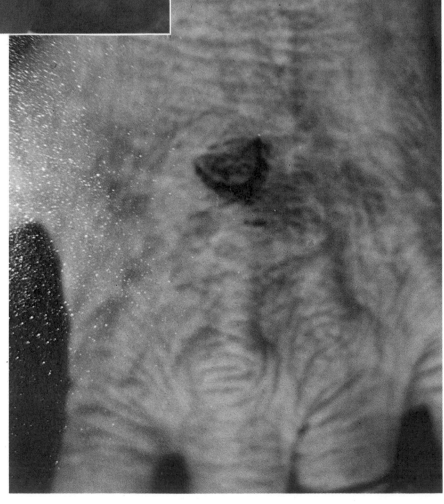

A CLOSE ENCOUNTER with an unidentified object can be a dangerous rather than an exciting experience, as three people discovered on a lonely road in Texas, USA, on 29 December 1980. On that evening when Betty Cash, Vickie Landrum and young Colby Landrum met up with a large diamond-shaped UFO on their way home, they had no idea that the event would change their lives. All three were injured by the encounter, and since that evening their health has continued to deteriorate.

When they stopped the car and got out to look at the UFO, the object was less than 55 yards (50 metres) away. It gave out so much heat that they were bathed in perspiration and their skin burned. The light that came from it was so bright that it hurt their eyes, and they were alarmed by its shrill beeping and by the bursts of flame it emitted. And this was only the beginning . . .

When the UFO departed, Betty drove Vickie and Colby to their home in Dayton. As she got out of the car Vickie said, 'My head hurts and I'm sick.' By midnight she felt worse. By that time both she and Colby had developed a condition similar to severe sunburn; they felt feverish and started to vomit. Later diarrhoea started and was uncontrollable for many days. They also experienced severe headaches.

Vickie attempted to treat their burns with

baby oil, but it took several days, and several bottles of oil, to bring the pain under control. She and Colby also consumed several bottles of commercial medicine intended to prevent diarrhoea, but without success. The headaches also refused to respond to any treatment. After three weeks the severity of their illness subsided, but the symptoms continued to recur over the following year.

Since their encounter with the UFO Vickie and Colby have been plagued by periodic outbreaks of skin troubles, as if they were more susceptible to infection than before. But the most far-reaching injury has been the damage to their eyes. Their eyelids became infected very rapidly, and have never fully recovered. Since the incident Vickie has had to have three new pairs of spectacles with successively stronger prescriptions to match the deterioration in her eyesight. Her eyesight is continuing to deteriorate and she still suffers from periodic eye infections; she fears she may eventually go blind. Colby too has experienced similar problems with his eyes, although he has needed only one new pair of spectacles since the incident.

Within a few weeks of the encounter Vickie had lost about 30 per cent of her hair, and had large bald patches on her head.

When her hair grew again it was of a different texture. 'It is frizzy,' she says, 'but more manageable.' Colby lost only a small patch of hair on the crown of his head; this, too, grew again in time.

Betty's injuries seemed even more severe than those of Vickie and Colby. 'The blinding headache that developed within an hour or so made me feel like I was going to die,' she said. She experienced a severe sunburn-like condition, and developed large water blisters, some as large as golf balls, over her face, head and neck. One of these covered her right eyelid and extended across her right temple. She also developed a long-term aversion to warm water, sunshine or other heat sources.

Betty had been an energetic woman. She ran a restaurant and a grocery store, and she had been planning to open a larger restaurant. Two years later she was still physically drained. In the year following the encounter she spent five periods in hospital, two of them in intensive care. Within four weeks of the encounter she had lost over half the hair on her head. Although it grew again slowly the texture of the new hair was not the same as that of the original hair. Betty has also been plagued with skin eruptions; many

Two months after her encounter with the UFO Betty Cash (left) had lost much of her hair. She was also suffering from skin blisters, nausea and severe headaches. A year and a half after the event Vickie Landrum (far left) still exhibited signs of facial burns and (below left) skin sores

Sickening waves

Electromagnetic radiation consists of waves of energy of varying lengths and frequencies spanning a spectrum from radio waves to gamma rays (right). Moving up the spectrum the wavelength decreases and the frequency increases. The spectrum also divides into ionising radiation (gamma rays, x-rays and ultraviolet) and non-ionising (infrared, microwaves, television and radio waves). It is ionising radiation that is potentially most damaging to living tissue. Exposure to ionising radiation can cause skin burns, nausea, vomiting, diarrhoea, loss of hair, lowered resistance to infection, headaches, fatigue, and other problems.

The sunburn-type injuries inflicted in the Huffman incident could be described as typical of exposure to ultraviolet radiation. They could also have been caused by x-rays or microwaves. The eye injuries could have been caused by any type of radiation, but they are most commonly seen in cases of ultraviolet exposure. Workers exposed to microwaves have also suffered damage to the tissues of the eye.

Microwave exposure produces symptoms similar to those of ionising radiation; it often produces an easily irritated skin such as Betty, Vickie and Colby experienced. If the microwave is pulsed,

gamma rays

x-rays

ultraviolet light

visible light

infra-red light

ionising radiation

microwaves

television

radio waves

non-ionisng radiation

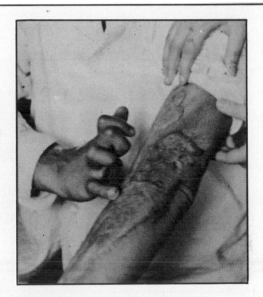

its effects are more harmful. Some devices that pulse microwaves also produce x-rays, and this combination could account for most of the injuries seen in the Huffman case.

Radiation damage is difficult to diagnose. Radiation burns (above) can be mistaken for more commonplace injuries such as sunburn. Even more difficult to predict are the long-term effects. Once exposed, an individual may develop diseases such as leukaemia up to 20 years later. Colby's grandmother Vickie is deeply worried about these potential future problems, and doctors can give her little reassurance.

of these are as big as a large coin and leave the skin permanently scarred.

Doctors are baffled by Betty's symptoms, and are convinced they are not connected with her earlier heart surgery. They have speculated that the symptoms exhibited by all three victims could have been caused by exposure to some type of electromagnetic radiation (see box).

Betty, Vickie and Colby not only suffered physical injuries from their encounter with the UFO; they also exhibit strong emotional disturbances as a result of their experience. Whenever they recount the events of that evening, or return to the place where they saw the object, they become very upset. Colby had terrifying nightmares for several weeks after the encounter, and during a re-enactment of the event set up by investigators he developed a high temperature and fever. 'He was so terrified,' said Vickie, 'I thought he would die of fright.'

Neither woman has fully recovered from the experience, nor been able to return to work. The consequent loss of income has been devastating for them. Even if they were not prevented from working by their poor eyesight and general debilitation, it would be impossible for them to work in the food service industry because of their continuing skin eruptions. Doctors are unable to predict when their condition will improve.

Betty, Vickie and Colby were not the only people to report seeing a UFO in the Huffman area on the evening of 29 December 1980.

Betty Cash, Vickie Landrum and her young grandson Colby Landrum a year and a half after they saw the UFO that changed their lives

Several residents of the small east Texas towns of Eastgate, Dayton and Liberty (all lying on an east-west line running from Humble, Texas, to the Louisiana border) reported seeing UFOs within two hours of the strange and terrifying incident at Huffman. The countryside in this part of Texas is

---

Early one morning in December 1967, Maryellen Kelley was outside her home in Mohomet, Illinois, USA, when she saw a large orange UFO. The object was about 40 yards (36 metres) away and flying about 50 to 65 feet (15 to 20 metres) above the ground. As soon as she saw the object, Mrs Kelley felt an electric shock go through her body. She developed a severe headache (which refused to respond to treatment), her face reddened, her hands and legs were burned, her eyes became bloodshot and her vision was affected. She also developed earache in her left ear, nosebleeds, pains in the chest and excessive thirst. Although her exposure was of short duration, her injuries endured for a long time. The incident was described in *Fate* magazine in May 1969.

In Finland in November 1976, 19-year-old Eero Lammi was knocked to the ground by a luminous ray from a UFO and suffered burns to the chest. His injuries were similar to those of a 20-year-old man from Tyler, Texas, who was hit in the chest by a luminous ray from a UFO in January 1979. His chest was marked by a large diamond-shaped burn for many months (right).

Burnt and bewildered

In August 1972, *Data Net Report* described how Osvaldo d'Annunzio (19 years old) was paralysed by a low-flying UFO, so that he was unable to run away. His face was severely burned, and he suffered afterwards from violent headaches. He commented: 'The cows in the surrounding meadows changed colour and did not resume their true colour until after the UFO's departure.'

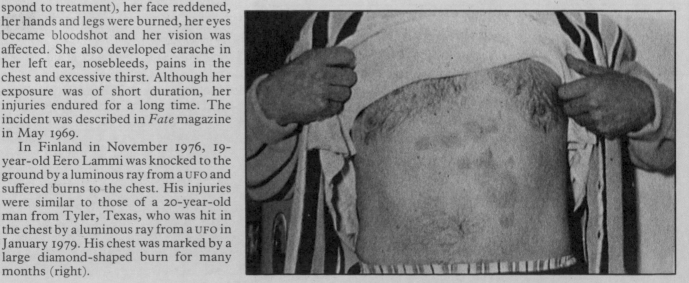

sparsely populated and dotted with forest and marshlands.

On the day before the Huffman event a number of residents of Ohio county, Kentucky, reported seeing strange objects in the sky. Two young observers were six-year-old twins Jason and Jesse Williams, who said they saw four silver 'triangle things' flying at low altitude; two of the things flew on together, while the other two flew off in' different directions.

Also on 28 December 1980 deputy sheriff Frank Chinn of Echols, Kentucky, told a local newspaper he saw 'an upside-down diamond' with flashing lights around the middle. His description of its shape, brightness and low speed corresponded with the description of the object seen at the Huffman incident. This was one of six UFOs sighted at about 5.30 p.m. that day.

A young Houstonian, Jan Moffett, believed she saw the same object seen by Betty and the others near Huffman. She was en route to North Dakota when she saw a big bright light coming down from the sky north of Houston. Unfortunately she lost sight of the object when it neared the ground, because it was obscured by the trees covering the area. Others also saw the bright light. A man and his 12-year-old son, who were travelling eastwards in the vicinity of New Caney, Texas, said they saw the object only a short distance away, flying about 150 feet (45 metres) above the road. When they accelerated to get closer to it, the object turned away from the road and headed north. According to these two observers, the UFO was bright, rectangular and flew slowly. It was larger than an aeroplane.

Betty, Vickie and Colby originally agreed not to tell other people about what they had seen, for fear they would be thought crazy. 'It was just too weird to mention,' said Vickie, 'but we didn't know then we had been hurt.' They eventually broke their pact of secrecy to tell the doctors who were treating them what had caused their injuries.

Vickie has been concerned to establish what really happened that fateful evening, primarily to ensure that Colby will receive the correct treatment and be able to grow up healthy. She is not concerned about, or interested in, other UFO sightings at the time. Betty shows rather more interest in the other sightings, but her continuing illness prevents her grasping the full significance of these events.

There seems to be no doubt that on the evening of 29 December 1980 the three of them encountered a brightly lit flying object and a large number of helicopters, and that as a result of this encounter all three have sustained lasting physical and emotional damage. In the past they used to make fun of people who claimed to have seen UFOs. They are still sceptical, but they no longer find it a joking matter.

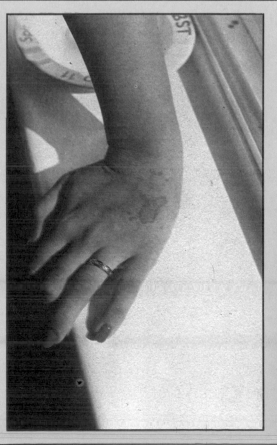

Left: in England a Plymouth girl was burned on the hand by the light from a UFO on 10 September 1981. This picture was taken two days later

In Canada, Steve Michalak was out in the countryside one weekend in May 1967 when he encountered a cigar-shaped object emitting a brilliant, purple light, near Falcon Lake about 75 miles (120 kilometres) east of Winnipeg. He received burns on his face and chest (below) and subsequently experienced nausea, vomiting, weight loss, weakness, diarrhoea, dizziness and blackouts. Mr Michalak eventually made a full recovery from the effects of the encounter, as did most of the other victims.

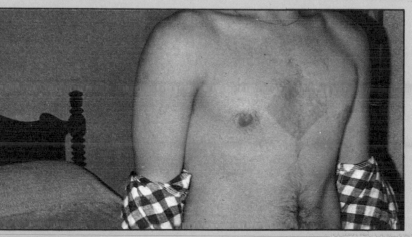

Five easy pieces

Hoax, hallucination or secret military operation? To establish exactly what happened at the Huffman UFO sighting in Texas, investigators produced the five possible scenarios which conclude this report

AS A RESULT of their encounter with a bizarre object on 29 December 1980 Betty Cash, Vickie Landrum and her young grandson Colby suffered serious injuries. Despite continuing investigations, a satisfactory explanation for the events of that evening had still not been found by mid 1982. Members of the Houston-based Vehicle Internal Systems Investigative Team (VISIT) called in to examine the case at first approached it with extreme caution. However preliminary investigations provided basic information of a kind that suggested the case merited serious attention.

Drawing on this initial basic information the VISIT members created a series of 'scenarios' of possible interpretations of the events of that night; these have formed the basis for extensive enquiries.

Scenario 1 In this scenario Betty, Vickie and Colby had set out to have an enjoyable evening at a bingo game. Disappointed to find all the bingo clubs closed, they were feeling let down as they drove home after a meal at a New Caney restaurant. The dark, lonely road also made them feel jittery, and

When Betty, Vickie and Colby encountered the UFO they counted up to 23 helicopters accompanying it. Some were CH-47s, the large double rotor type that so frightened Colby, others were smaller, faster single rotor craft similar to the ones shown here

they began making jokes about the lights of the distant aeroplanes they could see in the sky. One thing led to another, and soon they were saying that the lights could be UFOs. Confirmed scoffers, they decided to invent a UFO story to match those they had read in the newspapers. To make it seem more 'official', they added the helicopters; they then rushed home to tell their friends.

Scenario 1 was the starting point for the whole investigation. Until VISIT could be certain that this scenario was false there was no reason to proceed. And analysis soon showed that it did not stand up.

In the first place, all three victims had sustained serious physical injuries that had been verified by doctors. Furthermore a number of independent witnesses had also reported seeing the UFO and helicopters that evening. Interviews with friends and colleagues of the three victims failed to produce any indication that the story might be invented, or any suggestion that the three were prone to this kind of hoax.

In fact the three had made no attempt to tell their friends about the incident, fearing they would not be believed; nor had they approached the press. When the story leaked out and newsmen asked for an interview, this was granted free of charge. All three co-operated freely with VISIT even when this proved personally embarrassing.

Scenario 2 The three were driving home when they met a UFO blocking the road, making it impossible for them to proceed. This was not a chance encounter but a

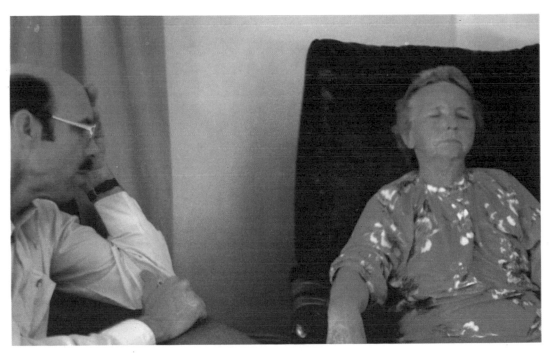

planned abduction, which may have lasted for as long as 20 minutes. While they were in the UFO the three victims had the idea implanted in their minds that government helicopters would fill the sky after the event, making them think they were involved in some kind of military exercise. In this scenario the UFO and the injuries were real, but not the helicopters.

Parts of this scenario stand up under scrutiny while others do not. Independent UFO sightings in and around the Huffman area, across Texas and in adjoining states during the same period suggest that the UFO was indeed a physical craft. The victims were certainly injured, possibly by the craft.

But no evidence could be found that an abduction had taken place. A few months after the incident Vickie agreed to undergo regressive hypnosis under the guidance of Dr R. Leo Sprinkle of Wyoming University. An authority on abduction cases, Dr. Sprinkle said he found no indications that Vickie had been abducted. Betty did not undergo hypnosis because her doctors feared it might put too great a strain upon her heart.

VISIT decided that there had been no abduction. Since other witnesses had also testified to seeing the helicopters, it was concluded that the only part of scenario 2 that was true was the part about the UFO and the injuries.

Scenario 3 In this scenario the huge UFO was carrying smaller UFOs and dispensing them near the city of Houston. Betty, Vickie and Colby happened along just in time to interrupt the operation and were accidentally injured. Rather than risk having the three observers talk about what they had seen, the UFO operators made them (by holographic means, mind control or hypnosis) see the smaller UFOs as helicopters. The UFO operators were probably unaware that the victims

Vickie undergoing regressive hypnosis under the guidance of Dr R. Leo Sprinkle, in an attempt to discover whether she had been abducted by UFO operators. Since no evidence of abduction was found, VISIT concluded that the idea of the helicopters had not been 'implanted' in the victims' minds

had been injured, and hoped they would accept the sight of helicopters as unremarkable, and say no more about them. (This scenario was suggested by an investigator for the Aerial Phenomena Research Organisation of Tucson, Arizona.)

Since the late 1960s there have been a number of cases in which it was not clear whether UFOs or helicopters were involved. At the Huffman event it appears that a UFO and helicopters were interacting in some way. The victims saw the helicopters at Huffman while the UFO was nearby and also after it had moved several miles away; other witnesses saw the helicopters without the UFO, or the UFO without the helicopters. As a result of all these sightings VISIT concluded that the helicopters were not camouflaged UFOs.

Scenario 4 Betty, Vickie and Colby encountered a UFO in trouble; it was operating an emergency system (the cone of fire) to overcome the problem and get it on its way again. Two hours earlier the same craft had been seen over Dayton and Liberty flying like a spaceship in trouble; it had been tracked on radar until it dipped too low to be seen, when a military team was sent to investigate. The team had CH-47 heavy lift helicopters to carry troops to cordon off a crash scene, and equipment to neutralise any problem; the smaller helicopters were gunships for protection. When the UFO regained control and made for the coast, the lead helicopters stayed close to it to collect data. Other helicopters held back, in case the UFO should try to land, or should crash.

Research for this scenario produced a number of other UFO sightings involving triangular or diamond-shaped objects, but only a few of these belched flames from the underside for a prolonged period. This seemed to support the idea that the Huffman

One day in April 1981 a CH-47 helicopter flew into Dayton, Colby Landrum's home town. As the little boy watched the aircraft fly overhead, he became very upset and agitated, because it was the same type of helicopter he had seen near Huffman the previous December. To allay his fears his grandmother Vickie decided to take him to the place where the helicopter had landed, in the hope that it would seem less frightening on the ground.

When they reached the landing zone they found a lot of other people already there, and had to wait some time before they were allowed to go inside the helicopter and talk to the pilot. Vickie and another visitor both claim that the pilot

Adding insult to injury

said he had been in the area before for the purpose of checking on a UFO reported in trouble near Huffman. When Vickie told the pilot how happy she was to meet him, because she was one of the people burned by the UFO, he refused to talk to them any further and hustled them out of the aircraft.

VISIT later located the pilot and questioned him. He admitted to knowing about Vickie's and Betty's encounter with the UFO, but maintained that he had not been in the area in December, and had had nothing to do with any UFO. Unless another pilot decides to speak up, it seems that the source of the helicopters reported at Huffman will remain shrouded in mystery.

UFO was in trouble. Moreover, people close to a UFO seldom suffer the dire injuries experienced in the Huffman incident, and this suggests that the injuries were caused by a system that was not operating properly.

One possible explanation for the helicopters is that a military team was co-operating with the UFO. If that was the case, it seems possible that similar incidents had occurred in the past, and that this was a fairly routine operation. It might also suggest that a NATO-like pact exists between the US government and the UFO operators, under which a craft in trouble might issue an emergency call for help. However, it has to be said that the US government refuses to acknowledge that UFOs exist, nor is there any evidence that such a mutual aid pact exists.

Scenario 5 In this scenario the whole affair was a government classified operation and was mistaken by the witnesses for a UFO encounter. The helicopters could have been transported to the Houston area from any base in the USA or central America, and could have been taking part in anything from an annual training exercise to some special operations simulation. The 'UFO' might have been a power plant, a weapons system or an electronic countermeasures system, and it might have been slung from a helicopter or flown by remote control. The injuries could have been caused by a powerful pulsed microwave system, or by exposure to some fuel, defoliant or other unidentified liquid.

As far as this scenario is concerned, the US government categorically refuses to acknowledge ownership of the helicopters seen over Huffman on 29 December 1980. Nor were there any commercial operations involving helicopters of the heavy lift type along the Gulf coast at that time. Since six witnesses have positively identified the helicopters, and since no one will accept responsibility for them, it must be assumed that this was a secret operation and that the welfare of the victims was of secondary importance. Vickie Landrum is quite certain that scenario 5 is the correct one. The UFO was not, she says, 'from outer space with little green men, that's for sure. If the government doesn't know about it, they better find out.'

VISIT has taken steps to make things easier for future victims of UFO encounters. When Betty and Vickie first sought help, they could find no one willing to take an interest in their case. VISIT has now produced a UFO Alert Card, which is distributed to the media and police within a 150-mile (240-kilometre) radius of Houston. Even when the women did find medical help, there was no information available to their doctors about injuries sustained in earlier UFO encounters. VISIT is now researching such injuries and hopes to produce a check-list for use by doctors and UFO investigators in future incidents.

In their initial attempts to get help after their alarming and damaging experience, Betty and Vickie could find no one willing to take an interest in their case. To make things easier for future victims, VISIT produced this UFO Alert Card, which is distributed to the media and police within a 150-mile (240-kilometre) radius of Houston

A night to remember

After Betty and Barney Hill had seen a UFO at close quarters, Betty dreamed she had been abducted and scrutinised by an alien species. But were her dreams based on fact? HILARY EVANS reports

IN SEPTEMBER 1961 BETTY HILL and her husband Barney were taken on board a spacecraft from another world, subjected to examination and given information by the alien crew members. That, at least, was what the Hills believed. Though their case is one of many, and more of the same kind are constantly being reported, it is uniquely important as one of the earliest, most fully documented and most thoroughly investigated. Whether their experience was just what it seemed, or some kind of fantasy, it is important that we should know exactly what happened to Betty and Barney Hill that night, for it is part of a widespread pattern.

The Hills lived at Portsmouth, New Hampshire, in the eastern United States. Barney, who was black, was aged 39 at the time; he worked as a mail sorter in Boston, a job he was glad to have, even though it was somewhat below his capacity, and involved not only night work but also a daily car journey of 60 miles (100 kilometres) each way. Outside his work Barney was active in

Betty and Barney Hill, who were returning from a short vacation when they claimed to have seen a UFO during a night drive along a lonely highway in New Hampshire. Two years after the incident they were both suffering from chronic ill health and nervous disorders. Betty was experiencing disturbing dreams, and Barney complained of stress, exhaustion and other anxiety symptoms

the campaign for civil rights for blacks; Betty, aged 41, was a child welfare worker. Both had been married before and had children by their earlier marriages, though the children were all living with their other parents. To all appearances it was a happy and successful marriage: the couple were popular and had many friends.

Late on 19 September 1961 the Hills were driving home after a short holiday trip to Niagara and Montreal. They were driving through the night because they had run low on money, the trip having been undertaken on the spur of the moment. They stopped for a snack at a roadside restaurant, which they left a little after 10 p.m. to drive on down the highway, US 3. During their journey that night the Hills passed not a single other car and saw only one other person.

What happened to the couple then was described by Betty in a letter to a UFO investigator five days later:

My husband and I have become immensely interested in this topic [UFOs] as we recently had quite a frightening experience, which does seem to differ from others of which we are aware. About midnight on September 20th we

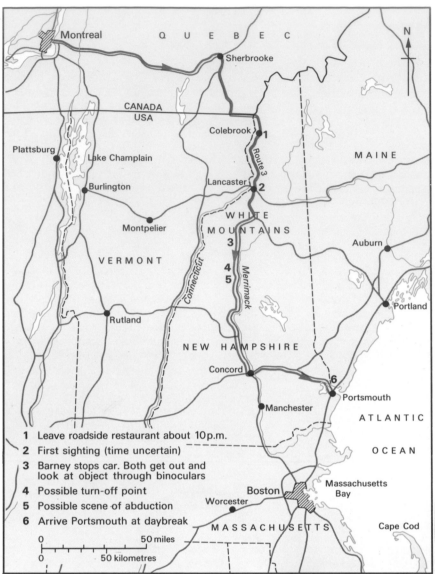

1 Leave roadside restaurant about 10p.m.
2 First sighting (time uncertain)
3 Barney stops car. Both get out and look at object through binoculars
4 Possible turn-off point
5 Possible scene of abduction
6 Arrive Portsmouth at daybreak

lights were on the wing tips.

As it glided closer he was able to see inside this object, but not too closely. He did see several figures scurrying about as though they were making some hurried type of preparation. One figure was observing us from the windows. From the distance this was seen, the figures appeared to be about the size of a pencil and seemed to be dressed in some type of shiny black uniform.

At this point my husband became shocked and got back in the car, in a hysterical condition, laughing and repeating that they were going to capture us. He started driving the car – the motor had been left running. As we started to move, we heard several buzzing or beeping sounds, which seemed to be striking the trunk of our car.

This letter, written to Donald Keyhoe of the National Investigations Committee for Aerial Phenomena (NICAP), effectively summarises what the Hills remembered of their experience. What it lacks is the emotional response of the couple. John G. Fuller, in his definitive account *The interrupted journey*, describes the event in such terms as: 'Barney was fully gripped with fear now', or: 'with all his energy he ripped the binoculars from his eyes and ran screaming back across the field.' While these may be honest descriptions of what occurred, we must not forget that they are a journalist's words, describing what

were driving in a National Forest Area in the White Mountains, in N.H. [New Hampshire]. This is a desolate, uninhabited area. At first we noticed a bright object in the sky, which seemed to be moving rapidly. We stopped our car and got out to observe it more closely with our binoculars. Suddenly it reversed its flight path from the north to the southwest and appeared to be flying in a very erratic pattern. As we continued driving and then stopping to watch it, we observed the following flight pattern: the object was spinning and appeared to be lighted only on one side, which gave it a twinkling effect.

As it approached our car, we stopped again. As it hovered in the air in front of us, it appeared to be pancake in shape, ringed with windows in the front through which we could see bright blue-white lights. Suddenly, two red lights appeared on each side. By this time my husband was standing in the road, watching closely. He saw wings protrude on each side and the red

Left: the route taken by Barney and Betty Hill on the night they saw the UFO

Below: the approximate place on highway US 3 where the Hills stopped their car and got out to look at the flying object, which Betty described as pancake-shaped, with windows in the front through which could be seen bright blue-white lights (right). The object also appeared to have fins tipped with red lights

was reported to him by others, and relating to events that had taken place some years previously.

It was not until 25 November, two months later, in the course of questioning by UFO investigators, that a 'missing time' puzzle emerged. Here are Barney's own words:

They were mentally reconstructing the whole trip. One of them said, 'What took you so long to get home?' They said, you went this distance and it took you these hours. Where were you? Well, when they said this, I thought I was really going to crack up . . . I became suddenly flabbergasted to think that *I realised for the first time* that at the rate of speed I always travel, we should have arrived home at least two hours earlier than we did.

For they had taken seven hours to travel 190 miles (305 kilometres), on empty roads, often at 65–70 miles per hour (105–112 km/h)

Disturbing dreams

Ten days after their return, Betty started to experience a series of disturbing dreams. At this date she had already written her letter to Major Keyhoe, quoted above, but had not yet been visited by any investigator; she had told friends and relatives about the experience and was not just puzzled but very disturbed by it. Not surprisingly, her dreams reflected her anxiety.

But they did more. While taking the UFO sighting as a starting point, her dreams seemed to continue the incident. They present a highly detailed account of happenings that, though bizarre, follow on logically from the sighting itself.

Betty's own account of her dreams is included as an appendix in Fuller's book. Unfortunately he does not indicate when the notes were made. Nor does he make clear how many dreams there were, and whether they repeated the same material, or whether some of the story was contained in each, as fragments that Betty later combined to form a coherent narrative. In other words, we cannot be sure that the smooth, continuous flow of her narrative was also a characteristic of the dreams themselves, or whether it was the result of her own re-telling of the dreams, in the process of which she must inevitably have imposed her own order and logic onto the dream material. Without questioning her sincerity and good faith, we must treat her account with caution. In the light of subsequent events, the coherence and detail of Betty's account of her dreams are of crucial significance.

The dream experience begins at a point immediately following the UFO sighting. Betty sees a very sharp left-hand turn in the road, which then turns back to the right. A group of eight or eleven men are standing in the middle of the road. Barney slows down,

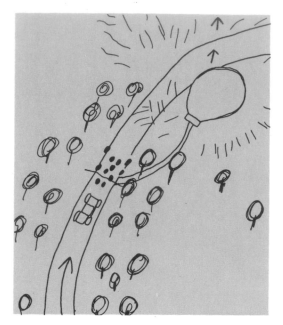

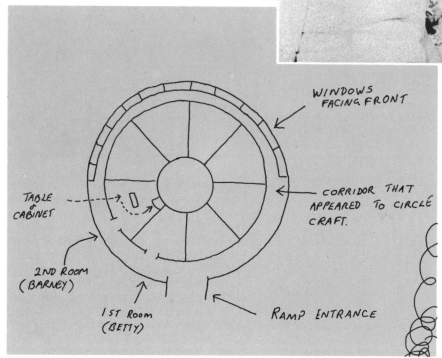

leader, who has returned to the room to watch the examination, clears the pain by waving his hand before Betty's eyes. She senses his concern, and from this point she loses all fear of him.

That concludes the testing, and the examiner leaves to help with Barney, whose testing is taking longer. Left alone with the leader, Betty examines the room and chats with him. He apologises for frightening her and offers to answer her questions.

They are interrupted by some of the men entering; after a brief conversation, the leader turns to Betty, opens her mouth, and touches her teeth as though trying to move them. He is puzzled by the fact that Barney's teeth are movable while Betty's are not; so Betty explains about Barney's dentures. This leads to a discussion of old age, which the man seems not to comprehend, for he asks Betty about time and how it is measured.

Betty asks for some proof of the incident;

and the motor dies. As he tries to start the motor, the men surround the car. The couple sit motionless and speechless: Betty is terrified. The men open the car doors, reach in and take Barney and Betty by the arm.

Next Betty seems to be walking along a path in the woods, with men ahead of, beside and behind her. Barney is similarly accompanied. She speaks to him but he does not seem to hear her: it is as though he is sleepwalking. The man on Betty's left, hearing her say Barney's name, asks if that is his name; she does not answer. He tries to assure her that there is nothing to be frightened of, no harm will come to them.

Soon they reach a small clearing, where a disc-shaped craft is parked: it is 'almost as wide as my house is long'. There are no lights or windows to be seen. They climb a ramp towards a door; reluctantly Betty goes in. They emerge into a corridor, curving with the shape of the disc. Betty is taken into the first room opening off the corridor, but Barney is led further along. When Betty objects, the 'leader' explains that only one person at a time can be tested in each room, and it will be quicker to examine them separately.

The men leave Betty in the room when a pleasant, reassuring man, who speaks English, enters; he is the examiner. He asks several questions about her age, her diet and so on. Then he makes her sit on a stool while he carries out a superficial inspection, taking samples of hair and ear wax, fingernail clippings and scrapings from her skin.

Next he asks Betty to lie down on a table. He examines her with a machine with needles on the end of wires, which, he explains, are to check her nervous system. During this test her dress is removed. With a needle 4 to 6 inches (10 to 15 centimetres) long the examiner carries out what he calls a pregnancy test, which consists of jabbing the needle into her navel. The is extremely painful, but the

the leader agrees and when she looks round the room and sees a book he says she may take it. Discussion of the book leads to questions about the Universe: the leader pulls out a kind of map from a case, on which are marked a number of stars. Betty tells him that she knows little about such matters, but there are others on Earth who do, and a meeting should be arranged with them. As she speaks, Betty is wondering whether she herself might be able to bring about such a meeting.

At this point some men return with Barney, who is still in a daze. When Betty speaks to him he does not answer. The leader assures her that he will be back to normal when they return to their car. They start to walk towards the door, and then one of the men says something that provokes an excited discussion. The leader takes the book away

Top: Barney shows his drawing of the spacecraft as he remembered seeing it, also with fins either side tipped with red lights, and members of the alien crew looking out of the windows. Although he had no conscious memory of being abducted, he was able after hypnosis to draw a plan (above) of the arrangement of rooms inside the craft, and a sketch of the area (top left) where the craft landed, showing the Hills' car on the highway and the group of spacemen (dots) who abducted the couple

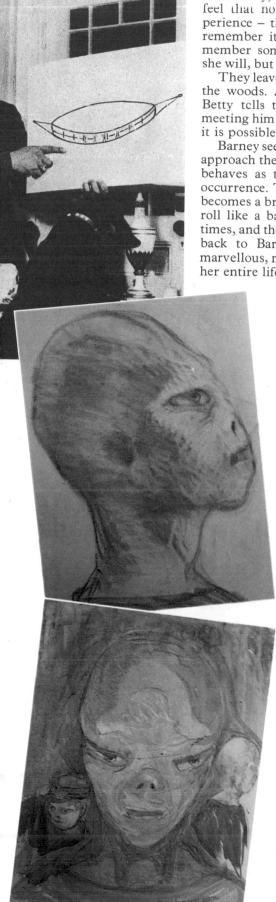

from Betty, saying that the rest of the crew feel that no one should know of this experience – that even Betty herself will not remember it. She insists that she will remember somehow; he agrees that perhaps she will, but he says nobody will believe her.

They leave the disc and walk back through the woods. All the men accompany them. Betty tells the leader she is happy about meeting him and begs him to return. He says it is possible, but he cannot say for certain.

Barney seems to become more alert as they approach the car, but shows no emotion and behaves as though this were an everyday occurrence. They get into the car. The disc becomes a bright glowing object; it seems to roll like a ball, turning over three or four times, and then sails into the sky. Betty turns back to Barney and says it is the most marvellous, most unbelievable experience of her entire life. Barney starts driving. So far

Left: artist's impressions of the alien crew members of the spacecraft, based on the Hills' verbal descriptions. In Betty's dreams, the aliens put the couple into separate rooms aboard their craft and carried out a physical examination of Betty; they took samples of her hair and ear wax, fingernail clippings and skin scrapings, and made tests 'on her nervous system' using a machine with needles

he has not uttered a word. She turns to him and asks, 'Do you believe in flying saucers now?' He replies, 'Don't be ridiculous!'

Intriguing though they were, Betty's dreams figured in the case only because they confirmed the impact made on her by the sighting. The investigators who visited the couple were concerned only with the waking experiences reported by the Hills. Walter Webb, an astronomer who served as one of NICAP's scientific advisers, was impressed by the Hills' testimony. In his report he wrote:

It is the opinion of this investigator, after questioning these people for over six hours and studying their reactions and personalities during that time, that they were telling the truth, and the incident occurred exactly as reported except for some minor uncertainties and technicalities . . . . I was impressed by their intelligence, apparent honesty, and obvious desire to get at the facts and to underplay the more sensational aspects of the sighting.

Fears, real and imagined

Significantly, Webb went on to observe:

Mr Hill believes he saw something he doesn't want to remember. He claimed he was not close enough to see any facial characteristics on the figures, although at another time he referred to one of them looking over his shoulder and grinning, and to the leader's expressionless face. However, it is my view that the observer's blackout is not of any great significance. I think the whole experience was so improbable and fantastic to witness – along with the very real fear of being captured adding to imagined fears – that his mind finally refused to believe what his eyes were perceiving and a mental block resulted.

In the course of the ensuing year, it was Barney's 'mental block' that gradually assumed overwhelming importance. His health deteriorated, and with it his mental state: his ulcer became more pronounced, he became exhausted and depressed. Seeking for a cause, it was not surprising that the Hills should wonder whether their UFO experience played any part in it. They suggested this to their doctor, who proposed hypnosis as a means of discovering more about the sighting and its effect on them. Already, during the investigation of their story, hypnosis had been proposed as a means of acquiring further data, so the Hills welcomed the suggestion.

But Betty had an additional reason for seeking what hypnosis might reveal: 'The moment they suggested hypnosis, I thought of my dreams, and this was the first time I began to wonder if they were *more* than just dreams . . . .'

Sensational information about 'alien visitors' emerged when Betty and Barney Hill's memories of their close encounter were probed by hypnosis. The Hills' revelations, particularly about the aliens' interstellar maps, have intrigued the experts

BARNEY AND BETTY HILL presented themselves at the office of Dr Benjamin Simon on 14 December 1963 to begin a series of hypnosis sessions that was to last seven months. Dr Simon was a practitioner of experience and repute, ideally suited for the task; his open-minded attitude enabled the troubled couple to present their stories in an atmosphere of sympathetic understanding, free from bias or prejudice.

It is important to remember why hypnosis was tried. In Betty's words:

We went to Dr Simon to get relief from the emotional trouble, and to determine what its cause was. In other words, we'd gone for medical help, not to find out about a UFO experience.

And the sessions were not part of a wider course of psychoanalysis: they were designed to see what relevance the alleged UFO sighting might have to Barney's physical and psychological state. So they do not give us a general picture of Barney's or Betty's psychological background. There are many questions we would like answered about the couple, about their attitudes to such matters as their interracial marriage, their previous marriages, their separation from their children, their involvement with social work and civil rights, all of which could have some bearing on how we evaluate their stories. But no such information is forthcoming: Dr Simon's probing, and his subsequent comments, were limited to the task in hand.

Each subject was hypnotised separately, with the other out of the room, one after the other. They did not hear each other's sessions at the time, nor the tapes of their own sessions. Only when Dr Simon judged that he had accomplished all he could and had brought the sessions to an end did he invite the couple to hear the tapes for the first time.

Making up for lost time

Above: Betty and Barney Hill, heads slumped, under hypnosis during their seven-month course of treatment. Their hypnotherapist, Dr Benjamin Simon (right), was concerned with 'the cumulative impact of past experiences and fantasies on their present experiences and responses' – not with the existence of UFOs. In an introduction to the published account of the case he is careful to say that hypnosis is a pathway to the truth 'as it is felt and understood by the patient'

Left: Betty and Barney are led to the mysterious craft by members of its crew. Betty felt great fear at this point – but Barney later insisted that he felt none

They chose to listen to them together.

All this was being done at the Hills' own instigation and, moreover, at their own expense. Apart from the emotional ordeal, seven months of sessions with a consultant of the highest qualifications must have cost a very great sum of money. There must have been an exceedingly strong motivation to encourage the Hills to shoulder such costs.

Under hypnosis the Hills independently told a story that matched the dreams that had so troubled Betty in the weeks following their supposed sighting. But with this difference: the histories were now recounted as the experiences of two people, each describing the events as seen from his or her individual viewpoint. During the phases of the story when the couple were together, each account confirmed the other; when they were separated, they had their own stories to tell, and told them with an immediacy and intensity that give a vivid impression of re-living an actual experience. Here is Barney:

I started to get out of my car, and put one foot on the ground. And two men were standing beside me, helping me out. I felt very relaxed, yet very frightened. They didn't say anything. I knew I was walking, or moving down the road from the position of where my car was parked. And I could see the ramp that I went up. . . . I could hear a humming sound that they seemed to be making. I was afraid to open my eyes. I had been told not to open my eyes, and it would be over with quickly. And I could feel them examining me with their hands. They looked at my neck, and I could feel them touching my skin right down my back. As if they were counting my spinal column. And I felt something touch right at the base of my spine, like a finger pushing, a single finger.

Betty's account was equally detailed:

They led Barney right past the door where I'm standing. So I said: 'What are you doing with Barney? Bring him in here where I am.' And the man said: 'No, we only have equipment enough in one room to do one person at a time. And if we took you both in the same room, it would take too long. So Barney will be all right, they're going to take him into the next room. And then as soon as we get through testing the both of you, then you will go back to your car. You don't have to be afraid.' . . . And they rub – they have a machine, I don't know what it is. They bring the machine over and they put it – it's something like a microscope, only with a big lens. I had an idea they were taking a picture of my skin. And they both looked through this machine. . . . Then they took something like a letter opener and they scraped my arm here,

Merely starstruck?

The American UFO sceptic Robert Sheaffer (right) has declared that the Hills' experience began when they misidentified the planet Jupiter as a UFO. Betty first saw a bright 'star' near the Moon; later a second one appeared and seemed to be moving. Jupiter and Saturn *were* visible near the Moon that night: had there been a UFO, Sheaffer says, Betty would have seen *three* 'stars'. Having satisfied himself on this point, Sheaffer dismisses Betty's other claims – such as that the UFO acted 'much like a yo-yo', had passed in front of the Moon in silhouette and flashed 'thin pencils of different-coloured lights, rotating around an object which at that time appeared cigar-shaped'. He cites other cases in which witnesses have produced fantastic misinterpretations of bright stars.

Sheaffer further questions the Hills' 'loss' of two hours. At various times the Hills have put the UFO encounter as occurring at around 11 p.m., between midnight and 1 a.m., and at around 3 a.m. Furthermore, Barney recalled that, as the UFO approached them, he drove extremely slowly; on the homeward journey he stopped at least once, for reasons he couldn't remember. Sheaffer insists that there is so much uncertainty in the times and in their speed of travel that there is no reason to believe in the 'loss' of the two hours – a loss that was 'discovered' only weeks later.

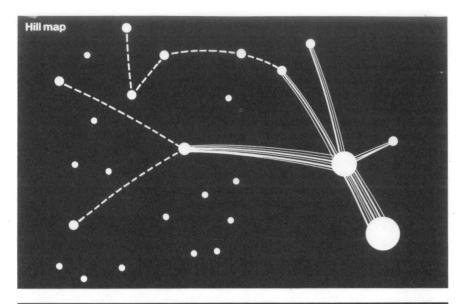

Hill map

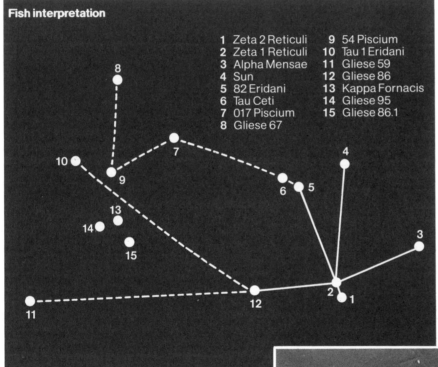

Fish interpretation

1	Zeta 2 Reticuli	9	54 Piscium
2	Zeta 1 Reticuli	10	Tau 1 Eridani
3	Alpha Mensae	11	Gliese 59
4	Sun	12	Gliese 86
5	82 Eridani	13	Kappa Fornacis
6	Tau Ceti	14	Gliese 95
7	017 Piscium	15	Gliese 86.1
8	Gliese 67		

I asked him where he was from. Because I said that I knew he wasn't from the Earth . . . and he asked if I knew anything about the Universe. And I told him no. I knew practically nothing. . . . And he went across the room . . . there was an opening. And he pulled out a map. . . . It was an oblong map. . . . And there were all these dots on it. . . . Some were little, just pinpoints. And others were as big as a nickel . . . there were curved lines going from one dot to another. And there was one big circle, and it had a lot of lines coming out from it. A lot of lines going to another circle quite close but not as big. . . . And I asked him what they meant. And he said that the heavy lines were trade routes . . . the solid lines were places they went occasionally. And he said the broken lines were expeditions. . . . So I asked him where was his home port, and he said, 'Where were you on the map?' I looked and laughed and said, 'I don't know.' So he said, 'If you don't know where you are, then there isn't any point of my telling where I am from.' And he put the map . . . back in the space in the wall. . . .

Betty drew the map to the best of her recollection, but with no names and no points of reference it was totally meaningless. However, in 1968 a schoolteacher and amateur astronomer, Marjorie Fish, realised that there must be a limited number of actual configurations of stars that would match up to the points of the map. She started by making a three-dimensional model of Betty's map out of beads and string and then set about seeking a match for it among the not-too-distant stars. After five years, she felt satisfied that she had found such a match.

The Fish map started a controversy almost as lively as that engendered by the Hills'

and there was like little – you know how your skin gets dry and flaky sometimes, like little particles of skin? And they put something like a piece of cellophane or plastic, they scraped, and they put this that came off on this plastic.

One of the practical applications of hypnosis is to bring into the conscious mind information that is stored in the subconscious – things experienced but not consciously noted by the witness. This was used to good effect by Dr Simon in the case of the star map Betty Hill said she had been shown by the 'leader' of the aliens. Dr Simon suggested that after the session, when she got home, she might care to try to draw what she remembered of the map. For, to judge from her account, it could be a valuable clue as to the origin of her abductors. In the session she said:

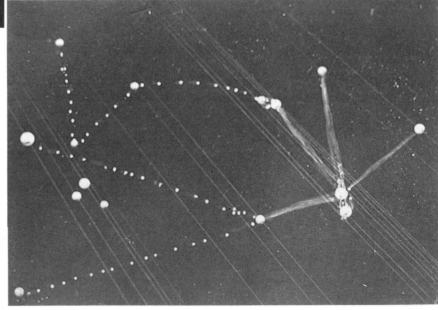

original sighting. An astronomer, Terence Dickinson, was favourably impressed and presented the case for the Fish model in an authoritative article:

Basically the Fish interpretation is a view from a few light years beyond the stars zeta 1 and zeta 2 Reticuli, looking back towards the Sun and the star 82 Eridani, which is about midway between us and the Reticuli pair. The 15 stars shown on the map are all basically like the Sun and could theoretically have planets like Earth. These are the types of stars some astronomers are currently examining in search of signals from alien intelligences. It is therefore a reasonable assumption that this type of star may be the only type on the map. . . . No other interpretation of the Hill map includes all of the solar-type stars within a specific area of space containing the Sun . . . and makes

Opposite: the home of the aliens? Betty Hill recalled being shown a star map something like this (top). The stars, seen from an unknown viewpoint, form unfamiliar patterns. A school teacher, Marjorie Fish, after several years' work arrived at this interpretation (centre). The aliens' home system, zeta 1 Reticuli, is about 37 light years from us. Marjorie Fish arrived at her result by making a model of stars near the Sun, using beads mounted on threads (bottom)

Above: the Hills' first close-up view of the aliens as they approached the couple's stalled car. This careful reconstruction of Betty and Barney's descriptions appeared in the UFO magazine Flying Saucer after their case had caught the public's imagination

sense in terms of logical travel between the stars.

The Fish model provoked much debate, largely related to the chances of finding such a pattern at random among the numerous stars in the neighbourhood of the Sun. By way of testing this, Charles W. Atterberg offered an alternative conjecture as to the region shown in the map. It is a measure of how debatable the findings are that the UFO sceptic Robert Sheaffer should find the Atterberg model superior to the Fish version, whereas Dickinson claims that it is more arbitrary in its selection of stars and contains several inconsistencies.

Additional support for the Fish model appeared in 1969, when a revised star catalogue, containing information that was simply not available in 1961, was published for the first time and confirmed predictions made by Fish on the basis of the Hill map. Though this is still not definite proof, it is

strongly supportive of the Hill-Fish suggestion. But the question remains of how much reliance can be placed on the recollections, by someone totally unversed in astronomy, of a map seen – under distinctly bizarre conditions – more than two years earlier.

The star map is the most tangible aspect of the Hill case, and lends itself to testing. For the rest, it is a matter of evaluating the Hills' personal testimony, and in the complete absence of any physical evidence – how valuable the book that Betty was offered would have been, if she had only been allowed to bring it away! – evaluation is limited to assessing the credibility of the Hills themselves. No critic has questioned their honesty and sincerity; rather it is their interpretation of their experience that is questioned. It is in this respect that our lack of information about the Hills' personal background becomes important. For, without questioning either their integrity or their intelligence, it is clear that there are factors in the Hills' personal circumstances that could be relevant to the way we judge their story. We have already noted such external factors as their mixed marriage, their previous marriages, Barney's state of health; there is also considerable evidence to show that Betty was a much more unusual person than she is presented as in, for instance, John G. Fuller's book *The interrupted journey*. (It is only fair to Fuller to say that much of this has come to light only after the publication of his book.)

Mixed blessings of fame

Barney Hill died in February 1969, five years after the sessions with Dr Simon: he died of a cerebral haemorrhage, as did his father before him. Since then, Betty has enjoyed the mixed blessings of fame. Her case has been featured in books and magazines, even presented as a full-length movie. She has made countless public appearances at lectures and conferences and as a guest on radio and television shows. Some time after the hypnotic sessions, she gave up her work and devoted herself full-time to 'UFO research'. She has become something of a celebrity, recognised on the most unlikely occasions:

At a recent lobster festival the man on the mike looked up, saw me and said: 'Welcome, Betty Hill! You've put us on the map with the greatest landing area for UFOs in the world!'

Cynically, one could say that she now has a vested interest in having people believe that her experience was genuine, but there seems little question that she is completely sincere in her belief that the abduction really took place.

However, she is no less convinced that a great number of strange events have happened to her since the alleged abduction.

The unended journey

The most famous of UFO close encounters, the alleged abduction of Betty and Barney Hill, continues even today. Do the extraordinary experiences in which Betty has subsequently been involved point to a psychological explanation of this bizarre case?

NOT LONG AFTER her UFO encounter, Betty Hill came home to find leaves piled inexplicably on her kitchen table. Among them were the ear-rings she had been wearing at the time of the sighting. Stranger and stranger incidents occurred over the years. There were unaccountable noises around the house, and remarkable things happened to appliances: wires pulled out of a central heating pump, a burglar alarm tripped off inexplicably, faults developed in electrical equipment such as the refrigerator, toaster, iron, radio set and television set, which just as strangely managed to right themselves. Betty finally claimed that her telephone had been tapped both by the Air Force and by some organisation calling itself the 'Federal Agency'. Her mail disappeared; she saw and heard prowlers; and she was visited by all kinds of strangers.

While for some of this there is external confirmation – neighbours did indeed see prowlers round Betty's home – most of it depends on her own personal affirmation. However, in connection with another of her

claims she welcomed other witnesses: this was her UFO hunting, which she does several nights a week, whether with visitors or alone. She told the ufologist Allan Hendry that she often saw as many as 50 to 100 UFOs a night in a 'special area' in New Hampshire. In an interview she told of a particular incident:

One particular UFO comes in almost every night. During the winter of 1976–1977, when I saw it often, it was quite spectacular – a sort of flattened disc with brightly coloured lights. One night in January 1977 it landed and turned on twelve big white lights around the rim. Under them there were two white headlights. I was out there one night with a retired military officer and his wife. When he saw the UFO, he got out of the car and started walking

Aliens in jackboots

At many points in the transcript of the hypnotic sessions, the latent fears of Barney (right) come to the surface. While recalling watching the light in the sky, he says: 'Betty! This is not a flying saucer. What are you doing this for? You want to believe in this thing, and I don't.' And a little later: 'I want to hear a *jet*. Oh, I want to hear a jet so *badly*. I want to hear it.' When the object is close enough to appear like 'a big pancake, with rows of windows', he says: 'Can't somebody come? Can't somebody come and *tell* me this is not there?' One of the men on board looks friendly, and 'I think of – a red-headed Irishman . . . because Irishmen are usually hostile to Negroes. And when I see a friendly Irish person, I react to him by thinking – *I* will be friendly.' But another figure has an evil face: 'He looks like a German Nazi. He's a Nazi. . . .'

Not surprisingly, considering he is black, Barney has a fit of terror: 'His *eyes*! His *eyes*. I've never seen eyes like that

before.' But after the abduction experience, when he is driving homeward, his former attitude returns: Betty asks him if he believes in flying saucers now, and he replies: 'Oh, Betty, don't be ridiculous. Of course I don't. . . .'

'A huge red ball, filmed coming straight down from the sky' (above left) and a 'double cylinder travelling along a beam' (left) – these are Betty Hill's descriptions of these objects, which she filmed with a Super 8 movie camera in New Hampshire, not far from where she lives

Left: Betty Hill reports frequent paranormal experiences and several sightings of UFOs each week. Sometimes investigators have accompanied her – and have reported that she misidentifies aircraft and street lights. She believes, however, that she has found a UFO landing site in New Hampshire and that this accounts for the fact that she sees so many strange aerial objects

towards it. Suddenly a large swirling mass shot out from the object. I don't know what it was, but it looked like a red ball rolling over and over and heading directly toward him. I jumped out and tried to film this with my movie camera. But then – I know this sounds incredible – a green light hit my camera and burned out the switch and the circuitry so my camera wouldn't work. When the officer saw this red ball coming at him, he turned and ran back to the car. The red ball stopped, rolled back to the craft, and disappeared.

But Hendry notes that 'a number of UFO field investigators have accompanied Mrs Hill to her special site, only to confirm that the lights in the night sky that Mrs Hill calls UFOs are only planes and streetlights', comments that others have confirmed; and he points out that 'she also related other tales involving robots, her neighbour's cat levitating, and a "militant" UFO that burned the paint on her car when she didn't leave the area soon enough to suit them.'

While it is fair to say that these bizarre incidents may be a *consequence* of her original experience, and do not therefore invalidate that experience, they cannot be dismissed as irrelevant. In a case that depends entirely on personal testimony, we must know just what kind of person is making the testimony. Psychology, not astronomy, will best help us to understand the Hill case.

We should note that the Hills' story contains many incongruous or inconsistent features. It is not clear, for example, whether Betty is communicating with the aliens in speech or by telepathy: sometimes one is suggested, sometimes the other. In either

case, the way the 'leader' used colloquial English is surprising in view of the ignorance they display in some matters – such as what 'yellow' is, or what is meant by a 'year'.

An example of seeming inconsistency is afforded by the Hills' statement that, in being abducted, they walked – apparently for some distance – through the woods with their abductors before reaching the clearing where the UFO was parked, whereas after the examination they were soon back at their car, from which they were able to watch the UFO's departure. Such details are not particularly important in themselves, but they serve to remind us that the Hills' story is by no means a precisely detailed and watertight narrative.

Sources of stress

In our search for an explanation, let us look at the Hills' psychological history. Barney's health deteriorated during the year following the sighting, but it was by no means perfect before it. Barney did not develop an ulcer in 1962 – the ulcer he already had grew worse. And an ulcer is notoriously the physical expression of psychological disturbance, usually stress. We have noted that both the Hills had had previous marriages and were separated from the children of those marriages; and, although their present marriage was to all appearance a happy one, it was none the less an inter-racial marriage in a society in which this was exceptional, and it remained a potential source of stress. Betty was involved in child welfare work, while Barney worked at nights, commuting 120 miles (200 kilometres) a day, and was involved in civil rights work: both these occupations were liable to produce anxiety.

Further, Betty had a history of psychic

experiences: she believed that psychic abilities were common in her family and that she herself had had traumatic precognitive dreams as a teenager. Curiously, this ability was shared by her adopted daughter. 'Actually,' Betty told Dr Berthold Schwarz, a psychologist with a close interest in UFOs, 'all my close family members have witnessed UFO sightings: my parents, my sisters and brothers, my nieces and nephews.' Poltergeist incidents of the type that occurred in the Hill household after the sighting were commonplace in her childhood home, where they were attributed to a 'ghost' named Hannah.

How does all this relate to their UFO sighting? Schwarz offers one possibility:

In Betty's abduction case, as in some UFO contactee examples, there is the overall impression that the involved individual is a unique type of person whose talents (e.g. the ability to rapidly enter a deep hypnotic trance, dissociative traits, and high quality psi potentialities), latent or otherwise, are necessary for the UFOs, or the forces behind them. . . .

But Schwarz's view begs the question of whether any external agency is necessarily involved. An alternative possibility is that there are no UFOs or any other external agency manifesting itself in that form but that the whole experience is a 'projection' from an internal source, Betty's own mind.

Many people have taken it for granted that Betty's dreams and the couple's hypnosis narratives are consistent with each other because both were derived from the same source – that is, an actual UFO encounter. But this is a naïve and unwarranted assumption – for it is no less possible that the stories recounted under hypnosis derive from Betty's dreams.

But the moment we focus on Betty's dreams as a record of fact, the insubstantiality of the case becomes apparent. What is

Two more of Betty's UFOs, filmed near the coast: a 'disc on edge, with a small remote-controlled object under it' (top); and 'three mushroom-shaped objects travelling together' (above). There are several military bases within 15 miles (24 kilometres). It is a rural area, with few street lights – but there is a fault line to the south, so ufologists may speculate on the possibility of 'earth lights' being responsible

the likelihood that they offer a reliable account of a factual experience? This is not what most dreams do; they are generally either total fantasy, or reworkings of material drawn from a whole variety of sources: the dreamer's daily life, books and television, wishes and fears. We must be wary of supposing that Betty's dreams are any exception to this rule.

Dr Simon, the Hills' hypnotist, never committed himself to a definite statement, but he himself put forward the possibility that Betty's recounting of her dreams had influenced Barney, who then relived them as recollections of reality. It is noteworthy that, though Barney's UFO examination supposedly took longer than Betty's, his account of what was done is far less detailed than hers.

Why would Barney fantasise? Probably because he was looking for an external cause on which to blame his internal trouble, just as all of us are apt to do. The UFO sighting offered a convenient scapegoat. So Barney took Betty's fantasy and used it, albeit unconsciously, for his own purposes. Dr Simon ruled out any question of conscious collusion, let alone deceit: whatever process was operating, it was completely on the unconscious level.

Dr Simon warned that hypnosis was not a royal road to the discovery of truth, and further evidence has emerged in later years to confirm this. Hypnotic regressions, in particular, have been shown in numerous cases to produce narratives that are nothing more than pure, undiluted fantasy. There is little evidence, on the other hand, for repressed experiences emerging as coherent, detailed and accurate narratives in dreams.

Inevitably, such an interpretation of the Hills' 'memories' of their abduction is bound to be pure conjecture. But it is not more conjectural than the hypothesis that the dreams and hypnosis stories are based on a real-life experience of a medical examination by beings from another world.

The UFO file

Reports of UFO encounters have been filed in every part of the world. We can learn a great deal about the nature of the phenomena by comparing the features common to the most interesting of these

Strange encounters of many kinds

ESTABLISHED SCIENCE has always tended to view the UFO phenomenon with scepticism. In his book, *The UFO experience*, Dr J. Allen Hynek, who was astronomical consultant to Project Blue Book (the US Air Force investigation into UFOs), tells the story of an event at an evening reception held in 1968 in Victoria, British Columbia, at which a number of astronomers were present. During the evening it was announced that strange lights – possibly UFOs – had been spotted outside. Dr Hynek continues: 'The news was met by casual banter and the giggling sound that often accompanies an embarrassing situation.' And, he reports, not a single astronomer went outside to look.

Even Project Blue Book attempted to explain away every reported sighting in terms of conventional science. It soon began to earn itself a bad name because many of its explanations were impossible to believe. In 1966 the US Air Force set up a two-year research project – to investigate, in effect, its own investigations!

The Condon Report, as it was unofficially known, was published in 1969 and stated,

Unidentified flying objects have intrigued the world for decades, but objective reports by experienced investigators rarely reach the mass media.

broadly, that since nothing valuable to science had come out of the study of UFOs, further research was not justified. This conclusion was reached despite the fact that about one in three of the 87 case histories studied by the commission remained unexplained in the report. After this the US Air Force relinquished responsibility for the monitoring of UFO reports and Project Blue Book was disbanded in December 1969. Since 1969 research has been largely left to private organisations, such as Ground Saucer Watch and Project Starlight International in the USA, and UFOIN (UFO Investigators' Network and BUFORA (British UFO Research Association) in Britain.

From UFO reports made over the past 30 years it has been observed that they occur in distinct waves, often called 'flaps'. The flaps of 1954 and 1965, when reports reached vast numbers, were particularly interesting. Featured below are two incidents from the 1954 flap. The third incident we describe, at Socorro, New Mexico, belongs to the smaller flap of 1964; it is a classic early example of an encounter involving humanoids.

What kind of sightings?

Astronomer Dr J. Allen Hynek, Director of the Centre for UFO Studies, USA. Dr Hynek has spent many years in applying the techniques of science to the study of UFOs

Dr J. Allen Hynek, while acting as a consultant to Project Blue Book, developed a system of classification of UFO 'types' which has become standard. He divided UFO reports according to the distance, greater or less than 500 feet (150 metres), at which the UFO was observed, and subdivided each of these two sections into three, giving six categories altogether.

The commonest sightings are of the 'distant' type.

Nocturnal lights Strange lights seen at a distance in the night sky, often with unusual features such as variations in the intensity of light or colour and sudden, remarkable changes of speed and direction of movement.

Daylight discs Distant objects seen against the sky during the daytime. The shapes vary considerably: cigars, spheres, eggs, ovals and pinpoints as well as discs are often reported.

Radar-visuals Distant UFOs recorded simultaneously on radar and visually with good agreement between the two reports. Dr Hynek excluded 'sightings' made solely by radar since false traces can result from a number of natural factors such as ground scatter – the signal is reflected from high ground – temperature inversions and even thick banks of cloud or flocks of birds. Radar-visual sightings are the most important

category of UFO reports as they give independent instrumental evidence of the sighting; unfortunately, they are very rare.

Reports of UFOs seen at close range are the most interesting and often spectacular; these are the famous 'close encounters'.

Close encounters of the first kind Simple observations of phenomena where there is no physical interaction between the phenomena and the environment.

Close encounters of the second kind Similar to the first kind except that physical effects on both animate and inanimate matter are observed. Vegetation may be scorched or flattened, tree branches broken, animals frightened or car headlights, engines and radios doused. In cases of electrical failure the equipment usually begins to work normally again once the UFO has disappeared.

Close encounters of the third kind 'Occupants' are reported in or around the UFO. Dr Hynek generally ruled out so-called 'contactee' cases in which the reporter claimed to have had intelligent communication with the 'occupants', arguing that such reports were almost invariably made by pseudo-religious fanatics and never by 'ostensibly sensible, rational and reputable persons.' But even these cases occasionally have to be taken seriously by scientists.

'We are not alone'

The UFO seen by Captain James Howard and the crew and passengers of BOAC Stratocruiser *Centaurus* on 29 June 1954 was not a saucer or a disc; it was, astonishingly, a shape that kept changing shape. The airliner had taken off from Idlewild, New York, bound for Newfoundland before making the Atlantic crossing to Shannon, then London.

The airliner was making its way steadily northeastwards when the radio crackled an order from ground control to 'hold' – a manoeuvre adopted when there is a hazard ahead. After half an hour's circling the skipper advised control that if he couldn't proceed he would have to return to Idlewild, as his fuel was low. After some delay permission was given to proceed and *Centaurus* went on automatic pilot at 19,000 feet (6000 metres), just below a broken layer of cloud and with a solid mass of cloud beneath it at 200 feet (60 metres). After some 20 minutes a glint of light suddenly caught Captain Howard's eye. On the port side of the aircraft he saw a large object of metallic appearance emerge from a gap in the clouds. Moving around this main shape were six much smaller objects, not unlike a screen of small destroyers escorting an enormous aircraft carrier.

A bizarre aspect of this remarkable apparition was that it seemed to be changing shape all the time. Captain Howard sketched on his knee pad the different forms he saw: they were a 'delta wing', a telephone handset, a pear. He has since said that, with its continual changes in shape, the object reminded him of a swarm of bees in flight. It was an estimated 4 miles (6 kilometres) from *Centaurus* and it maintained that position.

When Captain Howard turned to speak to his first officer, Lee Boyd, he found him already out of his seat, standing to watch the display. Captain Howard called up control:
'We are not alone.'
'We know.'
'What is it?'
'We don't know, but we've scrambled a Sabre from Goose Bay to investigate.'
'Good. Give me his frequency and I'll vector him in.'

A few minutes later the captain was in touch with the pilot of the Sabre jet fighter who, once he was in range, announced he had two images on his radar scope – one for *Centaurus* and the other, presumably, for the UFO. Then the unexpected happened: the six small objects manoeuvred into single file, bore down on the main object and appeared to merge into one end of it. Thereafter the size of the large UFO began to diminish until the Sabre's pilot announced he was overhead, at which point the object finally disappeared from the radar scope '. . . like a TV picture going off'.

Since about 1953, airline pilots have been required not to disclose to the public information about UFO sightings. In the case of *Centaurus*, however, many of the passengers had watched the display with amazement and the incident received wide press coverage. Researchers were fortunate in this, for this sighting falls into the important category of radar/visual cases. In this instance two separate radar sets were involved (at control and in the Sabre) plus visual observation by experienced pilots, air crew and some 30 or more passengers – only one of whom had a camera, and he was asleep!

'Luminous, silent and eerily still'

Nocturnal lights: Vernon, France, 23 August 1954

Vernon lies on the River Seine some 50 miles (80 kilometres) downstream from Paris; it is the point at which the Allied forces first crossed the river in pursuit of the German armies in 1944. Ten years later, and barely eight weeks after the Idlewild affair, the town was the scene of another significant event, which was witnessed by four people but received little attention in the press.

The sky was clear at 1 a.m. on 23 August 1954, with the moon in its third quarter and due to appear later that night and give only a faint light. M. Bernard Miserey had just returned home and was closing his garage door when he saw a giant cigar-shaped object hanging vertically over the north bank of the

river about 300 yards (275 metres) from him. This object, which he estimated to be some 300 feet (90 metres) long, was luminous, silent and eerily still. While the witness gaped at the phenomenon, a horizontal, disc-shaped object dropped from the bottom of the giant 'cigar', halted its free-fall, wobbled, turned a luminous red with a brilliant white halo and shot towards M. Miserey, passing silently over his house heading south-west.

This remarkable happening was repeated three times, then, after an interval, a fifth disc dropped almost to the level of the river bank before wobbling and disappearing at great speed to the north. While this last manoeuvre was under way the glow of the giant cigar began to fade and soon it was lost in darkness.

M. Miserey reported the incident to the police and was informed that two policemen on their rounds had also observed the happenings, as had an army engineer who was driving on Route Nationale 181 south-west of the town.

What was the meaning of the apparition M. Miserey saw? Was the large cigar-shaped object the 'carrier' of the smaller ones? Other UFO sightings have led many people to think this may be the case – including the Idlewild incident. The significant difference is that, whereas at Idlewild the smaller objects were assimilated by the larger one, at Vernon the small objects were ejected. But no conclusive evidence exists to establish what these objects in the sky actually are.

'Humanoids... and strange insignia'

Close encounter of the third kind: Socorro, New Mexico, USA, 24 April 1964

Below: Patrolman Lonnie Zamora whose close encounter is one of the best authenticated cases on record

At about 5.50 p.m. on 24 April 1964 Patrolman Lonnie Zamora of the Police Department in Socorro, New Mexico, was alone in his Pontiac giving chase to a speeding motorist who was heading out of town. Suddenly he heard a roar and at the same time saw a 'flame' in the sky, bluish and orange and strangely static as it descended some distance away. Fearful that a nearby dynamite shack might blow up, the patrolman gave up chasing the motorist and headed off over rough ground towards the point where the flame had come down.

After three attempts he forced his car to the top of a ridge and drove slowly westwards. He stopped when, suddenly, he saw a shiny, aluminium-like object below him, about 150–200 yards (140–185 metres) south of his position. Zamora said it looked like a car on end, perhaps 'turned over by some kids'. Then he saw two humanoid figures in white 'coveralls' close to the object. He estimated later that they were about 4 feet (1.2 metres) tall. One of them looked straight at him and seemed to jump. Zamora was wearing clip-on sunglasses over his prescription spectacles and couldn't distinguish any features or headgear at that distance.

The patrolman now accelerated thinking that, whoever the strangers were, they might be in need of help. The shape he'd seen was a

sort of vertical oval, and looking down he could see it was supported on girderlike legs. When the terrain became too rough for the car to go any further he radioed his headquarters to say that he was near the scene of a possible accident and would proceed on foot.

As Zamora left the car he heard two or three loud thumps, like someone hammering or slamming a door. These thumps were a second or two apart. When he was about 50 paces from the object there was a loud roar, which rose gradually in pitch. The humanoid figures were nowhere to be seen. At the same time he could see a blue and orange flame rise from the ground leaving a cloud of dust. Zamora beat a hasty retreat towards his car and as he reached it turned to see the oval shape, now horizontal, rising towards the level of the car. Frightened by the continuing roar, he ran on and dived for shelter over the edge of the ridge. When he realised the noise had ceased he raised his head from his hands and saw the UFO still in the air and moving away from him about 15 feet (4.5 metres) above the ground. It safely cleared the dynamite shack and continued to rise gradually, watched by the policeman, who was retracing his steps to the car. As he called up the radio officer he watched it accelerate away to clear a mountain range and disappear.

Zamora had seen a kind of strange insignia about 18 inches (45 centimetres) high on the side of the object and while he was waiting for his sergeant to arrive he decided to make a sketch of it.

Sergeant Sam Chavez was soon on the scene. Had he not taken a wrong turning he would have arrived in time to see the craft.

'What's the matter, Lonnie?' he asked. 'You look like you've seen the devil.'

'Maybe I have,' replied Zamora.

Zamora pointed out to Sergeant Chavez the fire that was still burning in the brush where the UFO had stood. When they descended to the site they found four separate burn marks and four depressions – all of similar shape – made, they assumed, by the legs of the landing gear. On three of the marks the dense soil had been pushed down about 2 inches (50 millimetres) and dirt had been squeezed up at the sides. The fourth pad mark, less well defined, was only 1 inch (25 millimetres) deep. When engineer W. T. Powers investigated the case he estimated that the force that produced the marks was 'equivalent to a gentle settling of at least a ton on each mark!' He also pointed out an interesting fact about the positions of the marks. Measurements show that the diagonals of a quadrilateral intersect at right angles, then the midpoints of the sides all lie on the circumference of a circle. Mr Powers noted that one of the burn marks occurred on the intersection of the diagonals and speculated that, assuming the linkage among the legs was flexible, this would mean the burn was immediately below the centre of gravity of the craft and might indicate the position of the blue and orange flame seen by Patrolman Zamora. Four small round marks were found within the quadrilateral on the side farthest from where Patrolman Zamora had stood; these were described as 'footprints'.

The Socorro incident was widely reported in the press and generated immense excitement throughout the world. The US Air Force's Project Blue Book usually ruled out UFO sightings with only one witness, but at Socorro Patrolman Zamora's story was so plausible that it was decided to carry out intensive on-the-spot investigations. This was one case in which Project Blue Book was forced to admit defeat: the apparition could

not be explained as any known device or phenomenon. Dr J. Allen Hynek admitted that he was more puzzled after completing the investigation than when he had arrived in Socorro. He commented, 'Maybe there *is* a simple, natural explanation for the Socorro incident, but having made a complete study of the events, I do not think so.'

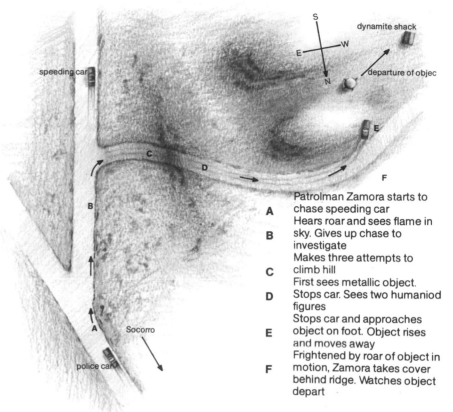

Patrolman Zamora starts to chase speeding car

A   Hears roar and sees flame in sky. Gives up chase to investigate

B   Makes three attempts to climb hill

C   First sees metallic object.

D   Stops car. Sees two humaniod figures

Stops car and approaches object on foot. Object rises

E   and moves away

Frightened by roar of object in motion, Zamora takes cover

F   behind ridge. Watches object depart

Below: one of the four impressions left by the UFO which landed at Sorocco, New Mexico on 24 April 1964. An engineer said pressure of 1 ton would have been needed to make the holes

The closest encounter ever

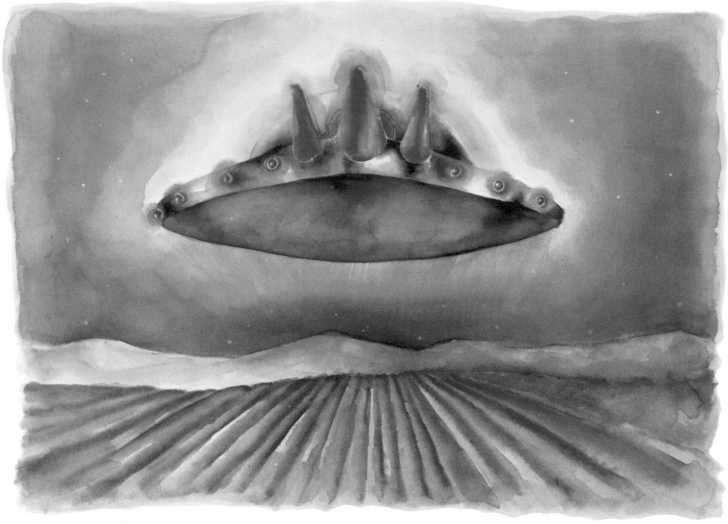

ONE OF THE EARLIEST reports of an alleged abduction by humanoids was kept secret for over three years because it was deemed too 'wild' by those who first interviewed the abductee. And in the early reports the witness was known only as 'A.V.B.' to preserve his anonymity.

This amazing case first became known when the victim wrote to João Martins, a Brazilian journalist, and his medical friend Dr Olavo T. Fontes towards the end of 1957. Apparently, the man with the strange story was a young farmer who lived near the small town of São Francisco de Sales in Minas Gerais, Brazil. Intrigued, Martins and Fontes sent the farmer financial aid to make the long journey to Rio de Janeiro, where the investigation began on 22 February 1958 in Dr Fontes's consulting room.

The story that unfolded was, the investigators felt, so astonishing that they decided to 'keep it on ice' in case a similar incident occurred that might corroborate any of the details. And they feared that if the account

One of the puzzling features of so many UFO incidents is their apparent pointlessness. Yet in 1957 a young Brazilian farmer was allegedly abducted by humanoids for a startling purpose: to have sex with a being from another planet, as if he were 'a good stallion' who would improve their stock.

became widely known there would be a rash of 'copycat' cases, which would end up invalidating this story. But a few details did leak out – fortunately in the right direction, for the outline of the tale reached the ears of Dr Walter Buhler in 1961, and he began to make his own detailed investigation.

The Buhler report eventually appeared as a newsletter and this, translated by Gordon Creighton and supplemented with editorial comments, appeared in *Flying Saucer Review* in January 1965. Very soon after, João Martin's account was published in the Spanish language edition – not the Portuguese as might have been expected – of the Brazilian magazine *O Cruzeiro*. Finally the full case, including the results of various detailed clinical reports, was included in *The humanoids*, a collection of accounts of encounters with UFO occupants, in 1969. At last the story that had been thought too 'wild' to be made known to the public was in print, and 'A.V.B.' was revealed to be 23-year-old Antônio Villas Boas.

'I am going to bear our child'

Close encounter of the third kind: São Francisco de Sales, Brazil, 15 October 1957

Antônio Villas Boas: his remarkable experience was at first concealed by UFO researchers because they considered it too wild

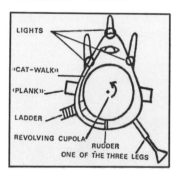

These sketches of the UFO were made by Villas Boas in February 1958 (above) for Dr Olavo Fontes, and in July 1961 (below) for Drs Buhler and Aquino of the Brazilian Society for the Study of Flying Saucers

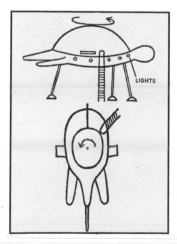

The actual abduction of Antônio Villas Boas was heralded by two unusual events. The first took place on 5 October 1957 when he and his brother were retiring to bed at about 11 p.m. after a party. From their bedroom window they saw an unidentified light in the farmyard below. It moved up onto the roof of their house, and together they watched it shine through the slats of the shutters and the gaps in the tiles (there being no ceiling proper) before it departed.

The second strange incident occurred on 14 October at about 9.30 p.m. when the Villas Boas brothers were out ploughing with their tractor. They suddenly saw a dazzling light, 'big and round', about 100 yards (90 metres) above one end of the field. Antônio went over for a closer look, but – as if playing games with him – the light moved swiftly to the other end of the field, a manoeuvre it repeated the two or three times the young farmer tried to get a closer look at it. Then the light abruptly vanished.

The following night, 15 October, Antônio was out in the field again, ploughing alone by the light of his headlamps. Suddenly, at about 1 a.m., he became aware of a 'large red star' that seemed to be descending towards the end of the field. As it came nearer he saw that it was in fact a luminous egg-shaped object. The UFO's approach brought it right overhead, about 50 yards (45 metres) above the tractor. The whole field became as bright as if it were broad daylight.

Villas Boas sat in his cab transfixed with fear as the object landed about 15 yards (15 metres) in front of him. He saw a rounded object with a distinct rim that was apparently clustered with purple lights. A huge round headlamp on the side facing him seemed to be producing the 'daylight' effect. There was a revolving cupola on top, and as he watched, fascinated, he saw three shafts – or 'legs' – emerge and reach for the ground. At this the terrified farmer started to drive off but after a short distance the engine stopped, despite the fact that it had been running smoothly. Villas Boas found he count not restart it and in a panic he leapt from the cab and set off across the heavily ploughed field. The deep ruts proved a handicap to his escape and he had gone only a few paces when someone grabbed his arm. As he turned, he was astonished to see a strangely garbed individual whose helmeted head reached only to Villas Boas's shoulder. He hit out at his assailant, who was knocked flying, but he was quickly grabbed by three other humanoids who lifted him from the ground as he struggled and shouted. He later said:

I noticed that as they were dragging me towards the machine my speech seemed to arouse their surprise or curiosity, for they stopped and peered attentively at my face as I spoke, though without loosening their grip on me. This relieved me a little as to their intentions, but I still did not stop struggling. . . .

He was carried to the craft. A ladder descended from a door, and his captors hoisted him up this with great difficulty – especially as he tried to resist by hanging on to a kind of handrail. But in the end they succeeded.

Once inside the machine Villas Boas found himself in a square room with metallic walls, brightly lit by small, high lamps. He was set down on his feet, and became aware that there were five small beings, two of whom held him firmly. One signalled that he should be taken through to an adjoining room, which was larger, and oval in shape, with a metal column that reached from floor to ceiling, together with a table and some swivel chairs set to one side.

A 'conversation' ensued between his captors, who made sounds like dog barks:

Those sounds were so totally different from anything I had heard until now. They were slow barks and yelps, neither very clear nor very hoarse, some longer, some shorter, at times containing several different sounds all at once, and at other times ending in a quaver. But they were simply sounds, animal barks, and nothing could be distinguished that could be taken as the sound of a syllable or word of a foreign language. Not a thing! To me it sounded alike, so that I am unable to retain a word of it . . . I still shudder when I think of those sounds. I can't reproduce them . . . my voice just isn't made for that.

Handled by humanoids

This strange communication ceased abruptly, when all five set about him, stripping him of his clothing while he shouted and struggled – but to no avail. (Apparently they stopped to peer at him whenever he yelled, and, strangely, although they seemed to be using force, at no time did they hurt him.)

The beings were all dressed in tight-fitting grey overalls and large, broad helmets reinforced with bands of metal at back and front. There were apertures through which Villas Boas could see light-coloured eyes. Three tubes emerged from the top of each helmet, the central one running down the back and entering the clothing in line with the spine; the other two curved away to enter the clothes, one beneath each armpit. The sleeves ended in thick gloves, which seemed difficult to bend at the fingers. The trouser part fitted closely over seat, thighs and lower legs, and the footwear seemed an integral part of this section, the soles being very thick – perhaps as much as 2 inches (5 centimetres). On his chest each being had a kind of breastplate or 'shield' 'about the size of a slice of pineapple', which reflected light, and the shield was joined to a belt at the waist by a strip of laminated metal.

The naked and shivering farmer it was a

pumped up and down. The alarmed Villas Boas watched the chalice fill with what was presumably his own blood. The creatures then left him alone. He sat on a soft couch contemplating the nightmarish situation in which he found himself.

Suddenly he smelt a strange odour, which made him feel sick. He examined the walls and saw metallic tubes at just below ceiling level. Grey smoke was coming through perforations in the tubes. Villas Boas rushed to a corner of the room and vomited, and after that he felt a little less frightened. Moments later there was a noise at the door, which opened to reveal a woman standing there. As Villas Boas gaped, the woman walked towards him. Flabbergasted, he realised she was as naked as he was.

The woman, said Villas Boas, was more beautiful than anyone he had met before. She was shorter than he, her head reaching only to his shoulder – he is 5 feet 5 inches (1.6 metres). Her hair was smooth, and very fair, almost white, and as though bleached. Parted in the centre, it reached halfway down her neck, with ends curling inwards. Her eyes were large, blue and elongated, 'slanted outwards'. Her small nose was straight, neither pointed nor turned up. She had high cheekbones, but – as Villas Boas discovered – they were soft and fleshy to the touch. Her face was wide, but narrowed to a markedly

Below: Villas Boas's impression of the inscription above a door in the humanoids' craft. In the statement he made to Dr Fontes, Villas Boas said it was 'a sort of luminous inscription – or something similar – traced out in red symbols which, owing to the effect of the light, seemed to stand out about 2 inches (5 centimetres) in front of the metal of the door. This inscription was the only thing of its kind that I saw in the machine. The signs were scrawls completely different from what we know as lettering'

chilly night outside, and no warmer in the craft – stood there quaking and 'worried to death'. He wondered what on earth was going to happen to him. One of the little creatures approached him with what seemed to be a sort of wet sponge, which he rubbed all over Villas Boas's skin. He said: 'The liquid was as clear as water, but quite thick, and without smell. I thought it was some sort of oil, but was wrong, for my skin did not become greasy or oily.'

He was now led to another door, which had an inscription in red over it. He tried to memorise this, although it meant nothing to him, being written in unknown characters. In yet another room one of the beings approached with a sort of chalice from which dangled two flexible tubes; one of these, with a capped end like a child's suction 'arrow', was fixed to his chin, while the other tube was

pointed chin. Her lips were thin, the mouth being almost like a slit. The ears were normal, but small.

The door closed, and Villas Boas found himself alone with this woman, whose slim body was the most beautiful he had ever seen. She had high, well-separated breasts. Her waist was slender, her hips wide and her thighs large, while her feet were small and her hands long and narrow. He saw too that the hair in her armpits, and her pubic hair, was blood red. He smelt no perfume on her, 'apart from the feminine odour'.

She approached the farmer and rubbed her head against his (presumably by standing on tip-toe). Her body felt as though glued to his, and she made it quite clear what she wanted. His excitement welled up. The sexual act was normal – as was the one that followed – but then she tired, and refused further advances.

Villas Boas recalled that she never kissed him, but once gently bit him on his chin. Although she never spoke, she grunted, and that 'nearly spoiled everything, giving the disagreeable impression that I was with an animal'.

When she was called away by one of the other beings, she turned to Villas Boas, pointed to her belly, and then pointed to the sky. These gestures instilled a great fear in Antônio – a fear that was with him still, four

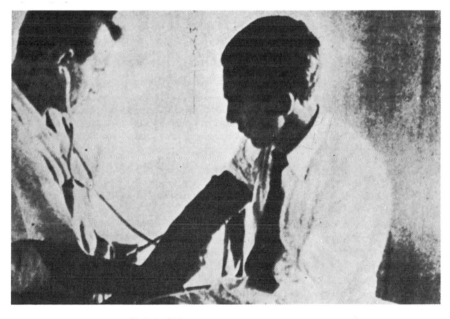

Villas Boas was examined by Dr Fontes in February 1958, four months after the alleged abduction. The symptoms he described suggested 'radiation poisoning or exposure to radiation', but it was too late for this diagnosis to be confirmed

years after the event – for he interpreted them as meaning she would return to take him away. Dr Fontes later calmed him by suggesting that she meant: 'I am going to bear our child, yours and mine, there on my home planet.' This led to speculation by the farmer that all they wanted was 'a good stallion' to improve their stock.

Then Villas Boas was told to get dressed, after which he says he was taken on a conducted tour round the craft; during this he tried to steal an instrument for a

keepsake, only to be rebuffed, angrily, by one of the crew. Eventually, he was invited to go down the ladder, and back onto solid ground. From there he watched the ladder retract, while the metal legs and the lights began to glow. The craft rose into the air with its cupola turning at great speed. With lights flashing it listed slightly to one side, then suddenly shot off like a bullet.

It was by then 5.30 a.m. and the abductee's adventure had lasted over four hours.

He returned home hungry, and weakened by his spell of vomiting. He slept through to 4.30 p.m. and awoke feeling perfectly normal. But when he fell asleep again he slept badly, and woke up shouting after dreaming of the incident. Next day he was troubled by nausea and a violent headache. When that left him his eyes began to burn. Unusual wounds, with infections, appeared on parts of his body. When they dried up they left round, purplish scars.

Mysterious scars

When Dr Fontes examined Villas Boas, he observed two small patches, one on each side of the chin. He described these as 'scars of some superficial lesion with associated subcutaneous haemorrhage'. Several other mysterious scars on his body were also noted.

In a letter to *Flying Saucer Review* Dr Fontes suggested that the symptoms described pointed to radiation poisoning, or exposure to radiation. Wrote Dr Fontes: 'Unfortunately he came to me too late for the blood examinations that could have confirmed such a possibility beyond doubt.'

On 10 October 1971 João Martins was at last officially cleared to write about the case for the Brazilian public. His account appeared in the Rio de Janeiro Sunday review *Domingo Illustrado*. His abridged account concluded with a statement that:

A.V.B. was subjected by us [Martins, Dr Fontes, and a *military officer* – whose presence was not revealed in the earlier reports] to the most sophisticated methods of interrogation, without falling into any contradictions. He resisted every trap we set to test whether he was seeking notoriety or money. A medical examination . . . revealed a state of completely normal physical and mental equilibrium. His reputation in the region where he lives was that of an honest, serious, hardworking man.

Martins also revealed that the interrogation at times bordered on harsh and cruel treatment, just short of physical violence, but Villas Boas never veered from his original story in any detail. The journalist concluded: 'If this story be true, it may well be that, somewhere out there in the Universe, there is a strange child . . . that maybe is being prepared to return here. Where does fantasy end? Where does reality begin?'

Sightings and side effects

Animals, countryside – and humans – may suffer physical reactions to a UFO visitation. Three such incidents are described below

THE 'REALITY' OF UFOS – whether they are 'nuts and bolts' craft, or some vision-like projection – is the subject of hot debate. But witnesses and participants in close encounters frequently report physical side-effects such as violent headaches, fits of weeping, and buzzing in the ears. In the cases that follow, zoo animals stampede and soldiers are paralysed in Malagasy while an Argentinian girl weeps for days after a UFO passes by – so just how 'unreal' can such alien craft actually be?

'A luminous green ball'

Close encounter of the second kind: Tananarive, Madagascar, August 1954

One of the most spectacular of all 'light in the sky' UFO fly-overs took place over the city of Tananarive, capital of Madagascar (now Malagasy) one day in August 1954.

Edmond Campagnac, head of Technical Services of Air France, was waiting with a group of people outside the Air France office on the Avenue de la Libération for the arrival of the air mail from Paris.

Suddenly Monsieur Campagnac saw a luminous green ball in the sky. It was descending, almost vertically, like a meteorite. Other people followed his gaze, and the object was seen to disappear behind mountains to the south of the city.

The time was 5.45 p.m. and dusk was approaching, although the setting Sun was still visible. While the group waited outside the Air France office, they were joined by scores of others on the streets as people began their journeys home from work.

The witnesses were still watching when an object of the same colour as that seen seconds earlier appeared over the hills near the old Queen's Palace, this time 'flying' horizontally and at a slower speed. The UFO curved past the government buildings, still appearing like a green ball. Soon it was descending even lower, almost to roof-top height, and heading along the eastern side of the Avenue de la Libération, just above the building opposite the Air France office.

As the light drew level with the group, they saw that it was in fact *two* objects. A lentil-shaped device was leading the way, and this was described as having the colour of an 'electric-green luminous gas'. Following some 100 feet (30 metres) behind was a metallic-looking cylindrical object, about 130 feet (40 metres) in length. While described by some as a 'cigar', others said it looked more like the fuselage of the contemporary Constellation aircraft shorn of fins, elevators, wings and engines. The surface of the cylinder reflected the dying rays of the sun, while behind it there splayed a plume of orange-red flame. Estimates of the speed of the objects were in the region of 300 km/h (185 miles per hour).

People stopped and gazed in amazement at the phenomenon, so much so that a pall of quietness hung over the city. The giant cigar and its lenticular companion were completely silent. Then there was another shock for the observers for, as the objects passed over the buildings, all the electric lights were extinguished, coming on again only after the objects had passed.

The strange aerial duo continued over the city towards Tananarive airport, then swung away to the west. Before passing from sight they skimmed over a zoological park where the animals, which were normally quite undisturbed by aircraft flying into and out of the airport, went into a panic and stampeded through fences. It was several hours before soldiers and police could round them up.

Not surprisingly there was a great furore in Tananarive over this invasion of Madagascan airspace, and an official enquiry was set up by General Fleurquin, the Air Force Commandant. This was conducted by Father Coze, director of the Tananarive Observatory. Father Coze had been at the observatory at the time of the incident and had himself witnessed the passage of the UFOs. He estimated that at least 20,000 people had seen the objects, and he and his helpers questioned more than 5000 witnesses. It is not known what happened to his report of this remarkable encounter. If it ever reached France, it certainly failed to arouse interest. Details were known only to a handful of French researchers in the early 1960s,

and to *Flying Saucer Review* in 1966, which received an account from Monsieur René Fouéré of the *Groupement d'Etude de Phénomènes Aeriens* (GEPA). But not a hint of the affair was known to the French public until 1974, when M. Jean-Claude Bourret broadcast his famous series of programmes on Radio France-Inter, transcripts of which appeared in his book *The crack in the Universe*, published in 1977.

'A shining egg'

Close encounter of the second kind: Malagasy Republic, May 1967

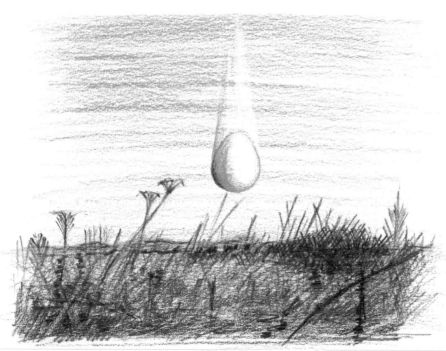

In May 1967 there was said to be another alarming close encounter in Malagasy. But it took 10 years before news of the incident reached *Flying Saucer Review* from the French research group *Lumières dans la nuit*. On this occasion, the reason for the delay was that the witnesses were 23 soldiers, their officer and four NCOs of the French Foreign Legion, and they were forbidden to discuss the affair. The eventual informant was a legionnaire named Wolff.

Wolff's platoon, which was on a reconnaissance exercise, had halted at noon in a clearing in the bush country. The troops were eating lunch when they all saw a bright metallic object resembling a 'shining egg' descend rapidly like a falling leaf, accompanied by a piercing, whistling sound, then thump into the ground. All the soldiers were 'paralysed' and, seemingly immediately, saw the object take off. But when watches were checked, the time was 3.15 p.m., which meant that three hours had passed.

M. Wolff claimed that the object was about 23 feet (7 metres) high and 10 to 13 feet (3 to 4 metres) wide at the widest part. It rose slowly at first, and then vanished at high speed, as though 'sucked up into the sky'. It left three marks in the ground that looked as if they had been made by legs, and a 10-foot (3-metre) deep crater, at the bottom of which was a sort of vitrified ring of coloured crystals.

None of the witnesses could recall what had happened during the missing hours, but for two days afterwards they all had violent headaches, with constant 'beating' in the region of the temples and a continual buzzing sound in the ears.

'An impression of goodness and kindness'

Close encounter of the third kind: Córdoba, Argentina, June 1968

The Motel La Cuesta is a well-appointed roadhouse, situated on Highway 20 that connects the town of Villa Carlos Paz, in the province of Córdoba, with eastern Argentina. The small country town is 500 miles (800 kilometres) to the west of Buenos Aires.

The motel's proprietor, Señor Pedro Pretzel, 39, lived at the motel with his wife and his 19-year-old daughter, Maria Eladia.

On the night of 13 June 1968, at about 12.50 a.m., Señor Pretzel was walking home when he saw, some 55 yards (50 metres) beyond the motel – and apparently on the highway – an object that he could not identify. It had two bright red lights, but could not be a car because it projected beams of peculiar intensity at the motel. This 'machine' was in view for only a few seconds. Puzzled and alarmed, Señor Pretzel ran to his motel and found Maria Eladia lying in a dead faint close to the kitchen door. After she had been revived she had a bizarre tale to tell.

Only a few minutes earlier she had said goodnight to her fiancé and had escorted some guests to the door; then she returned to the kitchen. Suddenly she noticed that the lobby was flooded with light. As she had just switched the lights off, she went to investigate. She was horrified to find herself face-to-face with a 'man' some 6 feet (2 metres) tall, dressed in a kind of diver's suit that had shiny, sky-blue scales. He was fair-haired, and was holding up his left hand, on the palm of which a sky-blue ball, or sphere, was moving about.

Maria said there was a huge ring on the fourth finger of the creature's right hand, which he moved up and down constantly in front of her. She was overcome by lethargy, as though strength was being drained from her. Light came from the creature's fingertips and feet and it seemed to Maria that the lethargic feeling was strongest when the light was pointed directly at her. But apart from this he showed no signs of aggression. Indeed, Maria remembers an impression of 'goodness and kindness' emanating from the being who, she added, smiled throughout the encounter. She said he also seemed to be trying to communicate with her, for, although his lips did not move, she could hear an unintelligible mumble that sounded 'like Chinese'.

After a few minutes – during which Maria stood transfixed in the presence of the humanoid – he walked, with slow, precise movements, to the side door, which was open. He went out and the door closed of its own accord. It was at that moment that Maria lost consciousness. Shortly afterwards her father discovered her on the floor.

Señor Pretzel reported the incident to the police, who promised to investigate it. As for Maria, she became extremely nervous and was subject to fits of weeping for some days after the affair.

Did Maria Eladia Pretzel witness a projected image – that of a 'man' in her kitchen – that was emitted from the UFO her father had seen on the nearby highway? If she had been witness to such a phenomenon, then it is possible that her father came on the scene just as the image was about to be withdrawn. Could the 'humanoid' have been a hologram transmitted by laser beams and projected against, say, the glass of the lobby window? (The intense beams of light seemed to have been emitted by the UFO, and it was presumably this light that first attracted Maria's attention.)

But however the strange and alarming effects were produced the questions remain: Why? And by whom?

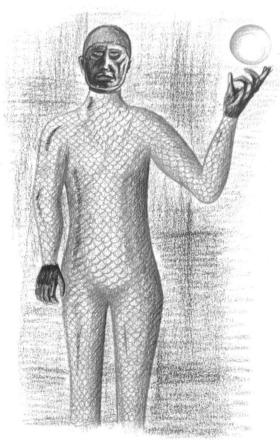

When light beams bend

Sometimes UFOS are reported to deflect light beams, defying known physical laws. Two cases have been recorded; one in Australia, and another, with many witnesses, in France

NEWCOMERS TO ufological research, accustomed to conventional physics, often throw up their hands in incredulity when they are confronted with reports of the extraordinary phenomena that occur during UFO sightings. Among the most remarkable of these are accounts of beams of light that stop short or make abrupt bends, without any evident absorbing, refracting or reflecting agencies to bring this about. The Trancas event, in Argentina, was a noteworthy example. In that well-documented case 'tubes' of light were extended from UFOS, bent into curves, and withdrawn. In the two cases discussed here, beams from torches and car headlamps were manipulated in an equally 'impossible' way.

'Gaseous lights of all colours of the rainbow'

Close encounter of the second kind: Bendigo, Victoria, Australia, 4 April 1966

The London *Daily Express* of 12 April 1966 carried a story in which it reported that a motorist named Ronald Sullivan, aged 38, had been cruising along near Bendigo in southern Australia under a moonlit sky when, inexplicably, his headlight beams bent to the right. In a statement to the police at Maryborough, near Melbourne, he said that he avoided a crash only with difficulty and, as he drew to a halt, saw a display of 'gaseous lights' of all colours of the rainbow in a field alongside the road. The display was followed by the appearance of an object that rose vertically about 10 feet (3 metres) into the air – and then disappeared.

When Mr Sullivan returned to the scene a few days later, he found that another motorist, Gary Turner, had been killed in a crash at the same spot the previous evening. Meanwhile the police had made their investigations and found in a freshly ploughed field 50 feet (20 metres) from the fence a circular depression about 5 feet (1.5 metres) across, and varying from 2 to 5 inches (5 to 13 centimetres) in depth. The police regarded Sullivan – a highly respected businessman – as a reliable witness, and noted that he professed not to believe in UFOS.

The *Daily Express* story ended there. The corresponding Associated Press message was more detailed: apparently, Mr Sullivan's encounter took place on 4 April 1966; he returned to the site on 8 April, and it was then that he learned of the fatal accident that had taken place on 7 April. A report in the *Melbourne Herald* added that he had driven to nearby Wycheproof where he had had his headlights checked – they were found to be in perfect working order – before going on to the police.

It was also revealed that the bent beams incident and the fatal accident occurred on a long straight stretch of road between Bendigo and St Arnaud, at a point 9 miles (15 kilometres) east of Bealiba, a small town nearly 130 miles (210 kilometres) north-west of Melbourne.

The information that was available left it a matter of speculation whether the bending of the headlight beams was accidentally caused by Mr Sullivan's car running into the UFO's 'force field' or whether, if the incidents of 4 and 7 April were connected in some way, the bending was the result of a deliberate action by a hostile agency – human or alien.

In a commentary in *Flying Saucer Review*, scientist Stephen L. Smith deplored the absence from the reports of important details such as the make of Mr Sullivan's car, the kind of dipping mechanism employed in its headlights, and the exact position on the beams at which they were bent. He pointed out that there were three possible explanations: that the beams were bent at source, that the bending occurred somewhere along the beams, or that the beams appeared bent through illusion or hallucination. Mr Smith wrote that his colleagues of the Cambridge University Investigation Group had suggested how an illusion might be brought about by the sudden extinguishing of the left-hand component of the headlight beam, which 'through its divergent character, would seem to have been bent to the right . . . [due] to a freak of reflection caused by the absence of dust particles by which headlight beams are normally seen'. If hallucination were the cause of the phenomenon, then was it spontaneously generated in the witness's brain, or was it caused by some outside agency – perhaps a force field emanating from the object he had observed?

'Beams that extended slowly'

Close encounter of the second kind: Taizé, Saône-et-Loire, France, 11 August 1972

The Centre for Ecumenical Meetings, Taizé – close to the landing point of what seemed to be an alien craft

People from all walks of life – most of them young folk – had gathered at the French spiritual centre at Taizé, some 6 miles (10 kilometres) north of Cluny, in eastern France, on 11 August 1972. Taizé is a Protestant monastery, and the gathering there was for celebrations organised by its founder, Friar Roger Schutz.

The events at Taizé in the early hours of 12 August 1972 were reported to the gendarmerie at Cluny, and afterwards to the French UFO organisation *Lumières dans la nuit*, for whom an investigation was conducted by a schoolmaster named Tyrode.

A group of about 35 of the young people had collected for discussions at a rustic open-air theatre situated among the visitors' tents near the crest of a ridge on which the community's buildings also stood. This site faced westwards over a gently sloping valley and a ridge known as 'la Cras', and successively higher ridges beyond that. The sky was overcast, and a light drizzle soon began to fall.

From the place where the earnest young debaters were grouped, a large ploughed field sloped down into the valley. A Monsieur F. Tantot, from Mâcon, a young man from Dijon and an Italian student were alerted at about 2 a.m. by Mademoiselle Renata, from Sardinia, to a 'star' that she could see descending. Before the others could swing round, however, she was already telling them that it had 'landed'. In a few moments, all the people in the theatre could see an object, seemingly stationary, on the slopes of la Cras, facing them and at the same level as themselves. All present had also heard the whistling noise as the UFO approached, and they could now see that it was bounded to the left by a field of cereal – its light colour showed the UFO up as dark by contrast – and to the right by a large tree standing on the ridge. The size of the UFO was estimated as 'larger than a coach' or at least 30 yards (30 metres) long.

All the witnesses now saw the UFO 'light up'. Seven yellow lights appeared in a row, then two orange ones outside and to the left of the object. After that, five of the yellow

A Position of object
B Position of witnesses
C Position of dark mass

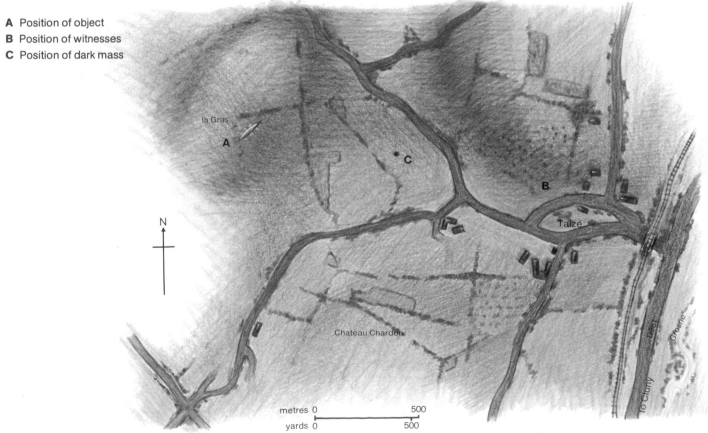

metres 0 — 500
yards 0 — 500

after 20 minutes, when the large beam to the left flashed several times.

By now the intrepid four had reached the middle of the field, and they became aware of a dark, haystack-shaped mass some 6 or 7 yards (5 or 6 metres) high, around which a point of red light moved in a haphazard trajectory. Between themselves and this mass, the witnesses thought they could see a hedge about 10 feet (3 metres) ahead of them – at a point where, they knew, no hedge existed. When a torch beam was shone towards the mass, the beam suddenly turned vertically upwards about 1 foot 6 inches (50 centimetres) from the hedge and, dispersing, was lost in the air. Subsequent attempts to illuminate the object, with all the torches the witnesses had with them, met with the same fate and, alarmed in the face of the bizarre unknown, the four were tempted to back off. However, when the lights on the UFO suddenly went out, only to flash back on again, and the three discs vanished into the big object, M. Tantot flashed his torch in its direction. As if in response, the largest beam from the UFO rose so that it shone directly at the witnesses. Dazzled, and feeling a surge of heat, they raised their hands to protect their eyes. Meanwhile, the UFO began to move away, until suddenly it accelerated and sped off towards Cluny. The time was 4.40 a.m. when it was lost from sight at Taizé.

lights began to emit beams that extended slowly towards the ground. What appeared to be cupolas were observed above the two light beams at the very left of the row. When discussing the phenomenon with M. Tyrode, some of the witnesses said they had the impression that the beams were pylons on which the object was supported. Indeed, it was as if the beams were made of solid matter.

At this point some of the witnesses, particularly M. Tantot and the man from Dijon, felt tingling in their fingers and knees.

While the 'solid' beams of light were extending to the ground, a train of red sparks was seen at the right-hand end of the object. These were soon extinguished, and where they had been there were now seen three small discs, each with two red points of light. These began to gyrate around the main UFO, and these manoeuvres went on until the end of the sighting.

At about 3 a.m. the four original witnesses decided to have a closer look at the big object and, armed with torches, set off across the field, watched as they went by the remaining 30 witnesses in the theatre. These were later able to report that the main beams were rotating around individual vertical axes. The beam second from the left suddenly grew brighter, and showers of red particles filled the air around the four and covered the ground. A row of what looked like portholes appeared in white light, only to disappear

Tantalising evidence: The New Zealand UFO film

One of the most impressive UFO sightings of all time took place in 1978 when a New Zealand television crew made two flights searching for UFOs – and actually succeeded in filming them

LATE IN THE EVENING of 30 December 1978 an Argosy freight plane set off from Wellington, New Zealand. Its skipper was Captain Bill Startup, who had 23 years' flying experience behind him, and the co-pilot was Bob Guard. On board was an Australian TV crew from Channel 0-10 Network: reporter Quentin Fogarty, cameraman David Crockett and his wife, sound recordist Ngaire Crockett. Their purpose was to try to film UFOs, for there had been reports of 'unknowns' during the preceding weeks in the region of Cook Strait,

which separates New Zealand's North and South Islands. They were spectacularly successful in the quest. So successful that, after the story had appeared in hundreds of newspapers and clips from the films had been shown repeatedly on television around the world – the BBC, for instance, gave it pride of place on the main evening news – critics and droves of debunkers lined up to try to explain what the television crew had seen, in terms ranging from the sublimely astronomical to the ridiculously absurd.

'Bright lights over the ocean'

Radar-visual: Blenheim, New Zealand, 30 December 1978

This spinning, luminous sphere was filmed by a New Zealand television crew on the night of 30 December 1978. The crew made two flights, looking for UFOs, on the same night – and, incredibly, saw them both times

The Argosy had crossed Cook Strait and was flying over the Pacific Ocean off the northeast coast of South Island when the excitement began. The television crew was down by the loading bay filming 'intros' with Quentin Fogarty when Captain Startup called over the intercom for them to hurry to the flight deck; the pilots had seen some strange objects in the sky. According to Dave Crockett, they had already checked with Wellington air traffic control for radar confirmation of their visual sighting.

Quentin Fogarty stated that when he reached the flight deck he saw a row of five bright lights. Large and brilliant, although a long way off, they were seen to pulsate, growing from pinpoint size to the size of a large balloon full of glowing light. The sequence was repeated, the objects appearing above the street lights of the town of

Kaikoura, but between the aircraft and the ground.

Dave Crockett, who was wearing headphones, received a call from Wellington control warning the pilots that an unknown target was following the Argosy. Captain Startup put his plane into a 360-degree turn to look for the unidentified object but the passengers and crew saw nothing. Control however, was insistent: 'Sierra Alpha Eagle . . . you have a target in formation with you . . . target has increased in size.' This time lights were seen outside the plane, but because of interference from the navigation lights of the plane, Crockett was unable to film. So First Officer Bob Guard switched off the navigation lights – and everyone saw a big, bright light. The plane was now back on automatic pilot, so Bob Guard gave up his seat for Crockett, who obtained a clear shot

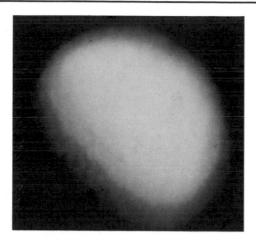

moonlight via cabbage leaves'. A more reasonable explanation was that the films showed a planet – but which one? One newspaper claimed it was Venus (left), another said it was Jupiter (right). But even the quickest glance at the planets themselves show these explanations to be unlikely. The *Daily Telegraph*, surprisingly, printed a strong condemnation of the Venus theory: 'The scientist who suggested that all [the television crew] were seeing was Venus on a particularly bright night can . . . be safely consigned to Bedlam.'

Rogue planets?

For a time it was thought that the New Zealand films might provide solid scientific evidence for UFOS.

Faced with this possibility, scientists were quick to react by putting forward a whole range of alternative explanations of what the object in the films might be. Some of their theories were wildly implausible – one even claimed the television crew had seen 'reflections from

Right and far right: two stills from the New Zealand television crew's film. The presence of the strange objects was confirmed by Wellington air traffic control, who saw their traces on their radarscopes

Below: Captain Bill Startup, pilot of the aircraft from which the UFO film was taken

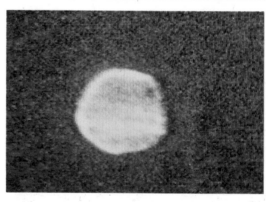

of the object with his hand-held camera. Dave Crockett has since explained that this changing of seats with the camera running was responsible for the violent shake seen at that point in the movie film.

After this, Bill Startup put the plane into another 360-degree turn. They then lost sight of the UFO, although Wellington control said its echo was still on the radar scope.

It should be noted that, although there was no room for a camera tripod to be mounted on the flight deck, the unidentified object stayed steady enough for David Crockett to be able to keep it dead centre in his camera viewfinder for more than 30 seconds.

As the plane approached Christchurch, the fuel gauge went into a spin, but the captain said that this occasionally happened and was not necessarily caused by interference by the UFO. At this point they were

tuning in on the UFO off Banks Peninsula and were out of touch with Wellington control. Christchurch control had the object on its radar scope but later, when Captain Startup and American investigating scientist Dr Bruce Maccabee asked to see the radar tapes, the Christchurch supervisor replied that they had been 'wiped' clean as part of routine procedure.

The Argosy landed at Christchurch and journalist Dennis Grant joined the team in place of Dave Crockett's wife Ngaire. They left on the return flight to Blenheim at about 2.15 a.m. on 31 December 1978.

Early in this flight the observers saw two more strange objects. Through the camera lens Crockett saw what he described as a sphere with lateral lines around it. This object focused itself as Crockett watched through his camera – without adjusting the lens. He said the sphere was spinning. Significantly, one of the objects swayed on the Argosy's weather radar continuously for some 4 minutes. Later, as the aircraft approached Blenheim, they all saw two pulsating lights, one of which suddenly fell in a blurred streak for about 1000 feet (300 metres) before pulling up short in a series of jerky movements.

True or false?

Were the objects 'flying saucers'? Many alternative explanations were put forward: the film depicted a 'top secret American military remote-control drone vehicle', plasma or ball lightning, a hoax, meteorites, 'helicopters operating illegally at night', mutton birds, lights on Japanese squid boats, 'reflections from moonlight via cabbage leaves' (at Kaikoura), while Patrick Moore hedged his bets with a guess of 'a reflection, a balloon or an unscheduled aircraft.'

One newspaper claimed the film showed the planet Venus, out of focus because it was filmed with a hand-held camera. Another offered Jupiter as a candidate; an amateur astronomer had enhanced the light values of the film by putting through a line-scan analyser and had identified four small points of light that could be taken to correspond to the positions of the four largest moons of Jupiter. Venus and Jupiter appeared in

completely. They definitely moved, varying between 50 and 100 knots (92.5 km/h and 185 km/h). I certainly couldn't identify them as anything. It's pretty inconclusive. They were purely the sort of radar echoes that constantly pop up. It is not unusual to get strange echoes appearing on what we call primary radar. They usually amount to nothing at all.

Nevertheless, the Royal New Zealand Air Force was concerned enough about the incident to put a Skyhawk jet fighter on full alert to intercept any other UFOs that might appear in the area. By the end of January, however, the fuss had died down and the New Zealand Defence Ministry stated that the radar images were 'spurious returns' and the unidentified objects 'atmospheric phenomena'.

What is the truth of the New Zealand affair? The film appears to be genuine; computer enhancement has not proved it to be a fake. It seems almost too good to be true that a television crew that had set out with the deliberate intention of filming 'flying saucers' should come up with such spectacular results; and yet it has to be assumed that the objects they saw were real enough to those who beheld them – and were not mere hallucinations. The case remains on file, a fascinating question mark.

Below: this unique frame from the New Zealand film seems to show the UFO performing an extraordinary feat of aerobatics – looping the loop in 1/24 of a second. An alternative explanation for this typical UFO behaviour: the hand-held camera was jogged

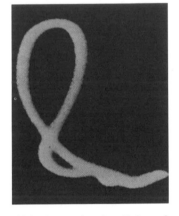

With the navigation lights of the aircraft switched off, the television crew was able to obtain this film of one of the objects. It pulsated from a pinpoint to the size of 'a large balloon'

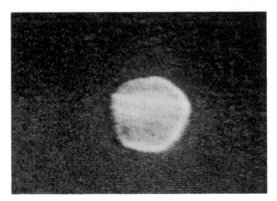

different regions of the sky; because the television crew were so vague about the position of the lights relative to the aircraft as they were filming them, it was impossible to make a positive identification.

One of the most exciting aspects of the incident is that it appears to offer independent instrumental evidence of the sighting both on film and radar. But even here there are problems. Although both ground radar and the Argosy's own radar picked up unidentified traces, the number of UFOs the television crew claimed to have seen – about eight – conflicts with the 11 reported by ground radar. And the crew actually filmed only one object. The radar controller at Wellington, Ken Bigham, was dismissive about the whole affair:

I managed to plot three of the echoes
for 20 minutes or so before they faded

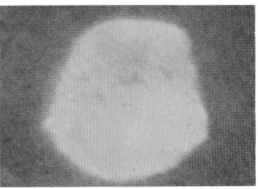

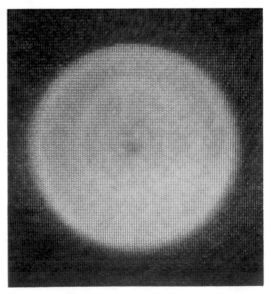

Aliens in the dark

UFOs are sometimes too aggressive to be ignored, especially when they leave physical evidence behind

THE UFO PHENOMENON often seems to veer into the realms of the psychic – indeed, some researchers believe UFOs to be from another dimension altogether. However, this view must be considerably modified when one comes across cases in which UFOs show up on radar screens, make deep marks in railway sleepers, or leave calcined stones behind as they did in these cases from England, France and Spain.

'Something is buzzing our airfield'

Radar-visual: Bentwaters, near Ipswich, England, 13 August 1956

THE NIGHT OF 13 August 1956 was a busy one for RAF and USAF air controllers and radar operators in East Anglia. Although some of the many inexplicable radar traces they obtained were probably spurious, others were undoubtedly from unknown objects. The sighting described here was stated by the USAF Condon Report as 'the most puzzling and unusual case in the radio-visual files'.

The main events began at 10.55 p.m. at RAF Bentwaters, near Ipswich, a station leased to the United States Air Force. A Ground Controlled Approach (GCA) radar

had been alerted by ground control, looked down and saw the fuzzy light flash between his aircraft and the ground. The UFO was heading towards Lakenheath, another RAF aerodrome leased to the USAF, and immediate warning was given.

For the record, there was no mention of a sonic boom at Bentwaters. Ground observers at Lakenheath saw the light approach, stop dead, and then move swiftly out of sight to the east. Some time after that two white lights were seen; they joined up and disappeared in formation.

Observers and radar operators of the

operator picked up a fast moving target 30 miles (50 kilometres) to the east, heading in from the sea at a speed of 2000 to 4000 miles per hour (3200 to 6440 km/h). It passed directly over Bentwaters and sped away until it disappeared from the scope 30 miles (50 kilometres) to the west. This overflight was not just a radar observation, however; a tower operator on the ground looking up saw a light 'blurred out by its high speed', while the pilot of a USAF C-47 aircraft flying over Bentwaters at 4000 feet (1200 metres), who

Lakenheath GCA and radar traffic control centre scopes testified to having recorded objects travelling at terrific speeds, stopping, and changing course instantaneously. After some hesitation the Americans at Lakenheath put through a call to the RAF.

The RAF Chief Controller at Bentwaters remembers USAF at Lakenheath telephoning to say something was 'buzzing' their airfield circuit. He scrambled a Venom night fighter from RAF Waterbeach, and his interception controller, with a team of three highly

few seconds, and in the space of one or two sweeps on the scopes, the object appeared behind the fighter. The pilot called out 'Lost contact, more help,' and he was told that the target was now behind him.

Meanwhile the chief controller scrambled another Venom fighter. The American witnesses said the UFO 'flipped over' and got behind the RAF fighter, which then manoeuvred to try to get behind the UFO. This information was given to the USAF-sponsored study of the UFO phenomenon under Dr E. U. Condon at Colorado University. Until the Condon Report was published in January 1969 the case had remained secret. A detailed study was carried out by Dr James McDonald, an upper atmosphere physicist at Arizona University. This was a sighting the Condon Report could not dismiss; indeed, it had to admit that 'the apparently rational, intelligent behavior of the UFO suggests a mechanical device of unknown origin as the most probable explanation.'

trained personnel, took over. The Venom was vectored onto the UFO and the pilot, who was accompanied by a navigator, called out 'Contact' when he could see it, and 'Judy' when the navigator had the target fairly and squarely on the fighter's own radar scope. The Venom closed on the target but after a

---

'Two very odd creatures'

Close encounter of the third kind: Quarouble, near Valenciennes, France, 10 September 1954

The small French village of Quarouble, not far from Valenciennes close to the Belgian border, was shaken by the events of the night of 10 September 1954.

At about 10.30 p.m., 34-year-old Monsieur Marius Dewilde was sitting reading in the kitchen of his little house. His wife and son were already in bed. The house was situated among woods and fields just under a mile from the village. There was a fenced garden in front of the house, and to one side of this there ran a National Coal Mines railway track between St Amand-les-Eaux and the giant Blanc Misseron steel works where M. Dewilde was employed.

Suddenly his dog started to bark and howl and, thinking there was a prowler or smuggler outside the house, M. Dewilde took his flashlight and ventured out into the darkness. He was instantly aware of an ill-defined shape to his left, on or near the railway line; he thought it might be a farmer's truck. Then, as his dog came up to him, cringing on her belly, he heard a sound to his right. He swung round, and his torch beam fell on two very odd creatures, each just over 3 feet (1 metre) tall and wearing what appeared to be a diver's suit. M. Dewilde said they seemed to

be shuffling along on very short legs. He noticed that they had very broad shoulders, but no arms and that they wore huge helmets. They were heading for the dark shape he had seen on the railway line.

Recovering from his initial surprise, the tough, taciturn steel worker ran to the garden gate with the intention of cutting off the interlopers from the path. He was about 2 yards (2 metres) from them when a blinding beam of light, the colour of magnesium flares, issued from an opening in the side of the dark shape. The beam struck him and he was stopped dead in his tracks, unable to move or shout; it was as though he were paralysed, he said. With a sense of horror he watched the two creatures pass within a yard (1 metre) of him, and on towards the still indistinguishable shape.

Suddenly the light went out and, recovering the use of his muscles, M. Dewilde set off after the small creatures. All he saw, however, was what appeared to be a door closing in the side of the object, which then rose slowly from the ground like a helicopter. There was a whistling noise, and M. Dewilde saw steam clouding up from beneath the contraption. After rising about 30 yards (30 metres) the craft – if that is what it was – set off towards the east, climbing and glowing red as it went.

Shocked, and in a highly agitated state, M. Dewilde woke up his wife, then ran off to the police station in the village. The policemen on duty thought he was out of his mind and sent him on his way. But he contrived to get access to the Commissioner who, after listening to his semi-coherent account, realised that this man – by now in a state of incontinence – was neither joking nor mad.

A detailed enquiry was set up by the regular police, the air gendarmerie and the

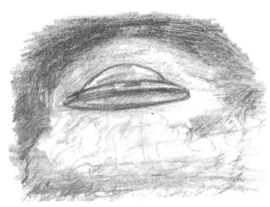

could not have been a helicopter (carrying contraband for example) because of the mass of telephone wires overhead which would have prevented a landing.

It was suggested by one journalist that M. Dewilde was suffering from the effects of a head wound, and had had an hallucination, but this theory was untenable in view of the discovery of marks, sharply and deeply cut, in the iron-hard wood of the railway sleepers where M. Dewilde said the object had stood. A railway engineer calculated that it would have taken a weight of 30 tons (30 tonnes) to have made the marks. It would have taken great heat to have produced the burnt and calcined ballast stones found between the affected sleepers, and this would have called for an extremely powerful hallucination!

Territorial Security Department. They were convinced that the witness was not lying. They were convinced, too, that the object

'As big as a jumbo-jet'

Radar-visual: Valencia, Spain, 11 November 1979

On Sunday evening, 11 November 1979, a Supercaravelle of the Spanish airline TAE, on a charter flight from Salzburg to Tenerife, put down unexpectedly at Valencia in Spain. The flight had been four hours late in starting, and this extra delay was almost the last straw for the tourists on board the aeroplane. Fortunately, most of them were unaware of what had gone on outside – 24,000 feet (7000 metres) above the Mediterranean.

The incident began after the aeroplane had passed over Ibiza. In an interview with newsman Juan J. Benítez, the skipper, Commandante Lerdo de Tejada, said that a few minutes before 11 p.m. he was requested by Air Control in Barcelona to tune in to radio frequency 121.5 megahertz, an emergency wavelength. He picked up the hiss of the carrier wave but received no instructions. Before the captain could query this he saw two powerful red lights at the 'nine o'clock' position (to the left, or port side).

Commandante Tejada thought there was only one 'thing' carrying two lights. This object bore down on them at great speed,

coming up on their left, and a little behind them. He added:

When we saw them first they were at about 10 miles [16 kilometres]. Then they made towards us and literally 'played' with us at about half-a-mile [1 kilometre] . . . the object was moving upwards and downwards at will, all around us, and performing movements that would be quite impossible for any conventional machine to execute.

According to the captain the object seemed to be as big as a jumbo-jet. Finally, he said, the speed and closeness of this monstrous object were such that he was forced to perform a 'break' – a sharp turn to avoid possible collision – about 60 miles (100 kilometres) from Valencia. Air Control in Barcelona were informed that unidentified traffic was close by, and that the UFO had stayed near to the aircraft for eight minutes. After the 'break' the UFO followed the jet for another 30 miles (50 kilometres).

The controls and instruments of the Supercaravelle were not affected during the emergency. The automatic pilot did, in fact, fail – but that, said the captain, was not due to the UFO. Finally Manises Airport at Valencia was contacted and permission was requested to make an emergency landing. The Supercaravelle touched down a few minutes before midnight.

Señor Morlan, director of the airport, his traffic controller and other personnel confirmed seeing an extraordinary object with red lights over the airport.

Señor Benítez also found that there had been a vigorous response to the alert by the Spanish Air Force as military radars had picked up unidentified targets in the precise area where the TAE airliner was flying. The unidentified echoes persisted and two F-1 fighters were scrambled from Los Llanos five minutes after the Supercaravelle had landed. It is understood that visual contact was made – and that one of the fighters was subjected to a number of close approaches by the UFO.

UFO photofile

*When computer science has identified
the clever fakes, the smudged lenses and
the tricks of light, there still remains an
impressive collection of photographs
showing images in the sky for which no
universally accepted theory has been
advanced.*

Above: this impressive photograph was taken during the Gemini XII space mission on 12 November 1966. Analysis has shown that the UFO that appears on the right of the picture is a distant object – but the NASA Photo Evaluation Lab claims this is actually rubbish that has been discarded from the Gemini XII spacecraft itself.

Left: at about 9.10 p.m. on 25 August 1951 a group of five professors and a postgraduate student were relaxing outside the house of Professor W. I. Robinson in Lubbock, Texas. Suddenly they saw a formation of bright lights flying rapidly across the sky. The professors estimated their speed at around 1800 miles per hour (2900 km/h) at a height of about one mile (1.5 kilometres). Sceptics claim that the lights were nothing more than reflections from the bellies of flying ducks – but if so, they would have been flying at more than 125 miles per hour (200 km/h) – which is far too fast for ducks!

Above: this photograph was taken by a coastguard, R. Alpert, at 9.35 a.m. on 16 July 1952 from the control tower at Salem Air Base in Massachusetts, USA. The objects were reported to be moving at great speed. They appear much brighter in the photograph than they actually were because the aperture of the camera was set for the brightness of the surrounding landscape and consequently the UFOs themselves are overexposed.

But is the photograph genuine? The images are unlikely to have been caused by lens flares, as these almost always appear in straight lines. But it is reported that the picture was taken through a laboratory window – and sceptics have suggested that the objects could actually be reflections of lights inside the laboratory. Photographic experts, however, point out that reflected lights are rarely as opaque as these.

Right: this picture, published here for the first time, was taken by London photographer Anwar Hussein in the Spanish Pyrenees in July 1978. After finishing filming one day, he found he had left one of his lenses at the top of a mountain. The next morning, about 9 o'clock, he returned to look for it. Mr Hussein found the lens and took some pictures; his camera was set on motor-drive. At the time he noticed nothing unusual – except the brightness of the light and the uncanny quietness. Back in London, he sent the film to be developed – and received a worried telephone call from the lab, who pointed out the 'object' on the film and thought it must be a fault that had appeared during developing. On examination, however, the emulsion was found to be undamaged. This is typical of many of the best UFO pictures, which are often of objects that go unnoticed at the time of filming.